LIGHT OF DAY

Finding my way through love,
loss, and childhood cancer

LORNA MACKINNON DAY

I love you Sam

FOREWORD
BY KATE MCMAHON

Like a bolt of lightning, a single phone call can forever change life as you know it.

"I'm a radiologist," a man who introduced himself said. *"I've reviewed your daughter's X-ray and it appears that there is a very aggressive lesion on her right distal femur, near her knee --"*

"Wait. What? Are you saying that it could be - " I forced the last word out of my mouth, "- cancer?"

"Yes. Those are our preliminary findings. But we need to do more tests. We're going to need an MRI, a biopsy and some other imaging scans...."

My hearing faded out. The world spun in fractured white light, and I collapsed to the ground as if falling from heaven to hell.

The first round of chemo was a nightmare. They flooded my daughter's 12-year-old body with chemicals so dangerous they could burn the skin. The nurses wear PPE just to handle the stuff. My daughter got violently ill from it and sleep was interrupted around the clock from either her vomiting, her having to get up to pee or nurses coming in the middle of the night like benevolent vampires taking her blood. My daughter's long, brunette hair was gone within two weeks, leaving her bald and embarrassed.

What a perversion of the mind to believe that something so toxic could actually be the cure.

Then, I got another phone call that forever changed my life - for the second time.

"My name is Lorna Day," the woman said. "I heard about your daughter's bone cancer diagnosis and want to offer my support. I lost my son to cancer six years ago. I know I represent your worst nightmare."

I remember the words I chose to say back to her. *"Well, I might cause you pain as well…because I still have my child."*

That first raw exchange between two mothers' tortured hearts, warning of the potential risks and rewards of knowing each other is how my bond with Lorna Day was forged.

Getting to know Lorna took time. At first, it was sort of a one-way street with her mostly dispensing support to me, suggesting questions to ask the doctors and providing my family a sense of community within The Club No One Wants To Join. (The childhood cancer club.)

Early on, I learned that Lorna is a generous listener who doesn't hijack my struggles into her story. She only gives advice if directly asked for it. And by some miracle, she has the capacity in her broken heart to care about other peoples' kids struggling with cancer.

In the nearly five years I've known Lorna, she has shown up for kids with cancer and their families in ways I can barely believe. She cries with us. She celebrates wins with us. She surprises us with hospital visits and nurturing gifts. She hears our desperation, validates it, and hopes for something hopeful to come.

In 2023 I approached Lorna with a proposal. I'm a journalist and documentary producer, and wanted to apply my skills to raising awareness about childhood cancer.

Unlike adult cancers, the cause of children's cancer can't be traced to decades of bad habits, lifestyle choices or many years of exposure to environmental toxins. No, something goes terribly wrong with the genetic coding that causes a young person's cells to turn malignant. Cancer is the leading cause of death by disease for children under age 20 in the United States. In a room of 264 kids, one will have cancer. The good news is there are more than 500,000 childhood cancer survivors in this country. But they will inevitably experience side effects of the barbaric, antiquated treatments which may cause heart disease, hearing loss, liver failure, cognitive dysfunction or secondary cancers. Progress for improved therapies and better outcomes has been glacially slow for kids because pediatric cancer only receives 4% of the federal cancer budget. The rest goes to adults. The rationale for such gross inequity is that childhood cancer is rare. But so are kids, when compared to how many people in the total population are children.

With those disheartening statistics in mind, I proposed publishing a newsletter that could help the childhood cancer community with science news and tips for living well - while also raising awareness about the need to change the narrative that *children's cancer is rare, so it is less important than adult cancers.*

Lorna and I teamed up, and together, we created the Well ONE DAY newsletter. It strengthened our bond. Lorna is now a beloved, permanent pillar in my life.

Having a front row seat to watch how Lorna operates, I marvel at how a bereaved mother can be seen as such an icon of hope to parents terrified of becoming like her. She is the definition of spiritual alchemy: the transmutation of someone's soul energy from negative to positive.

By laying down the tormenting unanswerable question, "why" she had to lose her beautiful boy Sam to cancer, Lorna has chosen, "what now." She chooses this path to channel her son's brilliant mind. He was a deep thinker and obsessive problem-solver. (Just like his mom.) Lorna justifies Sam's life by letting others get to know him posthumously, warts and all. Sam was complex and human.

Together, Lorna and Sam's spirits are on a mission to change the landscape of childhood cancer and make it better for kids and families living with cancer and its aftermath.

WELCOME TO
LIGHT OF DAY.

The book you're about to read is proof that out of darkness there can be light. It is not just a tragic story about a boy who dies - it's about a boy who *lived well* and *lives on* in his impact on the world and through his mother. *Light of Day* gives kids like Sam, families like Lorna's, families like mine and anyone who wants to care more about us an amazing story full of heart, humor, plot-twists and surprises born out of truth, love and, above all: hope.

1

ROGUE ANGEL

My husband says I'm good at grieving. A sideways compliment, but not untrue. I welcome a good, hard cry, and some isolated hours to sit with my sadness. As Bob boasts about my healthy grieving habits, I worry it might cost me a few social invitations. I like to grieve alone. When the sadness comes around, I feed it by scrolling through photos while I lie on my son's bed. I turn on melancholic music, and I imagine being with Sam again. I've learned to resist the urge to stay strong in those moments, because I know I'll be stronger after the darkness subsides. Weakness comes first.

As the first anniversary of Sam's death approached, a slow smother crept into my throat and tightened around my heart. These were the sensations of August, the back-to-school activities, the warm blue skies and dry vegetation. It was football season and summer salads and switching the sprinkler on in the mornings and evenings. It was the sun setting after a blue-sky day of 85 degrees. It was beautiful things that caused me sorrow. As if it hadn't happened yet. As if I knew his death was coming again, and I was helpless to prevent it.

Exactly one year after Sam died, Bob and I found ourselves

on Natalie's college campus in Southern California, saying goodbye to our daughter as she started her freshman year. We shared hugs and tears, and I managed to save my heavy grieving for later, when I could be alone. Natalie carried a mix of emotions. She was grieving, too. But also, and appropriately, she was excited for this new chapter in her life. Bob and I were about to be empty-nesters too soon. However, we were abundantly proud of our daughter: her courage, her joy, her bright light.

Instead of driving the I-5 route back to Oregon, Bob and I headed east to explore the national parks of Utah. We made it to our rented cabin in Zion by the end of the day. My dear friend Staci had written us a letter and sent along a bottle of wine. She was holding us close from a distance.

I brought Sam's CamelBak hydration backpack to use on the hikes - one of his many things I was attached to. I had picked it up at REI after his oncologist recommended a slow two-week infusion of chemotherapy. He'd sent Sam home with a clunky black medical case to carry the chemo and a small battery-operated pump. Sam was in 7th grade at the time, and the case was big, awkward, and ugly. However, a bag of chemo fits perfectly into the belly of a CamelBak, and it's a slightly more fitting accessory for a middle school kid from Oregon. Once Sam finished his chemo regimen, he even used it for its intended purpose on a couple of family hikes.

The next morning, as Bob and I prepared for our hike, I zipped open the pockets of the CamelBak to insert some snacks, Chap-Stick, and a pair of sunglasses. As if it were waiting for me, I found one of Sam's prosthetic socks. He had carried special socks with him, using them when the blood flow of physical activity caused his limb to shrink slightly, risking an accidental prosthetic leg detachment. I tucked the sock back into the pocket so I could keep a little bit of him with me on the trail. As I closed the zipper, I noticed a small tag stitched into the side of the bag. I'd never noticed it before. It had one word: "Rogue." I froze and stared at it for a moment.

I'd been thinking of Sam as a rogue angel since he died. I imagined him in heaven, pressing against the boundaries to make his existence up there even more fascinating. He'd been going rogue throughout his life. Disappearing from the classroom, testing the rules of the field trip, redefining the goal of a camp game, all because something more entertaining lingered on the other side of those guardrails placed by adults attempting to keep children safe and orderly.

I was that mom, seen slinking away from the park, grocery store, or church social, with a sobbing child tucked underneath one arm, because Sam couldn't keep his inventions, plans, and escapades within the established boundaries. I felt the shame of spawning the problem child, for Sam had no diagnosable disorder to explain his misbehavior. So, I was the mom who couldn't keep her kid under control. I think differently now. I like to believe that Sam broke the rules for one reason alone: to get the most out of life.

From the moment he could move, Sam was in search of adventure. Every new environment was a place to explore. For me, it meant the leisurely mornings at the park to chat with my friends while the kids played were never all that leisurely. Inevitably, two minutes into a conversation I would say, "Wait, where's Sam?" He headed beyond the swing sets and sandboxes, venturing outside the familiar safety of the playground to find something magical.

Because of his tendency to ignore instructions, I volunteered for all of the preschool field trips. Once, his preschool class toured the kitchen at a local pizza restaurant with an indoor play structure. The kids watched the cooks make a pizza while I kept an eagle eye on Sam. He tucked his hands in his pockets, just like we'd talked about.

Following the tour, the kids were given one square of pizza for their preschool snack. With a few squares left in the pan, hands went up to ask for seconds. There wasn't enough for everyone to have a second piece, so the teacher said, "No, you only get one piece. Pretty soon you're going home for lunch, so this is just a snack."The kids were excused to the playroom with the multicolored ball pit, a large tunnel and slide, and a miniature Ferris wheel. The room was enclosed with plexiglass so parents could nibble their pizza slices outside and chat while still keeping an eye on their kids.

I was just a couple of minutes into a conversation with another mom before I scanned the room and said, "Wait, where's Sam?"His teacher was my good friend Staci. She helped me search for him. A minute or two later she returned with a wide grin. She pointed outside of the play area toward the table with leftover pizza on it. There he was, kneeling on a chair with his elbows on the table, eating all those remaining squares of pizza he wasn't supposed to have. My little rogue preschooler.

One day, when I picked him up from preschool on a December afternoon, Staci pulled me into the craft room. A large corkboard was overflowing with little Christmas angels, made from cardboard toilet paper inserts, with paper doilies for wings, and a sparkly golden halo just above their smiling angel faces. Right in the center was one that looked completely different, surrounded by the perfect angels of those who followed the directions. No toilet paper insert. No doily angel wings. Just a white paper face, and a halo hanging below it instead of above.

That angel belonged to Sam. Rogue Angel.

2

THE LUMP

"Sam, come here and let me see your leg again."

"It feels better, Mom. I'm fine." He darted in the opposite direction with Cedar, our red golden retriever, trotting alongside him.

"Just a quick second, I want to see something on your leg!" He begrudgingly walked over to the wooden steps at the front of the cabin and sat down.

"Natalie! Wait for me over by the tree trunk and try to find another good stick over there!" Sam and Natalie had been playing in the woods at my dad's cabin on the Hood Canal in Washington. They found a few sword-like sticks and created a battle scene after a morning of beachcombing.

"Ow, ow, ow, ow!" Sam stumbled out of the shrubs, leaving his role as victorious 13th-century war hero to get a little help from his mom. His left calf had found some sharp foliage, which scratched his skin over a large portion of his calf. Blood seeped out.

I took a close look while he insisted that I doctor his calf, which was only worth doing to help with his emotional regulation. I found an ace bandage in the cabin's first aid kit, alongside

Band-Aids, and a travel-size can of Bactine. In no time he was patched up and ready to play.

After I wrapped Sam's leg, his tears dried on his soft round cheeks and the sniffles subsided.

"Thank you, mom." Once the sores were thoroughly protected, my little wounded warrior ran back into the forest with his sister again. But something didn't look right about it. As I watched him play, I became fixated on his leg.

His left calf, the wounded one, looked thicker than the other leg. I didn't think he had the type of injury that could cause rapid swelling. It looked more like a strong calf muscle, but much stronger than his right leg. He's been riding his scooter all summer long, I thought; that could make one leg stronger than the other. Was it because of football? He had recently started his first season of daily football practices, so was surely developing new muscle, but the lopsided appearance was odd, and while the play and conversation around me continued, the thoughts in my mind started running around with nowhere to go.

"Just let me look at your leg a minute."

I knelt down and wrapped my fingers around his calf, expecting to feel a strong muscle between my fingers and extended thumb. Just under the skin was something firm and not at all like the feeling of muscle. It was hard like a bone. That strong-looking calf felt like a smooth stone from the shoreline below us, covered by healthy young skin. I pressed my fingers into his leg, searching for edges and grooves under the skin, for some sort of clue that might help me define what seemed to be a subtle deformity in his bone. My brain didn't know how to inter-pret the sensation that came through my fingers, so it stirred up some emotional commotion that comes with an undefined threat.

Even when we don't yet know what's wrong, we usually know when something's not right. A wave of worry rushed through me and dampened the delight of our day. I couldn't reason it away. I disengaged. I sat on the wooden step, elbows resting on my knees, still focused on Sam's left leg while my heart beat into my throat with a pounding I couldn't ignore. This was a new kind of fear.

Something was wrong.

When I called the pediatrician's office on Tuesday after Labor Day, it almost seemed silly. "Hi. This is Lorna Day. I'd like to make an appointment with Dr. Moshofsky for my son, Sam."

"Sure. What's going on with Sam?"

"Well, his leg looks kind of odd. He has a hard lump on his left calf."

"Is he having any pain?"

"No."

"Has he had any recent injuries?"

"No, he seems fine. He went to school and ate breakfast. But I'd like to get it checked out."

I made an appointment for Thursday afternoon. For two days, I became obsessed with that lump. I stared at it below the hem of his shorts. I checked it when he went to bed at night. The fear kept rattling inside of me. I googled bone deformities in children. I spoke with my friend, Kirsten, on the phone and told her I was afraid of this strange bulge on Sam's leg.

"I'm sure it's just a worried mom sort of thing, but I can't help but think maybe it's cancer or something bad." As soon as I said the word, I wanted to take them back. I'd never heard of a bony lump indicating cancer.

"I'm sure it's nothing," she said, doing her best to comfort me.

We knew Dr. Moshofsky as a friend, so we called him Dean. As usual, he spent the first few minutes asking about Bob. Bob's life was quite interesting and busy. He was a commander at the Police Bureau at the time, also working as a football official in the

PAC 12 conference every weekend throughout the fall. It was the first week of September when we walked into this appointment, and Dean wanted to know his football schedule and whether he had any Oregon games. I was used to it.

Sam hopped on the table after confirming that he wouldn't be getting a shot.

"See, it's weird. Right here." I showed Dean where to palpate. "It looks like a muscle but it's really hard." I watched his face for signs that would settle me. The slight nod, the lifted eyebrows, and a one-sided smile that says *Ah…I know what this is. It's nothing to be worried about.*

"OK," he turned toward me and tempered his tone. "I want you to go over to a nearby building and get an X-ray. I'll let them know you're coming. Then, come back here. I'll have them send the results and we can go over it together."

"Ok" I said, still telling myself this was just protocol. Sam jumped off the table and we walked out of the exam room. I told him the X-ray wouldn't hurt and we'd need to come back after.

Then Dean said an alarming thing, as if I knew what he knew, "He has no idea what's going on. That's good."

I didn't ask what that meant because I didn't want to know. I was still telling myself it wasn't a big deal. Sam might need surgery. Or maybe he'd need to quit football. The conversation in my head continued, telling me there must be a non-life-threatening explanation for the bulge in his leg. This voice was competing with a current of fear growing inside of me.

A tremble took over my core and I called Bob from the waiting room at the X-ray clinic. I'm sure he heard the fear in my voice when I told him what was going on. "Dean sent us to get X-rays so we're in the waiting room for those now. I don't know why, but I'm getting really nervous." I told him we would return to the pediatric clinic after Sam received the X-ray to get an explanation.

"Did he give you any idea about what it might be?"

"No. He just seemed kind of serious about it."

We both sat silent for a moment.

"I can leave work now and I'll meet you there."

Within 30 minutes, Bob, Sam, and I were sitting in the pediatrician's waiting room again. I continued to tremble with my arms crossed over my stomach as if I needed to be the one to hold myself. Sam watched an animal show on the waiting room television and I was relieved I didn't have to engage with him. Dean came to get us, and suggested Sam stay put. One of the ladies at the front desk could watch him. At the end of the day now, there was no one else in the clinic. He shut the door after us in the small children's exam room. I sat on the edge of the only chair. Bob leaned against the wall.

"The radiologist sent over the images." He took a breath. A bright white screen hung on the wall and Dean pulled a copy of the X-ray of Sam's lower leg bones from a manilla envelope and secured it to the flat light.

"So, this is the area we are looking at. You can see how the bone doesn't have a clear edge to it."

We looked closely to understand what he was talking about. He faced us with a finger pointed at the mass and said, "This is a tumor. And it's cancer."

I grabbed my stomach again and bent over in my chair. I didn't cry, or scream, or gasp. I froze. Seconds went by. Bob slid down the side of the exam table and onto the floor. He put his head in his hands. I moved to the floor too, and so did Dean.

Following a moment of silence, Dean assured us, "I'm going to make a couple of calls. To find the very best doctor." He put his hands on our shoulders and we prayed together.

After Dean said, "We'll have to do some tests to confirm this. There's a chance we're wrong, so I recommend you don't say anything to Sam or Natalie until you have a firm diagnosis from an oncologist."

"Ok." I managed.

"That bone is probably very fragile, so he shouldn't play football this week or do any contact sports."

"Ok." Another pause of silence. There was nothing else to learn.

Still sitting on the floor, Bob pulled out his phone and called his mom. "Mom, we're at the doctor with Sam. It looks like he has cancer." Then he started to cry.

Bob hung up the phone and looked at me as if it was time to leave. Lifting my gaze I said to him, "I just need another minute before I can face Sam."

3

COMPASSION

As I have tried to come to terms with the best way to share Sam's story and what his life meant, I realize it's not just his story. It's also my story. And it's Natalie's story and Bob's story as well. Eventually, we would all need to find a path back to a life we could claim as our own. We'd each have to observe, even choose, how Sam's life and the tragedy of our loss would become integrated into our own hearts and souls. For most of my life I've been somewhat shy and generally won't talk about myself unless I am asked. However, it seems important to write about the ways in which I was both molded and shattered by the honor of being Sam's mom.

As a kid growing up in Shoreline, Washington, I learned empathy and how to advocate for others, especially those with disabilities. I learned this from my sister Cathie, who has cerebral palsy, or CP. CP is a type of brain damage to the part of the brain that controls one's muscles. In most cases, the damage occurs before birth, and the cause is usually unknown. Most people with CP have uncontrollably tight muscles, impacting their ability to move with intention. Cathie's version of CP left her somewhat floppy and slow, like a child powered by a low battery.

At home Cathie and I played games with pieces she could handle like Connect Four and Sorry, instead of Operation where the best fine motor skills won. Sometimes we played with our stuffed animals or dolls in the dresses my mom had sewn. My doll's dresses had buttons, and Cathie's had Velcro. When we played school, I was always the teacher telling her what to do.

Cathie and I went to the same preschool. My classroom had large wooden blocks to play with, and pieces of carpet arranged in a circle. That's where I learned stories like *Brown Bear, Brown Bear, What Do You See?* And *The Very Hungry Caterpillar.* Actually, I don't remember much about it. My sister's class was more interesting. It had fewer kids than mine, and a lot more things were made of wood. Cathie moved around her classroom like she did at home, rolling in a sitting position with her legs out in front, like a mermaid might do if she had to move on land. When she stopped to play on the floor, her legs moved into a W position with her feet sticking out on either side. She couldn't walk. I remember her red plaid pants, her thin blond hair and rosy cheeks.

Cathie learned to walk when she was seven. At times she used a walker. She wore braces on her feet to keep from dragging her toes across the floor. Before she got her braces, my dad duct-taped the toes of her shoes to make them last longer. Cathie was also dyslexic. And she had ADHD. She was hyperactive in slow motion. Cathie has always been able to laugh at the absurd outcomes of her disability.

We went to a camp for kids with physical disabilities when she was 13 and I was 15, barely old enough to be a counselor. I was younger than some of the oldest campers.

The first day of camp rattled me. Though I was comfortable around people like my sister, I had no reference for older kids who couldn't walk or talk or consume regular food. Two campers, Donny and Mindy, ate their meals in the building where the older girls stayed because it was less stimulating than the lively mess hall. They were both 17 years old. Mindy lay reclined in a hot pink cot while Donny sat up in his wheelchair with supports to keep his head upright. Both had towels around their necks to wipe food off of their chins. A counselor for each camper sat with bowls of puree, spoons, and extra towels. Time after time, food was spooned into a mouth, then wiped with a towel as it spilled out the corners. The two counselors chatted with ease, inclusive of the campers who could not chat back. For Donny, a stomp of his right foot said yes, and a stomp of his left foot said no. Mindy looked up to say yes, and her eyes gazed down or away to say no. Say something funny at the right time, and the contents of Mindy's mouth might spew. The counselors knew how to dodge the projectiles, as laughter was essential to every good meal.

Sitting in that space, I felt my throat tighten, and a desire to separate myself. As casually as I could, I got up and walked down the hallway to the bathroom, shut the door, looked at myself in the mirror and watched my own tears pool in the base of my eyes. I grabbed a bit of toilet paper to dab them clean and took a deep breath. *Come on Lorna, you can't cry in front of people here. Stop it!* I expected camp to be full of cute young kids in wheelchairs, or walkers with slow speech and silly giggles. I wasn't sure I could handle this, but I had a whole week ahead of me. Over the next couple of days, a mixture of empathy and insecurity drove me to fulfill the responsibilities of an upstanding counselor, and I hoped others would notice. "Would you like to go to the art room?" "Can I get you a cup of juice?" "Can I sit with you at lunch today?" I buzzed around asking campers how I could be helpful.

Two days into camp, I found Donny sitting alone near the mess hall during free time. There were no other kids in need at the time, so I approached him and asked if he wanted to go somewhere. He tapped his right foot *yes*. I ran through a thorough list of activity options, eager to raise my heart rate pushing this growing 17-year-old wherever he wanted to go. Donny raised his arm in the direction of the camp boundary line, his head cocked to the side and glossy straight brown hair hanging over his brow.

I pushed him in the direction he pointed as far as I was allowed to go. Another 20 feet away was a telephone booth, and Donny continued to point at it.

"Do you want to call someone?" I asked him.

His right foot tapped *yes*.

"Well, we're not really allowed to use the phone here."

I heard a grunt.

"Do you want to call home?"

His right foot tapped.

"Well....hmmm. Donny, I don't think we can call home. But maybe we can write a letter. Would that be ok?"

Donny stomped *yes* three times.

"Ok, let me go find some paper and a pencil."

Through Donny's smiles and the sparkle in his eye, his right foot and left foot taps, I learned his favorite camp song and that he loved it when campers sang on the bus. I learned he was looking forward to the dance and he wanted Mindy to be his date. He needed help asking her. I learned that he thought Ian and Jay were hilarious and the spaghetti dinner mediocre. I wiped the saliva moving from the corner of his mouth to the tip of his chin. I helped him drink a glass of orange juice and found a way to mail his letter.

It was my favorite hour of camp.

I don't know whether Donny or Mindy considered their lives to be one of suffering. Once I stepped in - though it was with reluctance - I liked what it did to my heart. This experience drew me toward the harder things in life. Human connection in the midst of the uncomfortable human condition was profoundly meaningful to me. So I looked for more.

4

THE BEGINNING OF SAM

Love for my kids came easy, but it also took effort, frequent naps, and regular consultations with friends a few steps ahead of me. Early motherhood set the stage for what would happen later. It tested my patience, my knowledge, my self-esteem, my life skills, and my identity. But the greatest challenge of being a mom came from coping with the persistent pain in my heart. It ached when they failed or faced rejection. The deep well of love I had for them is what helped me persevere.

When Natalie was born, love was redefined. She showed us her dimples on her first day of life. I had never seen a more beautiful baby. After that, I spent hours staring at her rosebud lips, and marveling at the grip of her dainty fingers.

Before Natalie was born, I had developed friendships with many more kids with disabilities. I went to college to become an occupational therapist, then worked closely with parents of newly diagnosed infants and preschool children while they grieved. I felt privileged to be a part of a support system, but from a distance. Shortly before I got pregnant with Sam, a physical therapist friend of mine suggested I take a course in infant massage. This class was one of those experiences that stirred up something inside of me, just like my younger days as a counselor at Camp Casey. I read and re-read my binder and the recommended books full of information on the elements of bonding and attachment, the power of skin-to-skin contact and the benefits of massage for the infant born with a disability. Once I became certified, I taught multiple group classes in the living rooms of friends with healthy babies developing normally, and heart-weary mothers whose infants would never walk or talk like other children. Their love overwhelmed me.

When I became pregnant with Sam, Natalie was 17 months old, and I wanted another baby just like her. I was having a boy, and it took me a minute and a few shopping trips for cute baby boy onesies to settle into the idea of a son. Once Sam was born, I had an idea about the kind of mother I wanted to be.

I gave Sam his first massage when he was ten days old. It was a warm July evening, Bob was working the night shift, and Natalie was asleep. With my laminated reference page, my food grade toxin-free massage oil, my just-right squishy pillow, and my very own newborn baby, I began a new ritual. His peaceful sweet stares and relaxed movements let me know when I could begin respectfully. I laid him face up on our overstuffed blue couch, perfectly cradled by a bunched-up baby blanket. I unsnapped his soft cotton full body onesie and pulled his legs out first. I was careful to read his cues: eye contact, steady breathing, and the tuck of his chin signaled contentment - an acceptable moment to begin. I paused at signs of discomfort like when his head turned away or when a bout with the hiccups emerged. I relished the intentional act of communicating and bonding with his perfect baby body. Massage was my secret ingredient for raising a harmoniously healthy human.

"Relax...relax...relax." I cradled Sam's leg and gently bounced it up and down, letting the muscles of my face calm. During the training I was skeptical that an infant could learn to relax with verbal and tactile cues.

Three weeks into our baby massage routine, he did it. While his gaze was fixed on mine, Sam's body stilled. "You did it!" I whispered with a bright big smile to let him know something lovely had just happened. Affirmation of an accidental rest taught him that he could control his body. We repeated the same bonding routine multiple nights a week. By the time he was six weeks old, my perfect baby boy could relax on cue. That was the kind of mom I wanted to be. Bonded and loving, with above average resources for raising emotionally healthy humans.

As Sam turned mobile, I became suspicious that he had been hard-wired with a curious adventure-seeking personality, and more intense than I was prepared to parent. Natalie, two years ahead of Sam, made Bob and I look good. Though she was an adventurer too, she followed the rules and had fun with every kind of playmate regardless of their gender or interests. Her dimples and ultra-blonde hair made people smile. She thought birthday parties were more fun than Disneyland, and that school existed to fill her days with joy. If we'd had only Natalie, we could have written a parenting book. At least it felt that way.

Once Sam was able to explore on his own, I recognized a similar adventure-seeking spirit, but without the capacity to follow reasonable rules. I regularly found myself exiting child-friendly spaces with visible sweat on my forehead, and a ponytail turned bird's nest. With Sam under one arm, climbing over my shoulder, or pulling away like a cat on a leash.

"You just need to be consistent," said the parent with a little girl like Natalie.

"He's just a boy," said the mom whose son was Velcroed to her hip. In the library, the grocery store, the indoor play structure, the local pizza place, other parents had somehow cultivated self-controlled, mild-mannered children, who behaved in public day after day, week by week, and in every season of their emerging toddler lives.

I felt like I had failed at being the kind of mom I wanted to be.

Sam got kicked out of preschool when he was four. Well, he didn't *exactly* get kicked out. My parent-teacher conference was taken up with brainstorming strategies for redirecting Sam's misbehaviors, like not staying inside his carpet square at circle time, and refusing to share the three Tyrannosaurus Rexes. Sam insisted he could learn the ABCs and memorize the words to *The Very Hungry Caterpillar* while simultaneously building the most incredible Duplo castle his classmates had ever seen. There was too much to discuss in one meeting. The teacher scheduled a follow-up. By the time we were wrapping up session two of how to manage Sam, I feared he was not only a burden to the school, but he was also starting to develop a bad kid identity. I pulled him out of the school, and cried for days. We visited three other preschools who told me they didn't have the support Sam needed. I was beginning to realize my plans to go back to work might have to be delayed.

Finally, I took Sam to a counselor who verified that he didn't have ADHD or any other diagnosable condition. He also confirmed that Sam probably could learn the circle time lesson while still building a Duplo castle. Following the rules was going to be a challenge for him, but getting the most out of life might very well be his superpower, if only the grown ups would let him take the lead.

As Sam grew through his preschool years, I continued to massage him following an older child version we called the *Seed and Plant* massage. A set of strokes for the back, paired with a story about a farmer planting a garden. "First, the farmer tills the soil." I started with long smooth strokes down his back while he lay face down on his bed. "Then, he makes holes in the ground," my fingertips drew circles along his spine.

"Then, he plants the seeds. Sam, what kind of seeds?" I said with my most calm bedtime voice.

"Thpider theeds, and thlug theeds, and cutworm theeds!" He laughed. Sam had observed my disdain for some invasive cutworms. I plopped those little wigglers into a plastic container with squeamish repulsion.

"Ewwww." I reacted.

He giggled every time.

Every night, Sam melted into my torso like warm Silly Putty while I read his favorite books, then giggled when I squirmed at the mention of those creepy-crawly *cutworm theeds*. There was no better feeling than the loving trust and affection of my kids. No matter how much Sam challenged his teachers, I believed I could provide what he needed most, because I loved him the most. This was the kind of mom I wished to be.

During Sam's preschool years, I learned that being self-aware is a different skill than having self-control. Sam excelled in self-awareness but his poor self-control emerged when he felt let down, and he could not always make the right choice. If he lost a game of Chutes and Ladders, or if Natalie got to go to a friend's house because she'd cleaned her room and he hadn't, or if today's movie was High School Musical again instead of Star Wars, Sam didn't handle his anger well. A loud and emotional *WHAT?* was followed by a slammed bedroom door. One year, we replaced our 1964 hollow bedroom doors with nice natural wood solid core doors, except for Sam's. He got another hollow core door.

To deal with disappointment, Sam created strategies for making things go his way. I remember his first play date, with a new boy in the neighborhood named Will, aged five, and one year older than Sam. I sent the boys downstairs to play in our new tri-level home so their kid noise wouldn't shred my nerves while I cooked dinner, or folded laundry in front of a mildly inappropriate sitcom. I could still hear what was going on.

After the boys bounded downstairs, I was still able to overhear Sam's content warning for a successful playdate. "Will," he said with a mildly commanding tone, "don't do anything to make me mad, because if you make me mad, I might hit you or push you and if I do that, I'll probably get a timeout, and I really don't like timeouts." Will agreed, and they had a lovely time.

Not all playdates were that successful. Sometimes I had to intervene, or send someone home, or apologize with cookies. Sometimes I pretended nothing had happened.

"Mom, I just get so mad sometimes, and I can't control myself," he once told me after shoving a kid at preschool who was about to kill a bug.

At the end of second grade, the whole family went to see a counselor for parenting help. He told us that Sam needed practice dealing with disappointment, and he gave us a specific assignment to repeat several times before we came back. He directed us to give something to Natalie that they both wanted. Like a big handful of M&M's. But first, we were to say: "Sam, I'm going to give Natalie 20 M&M's and I'm only going to give you five, can you handle that?"

"Sam," the counselor looked at Sam's wide eyes, "When you hear those words, *can you handle that?* it's your cue to practice staying in control." Sam listened while Natalie's dimples gave away a subtle smirk. The counselor then explained to us how Sam would be rewarded with even more M&M's than Natalie if he managed to stay cool. No slamming doors, no yelling, no spilled candy on the floor.

We practiced dozens of times over the next few weeks with M&M's, glasses of juice, quarters for the arcade, and several other coveted treats. Little by little Sam was learning to cope with disappointment.

Then, he was diagnosed with cancer.

5

SARCOMA

The surgeon explained the details with a measured tone and careful words. Ewing sarcoma is a bone cancer that shows up in kids most commonly between the ages of 10 and 20. It's aggressive. Sam needed to begin chemotherapy soon.

The treatment would be difficult. Sam would undergo high doses of chemotherapy for several days at a time, with each cycle requiring hospitalization. Because the tumor was embedded in his bone, surgery would involve removing a portion of his fibula, the smaller bone below his knee. Apparently, the fibula is not an essential bone. That was good news. It meant he could keep his leg. "If you're going to get Ewing, the fibula is a good place to get it." It was one of the optimistic phrases we would repeat to each other, first in the hospital elevator, and again in the car, then on the phone to family members, and on our newly launched Caring-Bridge site, intended to keep our friends informed and hopeful.

I recorded Dr. Harvey's comments in my pocket-sized purple notebook. Someone had warned me I would get overwhelmed and forget most of what the doctor said, so I should write it all down. I wanted to understand everything, down to the most minute detail. However, I obeyed the doctor's orders to not go searching for answers on the internet. I thought that maybe if I followed the rules, Sam would be fine.

Sam sat cross-legged on the paper-lined exam table. He heard the doctor's words but I don't think he was listening. He understood the cancer in his leg would require medicine that would make him feel bad. That's about all he was able to glean from the appointment. We honored his boundaries and kept the information to a minimum.

This appointment left me dizzy, searching for a positive emotion to grab ahold of. Like a cruel game of Pin the Tail on the Donkey, I spun in disorientation, trying to pin my hopes onto a fact or encouraging statement; but the rules of the game kept changing. This dizzying and nightmarish reality left me wishing for some sort of parenting angel to appear, offering me step-by-step guidance on how to mother a child with cancer. My attention split in two: part of me was straining to absorb the influx of medical information, the other focused on every non-verbal sign of anxiety Sam might reveal. I wondered how much he was hiding. Or maybe he was fine, and I could handle fine. But at some point, he wouldn't be fine, and I wasn't sure how to prepare for that.

The nausea-inducing electrical buzz running through my body after that first appointment needed to stay hidden, so I could be fully present for Sam. He was quiet and not obviously terrified, so I tried to fake my best non-verbal *it will be fine* attitude. I wanted Sam to stay a kid a little longer.

After the appointment with the surgeon, we called Natalie on the drive home to check in. She had gone to a friend's house after school, which would soon become a routine. I didn't share much, and maintained my *everything is fine* tone with her too. Natalie was not an anxious kid, so it wasn't all that hard. Mid-conversation, Sam blurted from the backseat, "Hey mom, hand me the phone. I want to tell Natalie something!" I hesitated, but his eyes were bright, and his tone suggested he wasn't about to disclose disquieting medical details to his older sister.

He started talking before the cell phone was in place. "Hey Natalie, guess what? I got Dry Bones on Mario Kart!" I could hear Natalie's elation through the phone. For days now, the animated character Dry Bones had been ceaselessly taunting them in their game. Sam and Natalie discussed their game strategy from inside their childhood bubble, still uncontaminated by cancer. I let some air out of my lungs.

"Hey mom," Sam pulled the phone away from his cheek, "Can Elise and McKenna come over to play Wii with us tonight?"

"Yeah, sure." I said quietly.

Appointments continued daily, followed by more tests, complex medical jargon, and unfathomable possibilities. Little by little, one by one, Sam began to ask questions. They were brave questions. I wished he didn't have to be so brave. Even more, I wanted to be brave enough to answer them. I needed to be thoughtful and deliberate. I needed to let him know how well I understood and how much I cared. I needed to tell him the truth in a way that made him feel safe.

The intensity of what was required in this moment stopped me. I needed Bob.

When Bob and I met, he was a police officer and the first person I knew who carried a cell phone. He drove a green Acura and I thought it was a little flashy. His hair was bright red and he wore a brown leather jacket. I didn't know any police officers, so I wondered if they all carried cell phones and drove fast cars and wore leather jackets.

I met Bob and his friends because I had a roommate named

Kim, who was exceptionally bubbly and social. She'd recently moved to Portland for a job. Kim worked with a local gal who had a bunch of friends, and the two of them decided to invite everyone over for an evening at our house.

Bob told stories about singing Neil Diamond songs at a recent wedding. His strong voice delivered such a comedic recap that the room overflowed with loud laughter from bent over bellies. My face was soaked with tears. Bob was the funniest person I had been with in years. At the time I needed some laughter in my life, so I started hanging out with him.

We didn't date right away. I planned to move back to Seattle after OT school, and a funny police officer with red hair wasn't on my list of men I'd change my life plans for. But over the next few months, Bob took an interest in me, and in what I was learning and why it excited me. Occupational therapy was like a new religion. My professors were fascinating. It was more than an academic track; it was a way to observe life and live it with purpose. Bob was skilled at asking questions. I longed to share my new insights with someone who was genuinely curious. Three months after we met, at the end of another long phone conversation, he asked me out.

Bob was on the Mounted Patrol Unit when we married, a great fit for his highly sociable demeanor on the job. His horse's name was Speedy and they had the same color hair. Together they walked the streets of Portland keeping people safe and cultivating a culture of positive city living. Bob and Speedy knew the folks who were struggling - who had an untreated mental illness, who just got out of jail or rehab, and who hadn't seen their family for many years.

Over the years Speedy became a folkloric figure. Anecdotes were legion, like the time he consumed the blooms off an entire bouquet of long stem roses a woman was holding while she petted and hugged him with little respect for his personal space. One time Speedy was hit by a car, and he ran off toward Waterfront Park with Bob laid out in the middle of the street. No one cared much about Officer Bob, but that horse made the news and generated a massive influx of donations to aid in his recovery. He ate all the local organic apples he could handle.

When Bob was thinking about proposing to me, I told him I didn't want a big public display, but I did want him to put some thought and planning into it. One night on our way out to dinner, we stopped by the horse barn to check on Speedy. He offered to teach me how to feed his horse an apple. He opened up his hand, but no apple – but a ring – balanced on his palm instead. Speedy was the only one to witness the moment when we got engaged.

In our early years of marriage, Bob was promoted to different positions within the police bureau. He loved being a sergeant, but it took him to the night shift when the kids were toddlers. Our 1400 square foot house with hollow core doors and squeaky oak floors didn't allow Natalie and Sam and me to go about our day without a lot of rambunctiousness and clammer. Bob slept with earplugs and a noise machine, but rarely more than six hours at a time. He was often grumpy. I knew he loved his work, but working the night shift with a young family took its toll.

I was a good police officer's wife. Most nights I didn't worry. Once in a while, in bed while Bob was still at work, I had a bad feeling and struggled to fall asleep. I got angry the day he was stuck with a drug user's needle. He spent the day at the hospital and came home with a cocktail of anti-HIV medications, and a schedule of follow-up testing for the next year.

From time to time I went on ride-alongs. Mostly they were interesting and somewhat exciting. Ride-alongs helped me to trust he was taking every necessary precaution. He explained how he was trained to approach a vehicle, how he didn't enter certain situations unless he had backup, how it was safer for the victim and for him to park his car a few houses away from a domestic violence situation. I liked the officers he worked with. They watched out for each other, they spoke to their suspects respectfully, and they took pride in their jobs.

After doing his time as a sergeant, Bob took other roles in the department. He got promoted to lieutenant and was also assigned to lead the Hostage Negotiation Team. Technically, this was a day shift position, but he was on call 24/7. He often got called out in the middle of the night because someone had a gun and wouldn't come out of their house. Or worse, the person had a gun and was threatening to shoot someone. One time all four of us had to leave an Easter family gathering because a man was on a bridge threatening to jump. We abruptly loaded into his take-home police car and drove with lights and sirens on for 30 miles, straight to the bridge. Both kids fell asleep in the back seat. Once we got to the bridge, Bob had one of the new officers drive us home. The man decided not to jump.

Life with a police officer required flexibility, independence, and a steady demeanor - qualities I carried reasonably well. But childhood cancer presented a foreign landscape I was unprepared to navigate. I would need to depend on Bob, he would have to rely on me, and Sam would need us both.

"If I don't do the treatments, will I die?" asked Sam, slumped in our overstuffed beige armchair with a gray light emanating from the window next to him. His words made the silence in the house even duller and deeper, in contrast to the happy noise of my kids' normal banter, and a question a kid should never have to ask.

I was tempted to put him at ease by dodging reality. I wanted to protect him the same way parents want to protect their kids from the trauma of violence or abuse. I wanted to say, *Let's not think about that, Sam. You're going to be just fine.*

In a tender quiet voice Bob responded with the simple, painful truth. He said, "Yes, Sam. You could."

"Ok. I'll do it," Sam said.

Later I told people how brave he was, and friends admired and praised him for it. But looking back, I don't think Sam cared whether people thought that or not. He wanted to live, which meant football at recess, sleepovers with friends, and new levels on Mario Kart Wii.

6

FAITH

I was raised in the Christian faith, and embraced it as my own, when I was quite young. Through adolescence and my young adult years, I experienced a soul-shaping love for God and a deeply spiritual life. I felt safe with like-minded friends and admired those who appeared to have an undaunted faith and continual joy. As a reflective person, I was also subject to a skeptical inner voice. Some of the doctrines and practices of my faith didn't seem to align with my own life experience, or of those I paid close attention to. I was a quiet skeptic, trying to embrace the beliefs of the people I admired. So, even though my faith satisfied a core spiritual longing, I lived it with some apprehension. I was afraid of rejection for my hesitancy to accept the common views of respected Christian leaders. In my faith experience, there was obvious paradox, complexity and wonder. Without really identifying it, I wrestled with the certainty in traditional Christianity. If I'd known a leader who could have affirmed my sense of wonder and a bigger lens for truth in my younger years, I might not have felt so alone.

During my stay-at-home mom years, the women's Bible study at my 2000-member church became the center of my social and spiritual connection. A friend asked me to lead a study group, even though I'd never been a regular group member, and I didn't have much experience studying the Bible. It turned out that I could lead Bible study without actually studying the Bible because our group of young moms would happily spend our small group time sharing prayer requests and personal stories. We talked through our marital, parenting, and mental health struggles, as well as our extended family dynamics. It was a mom/wife support group of sorts, more than a study of the Bible.

In year two, I wanted to be a more responsible leader, so I decided to take the study part more seriously. For hours each week, I dedicated myself to reading passages, examining commentary, and taking notes. I did this late at night, after the kids went to bed. Up until that time, I had found reading the Bible quite boring and confusing. Several weeks into a deep dive into the Book of Matthew, my spirit stirred in a way I'd never experienced before. The characters became human. The women seemed familiar. Stories prompted my curiosity, and I spent extra time connecting dots from the Old Testament to the New, from one gospel to another. I passionately shared my revelations with the study group, a fresh way of thinking about tired teachings. An attitude of wonder made me curious and kept me engaged about prominent passages I'd heard preached a dozen times.

My enthusiasm got noticed by the church's leadership. I was invited to write study notes for the other leaders. My church wrote their own curriculum, mostly for our women's groups. In addition, a handful of churches around the country purchased our materials for their women's groups. After six months of leading the Bible study, I was asked to join the 25-member curriculum writing team. Even more flattering, I was also invited to join the pre-writing team, a six-person core team of exceedingly bright women who generated an outline for the writers to follow during the summer-long process of curriculum development.

After my first meeting, I just about quit. Driving home, I was certain the other women had made a mistake and would soon realize I wasn't cut out for Bible study curriculum writing. Memories of my younger days of academic mediocrity overwhelmed any enthusiasm I had about studying the Scriptures with the church leaders I admired. But I didn't quit. And, one step at a time, I learned how to study well. After a thorough reading of the text, I learned to observe the details, cross reference and cautiously interpret, and tested out my theories with careful consideration of the words on the page and commentary by others. Through this method, I grew to delight in observations that invited mystery instead of assumptions. I noticed how often God's response to the questions from a struggling human heart rarely brought clarity. There were so many unanswered questions. Those stories brought me comfort.

When I was asked to teach for the first time, we were studying Ecclesiastes. Most of the women in my small group disliked the book, but they liked each other, so they kept coming back. It's understandable. The book begins with words of King Solomon, who declares, "Meaningless! Meaningless! Utterly meaningless! Everything is meaningless!" I loved it.

To me, the reflections of King Solomon at the end of his opulent life were real and raw and honest. I find that life mimics the stories and teachings of the Scriptures, and not only for those who share my faith tradition. Like Abraham, we need a place to belong. Like David, we can be unrestrainedly good and recklessly passionate. And like Solomon, we can find emptiness in a life of folly, and deep satisfaction in a life of purpose, compassion and friendship. "I hated life because the work that is done under the sun was grievous to me. All of it is meaningless, a chasing after the wind." (Ecclesiastes 2:7) Solomon found the human heart needs to grieve just as much as it needs laughter, and this passage put words to my experience as a human.

When we studied Ecclesiastes, I spoke from my heart at a podium on a small stage in a large room for a full 25 minutes, wondering if someone there might object to my words. But the women were attentive, and the buzz of sharing new insights added energy to my delivery.

My church gave me a voice and supported me as I learned to use it. Yet I also found myself disturbed by the overly-controlled nature of the church dialogue. I questioned commonplace assumptions about God. We hear things like: "God is in control" "God won't give me more than I can handle." "I guess God gave me this trial because he wanted me to learn something." Every time I heard another platitude about the nature of our suffering and healing, a quiet speculation lingered. I wished others would wonder with me, rather than conclude God's intention had certainty. The rules, political positioning and too-easy assurances left me feeling restless and resentful. I wrestled. I wanted to be accepted, to be spiritually mature, but my ideas were often at odds with the teachings of the other leaders.

I am quiet and small and I have good manners. The thought of stirring up controversy is mildly traumatizing to me. But my internal dialogue had an aggressive side too. A shout-out- loud sort of conviction. I toned it down and tried to be content. But I wasn't. I longed for a deeper life.

I was 40 when Sam's cancer showed up. The stay-at-home mom phase had lasted much longer than I had expected or intended. At the time, I was beyond eager to get back to my career as an occupational therapist, but I didn't quite know how to make the transition. Not when my family and my church community still expected me to fulfill certain roles.

My days were becoming increasingly unsatisfying. I cried more and smiled less when my hours were filled with endlessly mundane household chores. I needed to grow outside of the church. My spirit needed room to breathe and to engage with the world in interesting ways. I wanted to do more and talk less because contemplation and discussion are incomplete without some sort of engagement, and the world around me was suffering while I went to Bible study. I struggled to find contentment in life, then struggled with guilt about not being content. I had such a nice family in a comfortable, safe neighborhood and friends I could trust and have fun with, but my daily yearning for something bigger needed more than a tidy home and a gratitude journal.

Just before I turned 40, I stepped into a volunteer role as an advocate for sexual assault survivors. I took midnight calls from hurting women in fear of their perpetrators, and distraught girls who woke up on a stranger's couch to discover they weren't wearing pants and had no memory of what had happened to them. I was sometimes called to the hospital to sit with a young woman as she endured a forensic rape exam. I answered their questions, I fetched warm blankets, I held their hand during the painful parts and I stood by them while the police officer asked uncomfortable questions. I was expertly trained, yet continually afraid of letting these women down when they were at their most vulnerable.

One particularly difficult hospital visit was with a patient who had autism. The medical staff repeatedly misunderstood her signs of distress. I tried to help her communicate her needs. A nurse gave her a shot while the patient was still standing, and then the nurse quickly left the room without a backward glance. I caught the young woman as she fainted, and still the nurse didn't look back. The work was emotional, and often dark, but somehow I finished my shifts with a greater sense of gratitude and sorrow than when I started. There was a sacredness in caring for another person in their hour of darkness that expanded the capacity of my heart.

Occupational therapy was the perfect profession for me. Before I was a parent, I helped kids with cerebral palsy, sensory processing disorder, or Down Syndrome. I loved to see them learn new skills through play and creativity. I believed I was good at this work: I was made for it, and I needed to return to it. After a few uncomfortable conversations with Bob, we both began to see how vitally important it was for me to go back to work. It would require cooperation. We'd need to navigate getting our kids to and from school and determine which one of us stayed home if one of them got sick. I wondered if Sam would be denied the attention he needed to grow up well. Though the bumps were inevitable, I sent out my resume and was soon hired at a highly regarded private therapy clinic, half-time.

By 40, I was a working, volunteering, Bible-teaching mom with a few hectic days I was sure to iron out in the next decade.

7
CONTEND

I f there were strategies for parenting a child with big ideas, strong negotiating skills, and a talent for verbal persuasion, I hadn't read the book. Even before he was diagnosed with cancer, Sam's notions about what he intended to achieve each day were much bigger than he was. After a quiet 30 minutes alone in his room, Sam would often propose a major building project, a large-scale community event, or an aspirational plan for humanity. "Hey, Mom! Can we build a giant catapult in the backyard?" I tried not to tell him no, because a yes bordered on lunacy. Ultimately, 95 percent of his big ideas resulted in disappointment.

Sam generated endless adventures within his own imagination. These episodes inside his mind were sort of like daydreaming, but different. He wasn't the kind of kid who would tune his teacher out while they taught math with jellybeans, or elucidated the foraging tactics of the African warthog. Sam was pretty good at paying attention when he needed to. His daydreaming was something else.

Sam called it going "deep in thought," which seemed to me like an appropriate term for child psychologists to use in a clinical evaluation of kids like Sam. *Sam is an eight-year-old boy with the ability to maintain a deep-in-thought state of mind for 30 minutes at a time.* At ages seven, eight, and nine, he went deep in thought on a regular basis. On long car rides or lazy afternoons, he could wander into an adventure crafted by his imagination, and then he would follow up with an inquiry into some grand plan sure to become an epic reality, and possibly a story for the local news.

Going deep in thought was an intentional leisure activity for Sam, in the same category as building a Lego Star Wars ship prepared for battle with quad laser cannons and a rear entry cockpit. He let the family know when he was going deep in thought, because an accidental disruption to his grand good-versus-evil story of childlike fantasy might bring on major disappointment and protest.

"Hey, you guys. I'm going deep in thought, so, could you not disturb me?" He would say from the back seat of the car on a long drive to his aunt's house. That little voice would yell from his room to make sure everyone could hear, "I'm goin' deep in thought!! Don't disturb me!" He was protective of his deep-in-thought episodes, and it made me smile every single time.

The results of the time he spent deep in thought ranged in content from placing himself in the center of a Marvel super hero saga, to starting the world's largest silly string fight.

"Mom, how old do you have to be to run for mayor?"

"Mom, I need you to buy me 80 D batteries and 40 light bulbs. I'm building something."

Once, he wanted to create a gym made of magnets. He thought people could come in and rent magnet shoes designed to repel the magnet floor, just like rental shoes at a bowling alley, so people could enter the magnet room to walk on air. There'd be music and obstacles and games to play. People would pay a lot of money to walk on air, and one day he would be rich. Even on the most difficult parenting days, I believed there was something remarkable about Sam's spirit. While I envied my friends with compliant kids who followed the rules and obeyed their parents, I suspected this deep thinking, boundary-pushing, idea-generating little boy of mine could be the kind of kid who would one day make a significant mark on this world.

After Sam was diagnosed with cancer, something changed. He hadn't yet started chemotherapy, but we were at the hospital day after day getting blood work or scans, and consulting with different doctors who offered us lots of information but no real answers. One day, as we were getting ready to head back to the hospital, he sat down on the bottom step of our tri-level's entryway with his new green school backpack on. He looked healthy and whole. He stared straight ahead without expression.

I watched him for a moment, and then asked, "Sam, are you doing okay?" He stood up and, with his head hanging low, walked right into me for a hug, his arms wrapped around my waist. He said with a shake in his voice, "You know the worst part of all this cancer stuff? Ever since it started, I haven't been able to go deep in thought." He started to cry quietly with just a few tears rolling down to his chin. I kissed him on the top of his head. He was suffering in ways I hadn't anticipated. I didn't know how to soften his reality.

Had he overheard the tearful phone calls to family, his pediatrician, or the specialists at the hospital? Did he sense the gravity of his illness when we talked with family or friends? Was he aware that Bob and I had been taking turns sitting on our bedroom floor with the door shut, crying? I had assumed he was distracted with the usual kid stuff. Dreaming big. Not worrying about what it was like to live with cancer.

Losing the ability to go deep-in-thought added a whole new dimension to the sadness and the fear. The cancer wasn't just a threat to Sam's life, it was also a threat to that persistent imaginative spirit that so beautifully defined him.

～

After all of the tests and scans and appointments with doctors, it was time to get started with chemotherapy. For these treatments, a port is surgically implanted. A port is a small disc-like device with a rubbery middle and a long thin tube, it's placed under the skin near the collarbone. The tube runs directly into a vein near the heart. Instead of poking a needle directly into a vein in an arm, a larger needle goes through the soft skin of the chest and into the squishy center of the device. Getting poked this way is called "accessing the port" and Sam would need to be accessed at least twice a week for the next nine months. This is how the nurses drew blood and administered anti-nausea medication, hydration, and chemotherapy for several days at a time.

As soon as the port was placed, my role as a mom morphed into a medical role, something for which I felt entirely unprepared. I had no training. There was no curriculum. I wasn't sure a mother's intuition would cut it.

"Will I have to get poked?" Sam began asking each time he had another appointment at the hospital.

I hated saying yes.

More of these mini traumas were needed to check the rest of his body for any signs of metastases, additional disease in his bone marrow, lymph nodes, lungs, or other bones. These tests determined whether he had a 75% chance of surviving or a 20% chance. Each little bit of information introduced the possibility of greater fear, or maybe a little bit of peace.

I carried a prescription of Ativan now, because after a couple of nights without sleep I called my doctor on his personal cell phone and told him, "Sam has cancer, and I can't eat or sleep." Ativan was for anxiety and those days when I might fall apart and not recover. Each new bit of information could dictate whether it was an Ativan day or not.

Sam was being brave, but three pokes in this one week recruited all the bravery he could muster, so, in clinic room number three, he turned to protest. The pale skinned nurse with cartoon scrubs on pulled out her age-appropriate tricks. For a nine-year-old boy, it was money. A one-dollar bill.

"I'll give you a dollar for every time you have to come in and get poked," she proposed. But a dollar didn't quite persuade him, because this kid who was newly diagnosed with cancer was receiving an influx of presents that could load up Santa's sleigh. Our home was filling up with Nerf guns, and baskets full of games he could play in the hospital while a giant cookie bouquet waited for grazers on our kitchen counter. Sam sat on the yellow, paper-covered exam table next to the story books written for much younger kids. He tossed the dollar back at the nurse and yelled, "You can keep your stupid dollar!"

Sam, we don't treat people like that, was the kind of thing I used to say. Now, I didn't know how to handle the situation and the absurdity of it all left me powerless. Tears dripped from his chin. Bob handed him some paper towel as comfortless as the room itself. I reached out to touch Sam on the crown of his head but he pulled away. I wanted to fix something. To make something better and to move past this awful moment and find relief. I wanted so much to give anything I possibly could to make this situation better for him. But my efforts didn't make anything better.

After being told that he would have to be held down if he didn't give consent, Sam finally agreed to be poked. He asked for more numbing cream and extra time to let it work. The nurse used the tiniest needle she had to insert a little Lidocaine just under the skin so the actual poke would not be felt. After a few more negotiations, the nurse rolled her tray of sterile tools nearer to Sam, to access his port. She held a large needle with one hand and felt for the port under his skin with the other. Sam held his breath, squeezed his eyes tight, and wrapped his fingers around my wrist. Thankfully, she accessed the port on the first try. Sam started to weep, hiding his face underneath his own elbow crease, still laying flat on the table. I rubbed my wrist where his fingernails had penetrated a layer of my skin. I wanted to hear him say, *Hey, that wasn't so bad.*

I didn't get anything I wanted that day.

The next time he needed to be poked was in the Nuclear Medicine Department in the basement of the main hospital. Nuclear medicine sounded very unsafe to me but we were at the mercy of a well-equipped hospital, so I figured I ought to trust them to inject Sam with the radioactive liquid needed for his full body bone scan. The test would determine if cancer had settled anywhere else in his body. The technician was kind and more personable than I thought a nuclear medicine technician would be, but she was not set up with the extra small needles for a child, so they called in a pediatric infusion nurse named Daisy. After 15 minutes waiting in another small room with no windows, Daisy showed up with a plastic fishing tackle box, decorated with Disney stickers. The box was full of needles, gloves, tubes for collecting blood, band-aids and such. Her name tag was also crowded with stickers. Daisies.

Daisy knew nothing of Sam's previous encounter with the nurse and the dollar bills, and I sensed no concern or caution from her. I, on the other hand, told myself to keep breathing deep and fake it through my new PTSD symptoms while my lungs tried to freeze as if it were time to take the fetal position under a table to hide from danger.

Daisy got herself set up for the poke. Sam lay down on the paper-covered bench while Daisy prepared the small needle for entry. He didn't protest. She placed her left index finger and thumb firmly on the skin over the port while hiding the needle from Sam's view. As she leaned in, Sam raised his hand up in front of her face like someone diverting traffic and said, "Wait a minute."

She pulled her needle away. I watched and wondered whether I should step in.

"Wait a minute." The world stood still for a moment. Then, as if he surrendered to the invasion *you may enter my body,* while insisting *but you will acknowledge my humanity first,* he took two deep breaths and closed his eyes. His body relaxed, reminiscent of our infant massage moments. He settled what was inside of him before allowing what needed to enter him. He then asked Daisy, "Can you count to three?"

"Of course." She counted, slowly and deliberately, and then pushed the needle through Sam's skin directly into that newly inserted port.

A brief and mild response came out of his mouth with a wide-eyed expression. "Ah!" It was done. Once again, he had a needle in his chest, connected to a tube inside his body, traveling down a vein near his heart. The outside world of cancer infiltrated Sam's body just as he seemed to contend with the cancer growing inside him.

Each day was its own dark passageway into the endless underground maze called childhood cancer. If only we could peer down the pathway to see what was coming next, Sam could choose his approach. Like setting eyes on an obstacle course before tackling it, or reading the trail notes before a wilderness hike. Like scouting out the rapids before taking the journey in a raft. If only he could see the path ahead, he could navigate his way forward thoughtfully, with some semblance of control. Instead, we had to go about it blind, and tend to his bumps and bruises along the way.

Every port access needs to be deaccessed. After his tests, we were sent back to the pediatric oncology clinic to have the needle in his chest removed. This time, Sam was attended to by a less compassionate nurse. She spoke fast and didn't make eye contact with either one of us.

She placed her purple gloves on Sam's chest while he was visibly upset. "Here's how I do it," she announced, "One, two, three – out!" She tugged the needle out of Sam's chest and dropped it onto the metal tray – clink! And quickly taped a cotton ball to the open sore to stop the dribble of blood. Sam turned pale. His eyes went wide. He sat up on the exam table, crinkling the paper underneath. One hand grasped his throat, the other pressed his chest.

"Sam, are you okay?" I reached for him.

"I can't breathe," he gasped. "My throat feels tight." Tearful, he locked his gaze on mine. With urgency I looked to the nurse, who piped up blithely, "He'll be ok. It gets easier." I wanted to grab her by the hair and shove her out of our room.

Sam struggled to breathe. Several seconds went by. I wondered if I should push that big blue button on the wall to prompt a hospital-wide announcement, 'Code Blue in Room 6.' The nurse kept assuring me that he was just fine. Finally, Sam dropped his gaze, fixating on the white square tiles on the floor and managed to take a deeper breath.

When my own adrenaline rush subsided, I realized Sam had experienced a panic attack.

Over the next few days, I wondered if his unfortunate mistreatment by an inconsiderate nurse signaled the beginning of a chronic anxiety response to the unrelenting medical procedures. But I could also see that quietly, inside his mind, a new kind of strength was waking up. It was a grown-up strength, meant to emerge at a much later time in life. I wished he could take my grown-up strength. I wished he could endure this world like a naïve bear cub unaware of the dangers while his mom became ferocious, protecting him from all kinds of threat and hardship. But, there was no such opportunity to shield my boy from his terrible world. I could only be near him while he endured it. So, just like with nurse Daisy, Sam found his grown-up strength and began plotting his navigation plan. First, he needed to convince the nurses he was capable of doing their job.

Cancer kids are treated on the 10th floor where the hallway outside the unit looks toward the city. Inside the double doors you have to wash your hands, sign your name, and confirm you don't have a cough or a runny nose because bald kids with weak immune systems live in rooms with signs that say things like *Isolation Protocol* and *Nothing By Mouth*. You can't see the city from the inpatient rooms. Nurse Jill set Sam up for his first chemotherapy in Room 13. She radiated warmth and was easy to talk to. She educated us on the symptoms and the risks, and when to push the call button, or grab the bucket before puking. She explained how the drugs used for his chemotherapy were so toxic that any contact with Sam's bodily fluids – his vomit, blood or urine – might burn our skin. Most importantly for Sam, Jill taught us how to access the video games on the screen of the TV in the room.

After the set-up, Sam had two days straight of his chemotherapy, with Jill as his day nurse and Erin as his night nurse. He stared at a television, threw up, nibbled on saltines, and slept. When visitors came, he sometimes got out of bed to wander down the hallway, rolling the wheeled stand that carried IV bags of chemo and fluids. I followed him closely, worried if he moved too quickly, he might rip a tube out of the port in his chest. When I mentioned this, he became agitated and spoke loudly.

Jill was back on shift when Sam was ready to be discharged at the end of this round of chemotherapy. In addition to packing, and a final review of the paperwork, Sam had to be de-accessed from his port. Jill, in purple gloves, reached for some sterile gauze. Sam asked, "Hey, can I take this thing out myself?"

Bob said, "Sam, just let Nurse Jill take care of it for you."

Jill thought for a moment and said, "Sure you can, Sam." She walked Sam through the steps of peeling off the clear sticky patch which kept the device close to his chest. He winced but kept at it, moving at his own pace. Jill chatted as he peeled a centimeter at a time. Once the sticky sheet was finally removed, she showed Sam how to use two fingers to put pressure on his skin when the needle came out. His other fingers had to grab the butterfly wings on the device just right, to ensure the needle would retract as soon as it left his body. Sam pursed his lips and plucked the device from his chest. Jill intervened with gauze to catch a drop of blood. She discarded the stained gauze, and then added a bandage to the wound.

From that day on, Sam deaccessed his own port every single time.

8

A YOGA MAT

Like many other words and phrases lightly tossed around by the general population of non-cancer-fighting humans, self-care meant something different than it had before Sam's diagnosis and treatment.

Before cancer, self-care meant staying fit, getting a pedicure, and a good night's sleep. I considered myself a runner, which means I ran between two and five miles on a regular basis. I signed up for a few fun runs; I ran the 12-person, 199-mile Hood to Coast Relay a couple of times, and once I ran a half marathon. (My friend and I tied for third place in our age group, which was a thrill even though there was no fourth place.) I ran because I wanted to stay fit, and to my surprise those fun runs were actually quite fun.

I've always admired endurance athletes. Their strength and body structure is attractive to me; the way they stand strong with their hands on those slight graceful hips with no sign of squish between their small bones, slender upper body and solid legs. The physical and mental strength of endurance runners was something I coveted more than any other type of athlete. My small narrow frame might give the impression that I am fast. but

I lacked the internal drive to run for the sake of running, which made me feel disappointed in myself.

Real runners need to run. They crave it. There is a difference between a runner and a person who runs. I wanted to be a runner, but I was sort of faking it. When Sam got cancer, I quit running because the extra dose of energy needed to move through those two to five miles of pavement had been siphoned right out of me, and I stopped caring about being a runner.

A couple of weeks into Sam's treatment, his pediatrician called me to check in. I took my phone to the empty spare bedroom and shut the door. I spoke softly. Folded into a ball on the carpet floor my hollow, empty abdomen rested on my thigh. His voice was soft and intentional.

"Are you taking care of yourself?" he asked. I expected questions about Sam, not about me. I said nothing for a moment. It was as if the doctor had asked me if I was planning a fancy family vacation to Tahiti while my son was in treatment for cancer.

"Umm, well, I got some medication to help me sleep. I guess so." It mattered to me that he cared, but that was all I had to say.

Taking care of myself had not made it to the newly drafted to-do list, along with learning medical terminology, managing a detailed medication chart, or devising an adapted education plan to keep Sam from failing the third grade. I thought of nothing other than caring for Sam. The only addition to my list of Sam-centric tasks was Natalie, which especially in those first few weeks I rarely executed well.

Bob and I made sure Natalie was cared for by people she enjoyed while we were at the hospital. Sixth grade seemed too young for her to have a phone yet, but communication was key, so we got what became known as the Family Phone. We kept it in a drawer in the kitchen so that when Natalie went to bed she wouldn't be tempted to text inappropriate things to boys, a thing we had heard could happen. The Family Phone was pink.

Natalie hung out with friends who went to church and sang

High School Musical songs at weekend slumber parties. She had adults in her life who gave her hugs and made her laugh, and she demanded little. I managed to make it to her soccer games and Back-To-School nights, but I was anxious around other parents who didn't know how to talk to me. I had no desire to talk to them.

I used to be the quiet, unassuming type. I used to be the person people had to meet five times before they remembered they'd met me before. Now, at community gatherings I felt the other parents were whispering about me, the mom whose son has cancer. I didn't like that. I tried my best to be fully present, but meanwhile my brain was screaming at me to get back to the den because one of my cubs was in danger. I didn't know what *taking care of myself* meant, or how I could possibly prioritize it. The concept of stepping away from Sam while he endured the brutality of childhood cancer treatment to pamper myself or indulge in any way seemed impossible to do without disabling guilt.

"You'll be stronger for Sam if you are able to take care of yourself," the doctor nudged. Though I respected this man, and his wisdom and concern, I didn't want to take care of myself. What's more, I had no idea where to begin. Should I get a massage? Buy more vitamins? Get my hair done? I wasn't interested in going out with my girlfriends for a glass of wine. I was far from wanting to talk through what was happening, or how my heart was handling it, or how my spiritual life was taking shape in the midst of this traumatic event. I didn't understand how self-care could, or should, be a priority.

A few weeks into Sam's treatment, I started to get a sense of what caring for him would require. I learned the names of the different chemotherapies and corroborated with the nurses on how to dose his anti-nausea meds. I developed routines and even a wardrobe, with sweatpants that doubled as pajamas and slippers that doubled as shoes for our multi-day hospital stays. My morning coffee came from the Starbucks in the lobby along with a bacon, egg, and gouda biscuit. I found the small health food market on the ninth floor of the main hospital, and the cafeteria on the third floor, and I figured out how to take the stairs to avoid people on an elevator. I helped myself to warm blankets and fresh sheets behind the curtain in the hallway and I hit the silence button on Sam's drip pole when it started to beep. On Wednesdays, Sam played Bingo and on Thursdays at 6pm the cancer support non-profit provided us spaghetti and a Caesar salad in the recreation room. Saturdays were for watching football games and engaging with visitors who came to play Uno and Spot-It at the foot of Sam's hospital bed when he was comfortably doped up and hydrated. I got a handle on the routine of a mother whose son has cancer. That's when I considered self-care.

Yoga was attractive to me, a little bit like endurance running. I had never tried yoga and believed I lacked the flexibility to do it well, so it was one of those things I admired from afar. I avoided the risk of embarrassment that came with entering a yoga studio with zero experience. I decided to try a class at the neighborhood athletic club where we were members. I wore running shorts, and my favorite running shirt: white, with the cap sleeves and blue trim. All the other women in the class wore yoga tights and tank tops that didn't expose their bellies in the upside-down poses. I had set my mat down near the door in case I decided to ditch.

It wasn't horrible.

My hamstrings were tight, and the instructor seemed to focus on stretches that challenged me, instead of the ones that might impress anyone glancing my way. I disliked downward facing dog and hoped that was a pose they only did on occasion in case I decided to go back. At one point during the class, we faced the mirror wall in a lunge with our hands in the air, and while I looked straight at my own reflection to determine whether I appeared embarrassingly unyogi-like, I noticed a tag sticking out of the seam under the armpit of my shirt. *Oh shit.* My shirt was inside out, and the tag was one of those huge ones with multiple layers of washing instructions in five different languages. I held the pose and kept a straight face, but in the mirror, I scanned all the other faces in the room to see if anyone was staring at me, the inflexible newbie with the odd choice of clothes worn inside out.

A few days later, I was able to laugh with my friends John and Staci about my embarrassing introduction to yoga. I thought maybe a good laugh at myself every once in a while was an adequate approach to the topic of taking care of myself.

"Lorna, I do yoga on Sundays with Joan," John offered.

"You do yoga?" John didn't strike me as the yoga type of guy.

"I think you'd like her."

I bought some yoga pants at a discount store and arrived at Joan's yoga class the following Sunday afternoon. She was in her 60's and she had long, glossy-brown hair she wore up in a twisty bun with an artsy accessory. She had a tattoo of the Pi sign on her forearm. She was lovely. Small and thin with lean muscles and a flat stomach, she wore black yoga tights and a burgundy camisole like a dancer. She exuded elegance in the simplest of clothes.

Unlike endurance runners, Joan emanated peace instead of drive. She was graceful in the space while students entered the room with their mats, slipping their shoes off at the door and settling into a spot on the golden hardwood floor. Sunlight shone through the skylights above, warming the room. Joan greeted every person by name. She spoke to each with soft compassion as if each and every one arrived to yoga carrying some pain.

John introduced me. "Joan, this is my friend Lorna."

"Lorna." She repeated as if to slide my name carefully into her memory. "I'm so glad you are joining us today." The way she said it, I believed her.

Joan moved us into our asanas slowly and with clear, careful instruction. She blended the meditative flow of yoga with the precision of posture and breath, reminding our bodies we were meant to move with grace and strength. She affirmed her yogis throughout the class. "Oh, that's beautiful John. Yes, Cecilia, that's lovely. Sally, you're so graceful!"

"Lorna, that's beautiful." While Joan affirmed me, a touch of emotion swelled with my breath. For a few moments, I was attentive to my own body, my own tender soul. I noticed how this way of moving, breathing and being might serve to replenish my terribly impoverished spirit. In our final resting pose, tears started to fall from my eyes.

The safety and kindness of Joan's class lured me back. I needed more. My anxiety about being awkward and less than flexible subsided as I began to encounter a sense of belonging. Within a few months, I was attending multiple yoga classes at the club, and another at a different studio on Wednesday nights. I bought more tights and lightweight tank tops and I ordered my own pretty blue mat.

Yoga has its health benefits like stress reduction, improved sleep, strength, flexibility, and posture, all of which I needed now more than ever while dealing with the tumultuous realities of childhood cancer. But what surprised and nurtured me the most was how my time on my mat brought me back to myself. Like Joan caring for her yogis, I could tend to my own hurting soul with compassion.

Life had become dizzy. I lost myself. Like a child being dragged into one of those scary, spinning amusement park rides, I became disoriented. The well-defined roles I had previously invested in fell away - occupational therapist, volunteer advocate, humanitarian - everything that defined me became irrelevant as I was pulled into this other worldly reality where sick kids turn bald from their medicine. In yoga, I found the self I had lost. In the space and time and centering movement of yoga, I started to feel more kindness toward my own heart: *Ah, there you are.*

My favorite yoga teachers are strong and graceful. They lead us through asanas that also emulate our own inner and outer strength and grace. I love this about yoga. While many of my days were consumed with chemo vomit and restless nights and worry over Sam's spirit, his suffering and his survival, yoga reminded me that my kids needed a mom who could advocate for them and be present regardless of the circumstances. There is something about holding a pose. It made me want to embody an ideal of calm as I walked through the difficult days.

I settled into my downward dog pose. I craved the deep breaths that accompany a full sun salutation. I could create my warrior with confidence. I evolved.

Some poses are hard for me. Revolved half-moon reminds me that I am limited, awkward, and weak. I have so much room to grow. Other poses, like side crow, I can come close to mastering, while much of the class took a rest instead. I wondered, what else am I capable of? Good yoga teachers give their students freedom to flow with some individuality. They say, "Find *your* down dog." Or, "Take *your* vinyasa." I needed to find *my* best way of being me, even through the shadowy cold path ahead.

"I won't let cancer define me," is a phrase I began to hear more regularly. Though it's usually about the cancer patient, I was wrestling with being defined by my role as a cancer mom. Cancer is often spoken of as an enemy that evokes fighting language and a disgust for how it invades the flesh and soul of beautiful humans. A resistance to how it might succeed in creating a path of devastation rises out of the trauma. *Cancer will not win. Cancer will not define me.* But if resistance to being defined by cancer required more internal resources than I cared to muster, I just might let cancer define me. Not all identities are ones we choose. I could be a cancer mom, and I could do my best to fulfill that role with the kind of love, presence, advocacy, determination, and strength my son deserved.

After several weeks in Joan's class, I told her that my son was sick with cancer. She sighed and embraced me in the way only another grieving mom knows how. She shared that her own adult son had died four years earlier from a drug overdose. The Pi tattoo on her forearm was a symbol of his nickname. She still carried sorrow with her every day, but she lived with grace and strength. I thought deep down in the places I only give myself access to, if someday I lose Sam, maybe I'll be able to live with grace and strength like Joan.

9
SURGERY

Sam had surgery to remove his tumor and a portion of his left fibula. It was a damp January day, typical of Oregon winters. Bob and I were called back to the recovery room after Sam had been awake for a good 30 minutes. Sam lay on his side with an oxygen mask loose around his face. His eyes closed and his cheeks flushed. He was groaning.

"Hey, sweetheart, we're right here." I placed my hand gently on his arm and kissed his bald head. Even his eyelashes were gone now. The nurse told us he was doing great, but that was clearly a clinical assessment; she wasn't talking about how he felt. Her eyes moved back and forth from Sam to the patient monitor listing numbers in green, red, and blue colors next to their waveform lines recording heart rate, oxygen and blood pressure. She entered information into another screen in front of her and checked the bags of fluid and tubes leading to Sam's port.

"Hey Sam?"

"What!" He mustered an irritable response, his voice raspy from being intubated.

"On a scale of one to ten, what number is your pain at?"

"Fourteen!" Sam groaned.

We'd been told bone surgery is painful. Morphine couldn't reach that pain. Heavier drugs were needed. We expected this to be his only experience with pain that surpassed the one-to-ten scale.

Sam spent three dark and sluggish days in the inpatient surgery unit. He lay in a hospital bed, and he resisted the physical therapy exercise required to maintain mobility in his knee. No one told us how important it is to take deep breaths and keep the lungs clear after surgery, and Sam developed an infection and a high fever in the middle of the night.

When day three came, Dr. Harvey visited. He asked Sam to flex his foot at the ankle. The ankle didn't move. The surgery had caused some nerve damage, and the muscles needed to lift his foot weren't getting the message. This is called *drop foot*. While this condition can be permanent, we hoped it would fully resolve as the nerve healed over time. Sam was discharged with a child-sized dose of narcotics, a walker, and an orthotic boot to keep his ankle at 90 degrees. Recovering at home, he moved from the couch to his bed and back again for several more days. The mood in our home was as somber as the cloudy dark wintry skies over our heads. Sam remained sedentary, until a can of Silly String and a break in the clouds motivated an outing to the backyard with Cedar, who needed to engage his inner racehorse. I called those days *turn the corner days* - when the pain medications could decrease, or when Sam could finally keep some food down, or when he could leave the house to be with friends. They were a clear and substantial step toward recovery, and I didn't realize then how familiar those *turn the corner days* would become.

Ten days after surgery, Bob and I took Sam to his follow-up visit. I was anxious for an optimistic prognosis for his foot. If the news wasn't good, I hoped Dr. Harvey had a plan to fix it.

Instead of addressing the issue of drop foot, Dr. Harvey shared, "I've got some bad news. Sam's tumor is unusual." He explained how normal Ewing tumors deflate like a balloon with chemotherapy. A sarcoma surgery should remove the tumor, plus a layer of tissue around the tumor that has absolutely no cancer in it. That section of normal tissue is called the margin. However, as it got smaller, Sam's tumor developed spikes on the outer edge that invaded what was thought to be a clean margin. Without a clean margin, the cancer would likely grow again, in the same place it first took root.

"It's very likely there are still some live cancer cells in his leg. I'm sorry this isn't what you were expecting to hear."

I was only prepared to talk about the drop foot. I had dared to wonder if it would never resolve, and Sam would have to live with impairment. But this was a different discussion.

The doctor gave us three choices: Wait and see if the remaining rounds of chemo would kill the rogue cancer cells. Or, add radiation to his regimen. Or, amputate.

The room filled with a long gentle pause. The demands of the situation before us caught up with our racing hearts and minds. We talked about the options until we had no more questions to ask.

Dr. Harvey explained that radiation could cause the knee to become stiff, making it difficult for Sam to run or play sports. Doing nothing was the greatest cancer risk, but he would still have a functioning leg. We would then resume the drop foot conversation. We acknowledged that amputation presented the best option for getting rid of every cancer cell in his leg. Since Sam's tumor grew so close to his knee, the doctor wasn't certain whether he could save enough of the leg for a below knee amputation (BKA). A BKA allows for much better mobility than an above knee amputation. Dr. Harvey walked us through the functional outcomes of amputation, and the options for prosthetic legs with a good chance of near normal mobility.

"You can hardly tell someone has an amputation if it's below the knee. But it's going to be difficult." He talked about the possibility of Sam having a surgery called rotationplasty, which would reattach his ankle, heel, and foot to his femur, rotated around so that his heel would become a knee, and his foot would slide into a prosthesis. He was hopeful that a BKA would work instead, but the more dramatic option was still on the table. We had 48 hours to think it over.

Whether or not to amputate. The question turned my skin cold.

On the way home from the appointment, the unthinkable started to creep closer to reality. I began to realize it was Sam's best chance. But it was Bob who said it out loud. While Sam gazed out the window listening to music on headphones, Bob whispered, "I think we can survive without Sam's leg, as long as we get to keep Sam."

We didn't have to convince Sam. He agreed, amputation would most likely save his life. The next day, we called Dr. Harvey and told him of our decision.

Once the decision was made, Sam withdrew. He stayed in his room with the door shut, playing on his handheld screen or zoning out in front of the TV. He talked about it briefly and cried a little, but then he disengaged.

"I'm sorry I'm so irritable," he said, which only made me sadder. He shouldn't have to apologize for feeling angry about losing his leg. Every moment hurt. Our home felt like a dark movie on replay. We ached for some exposure to the light but there was no light to be found.

One afternoon while sitting in front of the TV, I passed by the recliner holding Sam, wrapped in a blanket pulled up to his nose. I put my hand on his head. He ducked and pulled away.

I said, "Hey, there. Is there anything I can do for you?"

"No! I just want everyone to leave me alone!" He pulled the blanket over his head.

"Hey, Sam, I'm just trying to help."

He peeked out from under his blanket with a scowl that both frightened me and compressed my heart. Sam was burdened with the kind of despair I couldn't soften with a kiss, an ice cream cone, or extra screen time. This wasn't the expression of a kid protesting what he believed to be an unfair punishment, or when he lost a soccer game, or became jealous because Natalie had something he wanted. It was an expression of a deeper, more profound struggle that wandered far beyond the boundaries of childhood grievances. A storm was brewing within his nine-year-old soul.

He erupted, "I'll never get to play sports with my friends again! I'll never be able to run with a wooden knee!" His words were thrown at me with as much force as his voice could access. But when he finally put words to everything he'd been holding in for three days, I understood his distorted perception. Now there was something I could do for him.

"Oh, Sam." I knelt down next to him. "You're not going to have a wooden knee." His eyes turned red with big tears. "Dr. Harvey thinks you can keep your knee. I don't really know exactly what it's going to be like, but I'm pretty sure you'll be able to run with your friends again." I reached out to him until he pulled away, which hurt a little because I wanted to be the one to make it better. I left the living room to give him space, and paced the kitchen.

Later, on the couch, I opened up my new white Apple MacBook. This was my first laptop. It made me feel smarter and more resourceful, like I had access to an immense library of resources, and it was just a matter of plunging in to eventually find the know-how that would change everything. There must be something inside the world of Google to give Sam hope.

And me.

I needed hope like I needed air. The difference between hope and air is you can stay alive without hope. The heart will keep beating and the organs will continue to do their work. Physiology allows for a hopeless existence. But, without hope, I'm not sure I would care to endure.

～

I googled *amputee runners* and up popped images of a muscular brown skinned athlete. His name was Marlon Shirley. A few clicks took me to the story of this Paralympic Gold Medalist in the 100 meter sprint. Google pointed me to a YouTube video, and within a few seconds my heartbeat grew lively.

"Here's my message to the world's fastest sprinters," Shirley taunted. "Watch out, 'cause I'm catchin' up," the athlete said to the camera from a dark lit room, with a voice unafraid to challenge his non-disabled peers. A heavy beat of the music intensified the video clip of this athlete densely muscled except for his foot: a striking metal blade I later learned was called a Cheetah Leg.

After watching the full four minutes twice, I went downstairs to tell Sam that I had found a cool video. I invited him to sit down on the couch beside me. Sam drew closer to see what was on the screen. I resisted bending down to kiss his bald head but it was so very tempting. I soaked in those four minutes of nearness and hope. We watched the video several times while his expression became brighter. His eyes widened. I could see and feel his mindset change. Within minutes, Sam started talking about himself in a new way. He asked if he could get a leg like Marlon Shirley's, and a personal coach and one of those parachutes that athletes run with to create resistance so they can become "really super strong and fast."

"One day I'm going to have one of those Cheetah Legs and I'm going to run even faster than all of my friends." Sam talked big, and I let him. I asked myself whether I should temper his expectations, whether it was good parenting to let him get his hopes up. But that hope changed everything, and I needed it too. Over the next few days, Sam stopped hiding under the blanket. He engaged with us again.

A few days later I heard him say, "Hey guys, I'm going deep in thought. Don't disturb me."

10

AMPUTATION

When the kids were five and three, I took them to a photography studio in their denim jeans and pastel shirts. Orange was a good color for Sam (and easy to spot him in when he went rogue) so I dressed him in a light orange polo shirt. Natalie wore a deep pink shirt with puffed shoulders. It wasn't until I had a daughter that I began to love pink. She had flowers embroidered on the cuffs of her jeans. They looked so clean and sweet. Inside the small studio surrounded by props and backdrops, I removed their bright white sneakers and socks to expose their expressive little toes for the photos.

It was one of those days when they got silly with each other. They ignored my direction, and every trick in the photographer's bag. I started to sweat and my voice had an edge. I worried this was a waste of money. Luckily, the photographer was ready for the spontaneous when my kids both dropped to the hardwood floor, Natalie in a crisscrossed leg position and Sam following her lead. Still giggling, Sam wrapped his arms around her bent legs and snuggled his head into her lap. Natalie folded over him like a chunky soft sweater. Sam closed his eyes with a smile while Natalie looked right into the camera, her ocean blue eyes sparkling, her dimples pronounced and cheerful. Tangled up together, collapsed over their happy little feet, the perfect photo revealed itself. The photographer then snapped the photo that to this day remains in its frame on my bedroom dresser.

Photos of my kids were rarely snapped in pre-set poses. Any directions about how to sit or stand, or where to put their hands and feet, were fully ignored for the greater delight of climbing and dancing and making funny faces. One thing was consistent: Natalie's attentiveness to her brother. She was always ready to match his energy when he popped up with delight to engage with the world.

I'd dress them in hand knit sweaters made by my mom and march them someplace outdoorsy for a DIY photo shoot in the late afternoon light.

"I want Sam to sit at the top of the slide with Natalie right behind, like you're going to slide down together." They ignored me.

"Natalie, stretch out on the grass. Sam, lay down next to her with your feet in the air." I should have brought jelly beans.

Sam would make a face and Natalie would laugh at him - click.

Sam spotted a farm animal and Natalie took his hand - click.

Sam sang a silly song and Natalie put her arm around his neck to sing along - click.

In every shot Natalie is leaning into Sam's exuberance, which he absorbed as part of his own orbit.

When Sam got sick with cancer, Natalie fled. Before Sam's diagnosis, she was a self-contained kid, easily contented, and rarely anxious. She found out her little brother had cancer during the first week of middle school. When Sam's days and nights became prone to throwing up, bad dreams, and a groggy sort of existence, something changed in Natalie, too.

Natalie loves happiness. She flocks to the fun. She fabricates jokes to cheer the downhearted. I tried to hide it but I'm certain she was aware of the times I was alone in my room with the door closed, sorrow dominating my heart, and hindered me from being fully present for her. When Sam started suffering from the effects of chemotherapy, she requested more afternoon and overnight visits to her friends. I was sad, but I realized Natalie needed a place where she could still enjoy freshly-baked cookies and a spontaneous dance party. Where no one was crying.

Vomit. Induced by Sam's chemotherapy. This bodily response distresses me so much, I'm uncomfortable typing the word. Natalie is the same. Some people, like oncology nurses, can deal with vomit just fine. Others are so repulsed we spend hours in recovery after witnessing someone losing their lunch. When she was anywhere near Sam throwing up, Natalie would tremble, and discomfort would overwhelm her.

She fully withdrew when Sam started carrying an emesis bag. She asked to sleep downstairs when she could hear his groans and coughs late at night on the days following chemotherapy. Natalie was losing her youthful sense of safety and peace. Then, we told her Sam would need to have his leg amputated.

Surgery was first scheduled for Valentine's Day. I tried not to think about how he would miss the frenzied fun of passing out superhero Valentine's cards with a candy heart attached. Instead, he was scheduled to have his leg amputated. But hope is adaptable, and I kept it in focus. By now I could hardly remember hoping for the drop foot situation to resolve. My new hope was focused on getting rid of all cancer cells, and saving Sam's knee.

Since Sam was still recovering from his last chemo, it was necessary to test his blood before surgery to see if his white cell count was high enough. Over time, the bone marrow gets tired of over-producing new blood cells on demand. Sure enough, his counts were still too low. Surgery was postponed.

That might sound like a good thing, allowing Sam to ambulate on two legs for as long as possible. But there is something deeply burdensome about anticipating an inevitable loss. Since Sam had turned the corner with his outlook, he wanted to get it over with and move forward. Heading into something terrible is sometimes more difficult than recovering from something terrible because recovery is where the work begins. We wanted to get the terrible over with. We were sad, worried, frustrated and afraid – and we were tired of being sad, worried, frustrated, and afraid.

Sam's surgery was rescheduled for March 4, 2011. On the CaringBridge web site, Sam's second grade teacher mentioned that it's the only day of the year that serves as a command - to *march forth*. But, how could Sam march forth with only one leg? I couldn't make sense of the irony at the time. It also seemed mysterious and meaningful: it was something to cling to, because belief in a deeper insight for what was happening helped me to find a way to exist in it.

On March 3, Sam's blood test results confirmed he was ready for the surgery. Instead of heading back to school for his last afternoon on two feet, we pulled his buddy Josh out of class for an hour of video gaming at the nickel arcade. I called my mom in Seattle, to give notice that she should begin the three-hour drive to Portland to be with Natalie. Mom arrived with a cookbook and grocery bags full of ingredients. "It's going to be all right," she said with watery eyes.

The next morning, my coffee pot began to gurgle. Surgery was scheduled for 7:30am. Bob and I were up at 5:00. Sam had to be out the door by 5:30am with nothing to eat or drink. He was still asleep. Sam wanted us to wake him just minutes before leaving so he wouldn't think about breakfast, and I wanted Natalie to sleep as long as possible on this impossible day.

I couldn't understand why Bob was talking so loudly while we fixed coffee and loaded the car. He asked me questions and gave directions like it was the middle of the day. I think Bob thought the kids would sleep through his loud voice the way they used to sleep through the vacuum cleaner when they were babies. We had this weird conversation where I didn't want to tell him to be quiet because we were already tense, so instead I exaggerated my quiet voice hoping he would get the hint.

"Did you pack Sam's iPad charger?" he asked in a vigorous voice. I whispered as if in church. "Yes."

"I'll put his backpack by the door for him." He continued, oblivious or oppositional to my hint that he should whisper. "I'll pack his blue blanket for him to have later today when he comes out of surgery." I nodded.

A bit more shuffling around the house with our awkward loud talker/quiet talker dialog, I heard Natalie shout from her bed. "Mom!? Moooom!" I rushed to her room, cussing inside my head. By this time, Sam was up and dressed, but Natalie was upset.

Since we were taking separate cars, Bob and Sam could leave without me, honoring Sam's wishes. Sam walked from his room to the front door with his green school backpack on. He made no eye contact and said nothing. He didn't whine or protest or cry. When Bob was ready, he and Sam walked to the car while I stayed back to be with Natalie.

I didn't want to miss anything. I wanted to be near Sam from the moment he walked into the hospital, and absorb the profoundly sad moments of his last few steps on his own two feet. But my sweet sad daughter was now awake and frightened too, and I needed to stay.

I sat at the edge of Natalie's bed and put my hand on her trembling chest. This had happened before, but only since Sam's diagnosis. She was weeping and shaking and holding her breath. I crawled into bed beside her and rested my hand on her heart.

"Take a deep breath." I whispered. "It's okay. It's going to be okay." I inhaled slowly and deeply, to encourage her to match her breath to mine. If only love expressed could lessen the pain.

"Breathe, breathe, breathe." Her trembling diminished and her whimpering subsided. I stayed with her until she was dozing back to sleep. Then, I crept out the door and headed for the hospital.

I drove through the darkness just before dawn. When I arrived, Sam had already been called back to the pre-op area. Each hospital bed was partitioned from the one next to it with a thin pale green wall. There were two chairs next to each bed for family members. In their beds with open curtains that offered little privacy, kids looked out with wide-eyed expressions. I wondered what they were in here for. A heart defect? A tonsillectomy? Tubes in their ears?

Then Dr. Harvey came in. He seemed confident and focused, as if he were the most alive just before the sun came up. Bob immediately informed him that Sam didn't want any small talk today. He said that sounded just fine to him. He wasn't really a small-talk kind of guy anyway. He examined Sam and put an X with a circle around it on his left leg, so he wouldn't accidentally remove the wrong one. I wondered if that had ever happened.

Despite my growing nausea, I got these words out: "Dr. Harvey, even if you don't find more live cancer cells in the follow-up biopsy, we're not going to regret this decision." He nodded, gazing down. "That is really good to hear you say," he replied, looking up at me with warm eyes. "We have no way to know if this is essential or not. But I think it's the safest thing to do."

After prepping Sam, a process that was painstakingly slow, the nurses and the anesthesiologist came to roll him away for surgery. We walked alongside his bed on wheels to the "kiss corner" where family members wave goodbye. Bob swiped his hand over Sam's head and gave him a peck on the forehead. "We love you, buddy. You've got this."

"I love you Sam. We'll see you when you wake up." My tears emerged as the words came out of my mouth.

"I love you guys, too." The anesthesiologist pushed the drugs through Sam's IV as they rolled him down the hallway to the OR. We watched until the double doors closed behind him.

We spent the next nine hours in the family room down the hall from the regular waiting room with friends. Pastors, family members, and the near-and-dear all showed up to spend time with us. They brought food and conversation to the interminable waiting and wondering. The distraction was good for both of us and I hardly wept at all.

As expected, the surgery was complicated. For Sam to keep his knee, they would have to take soft tissue from his foot and move it up to the space below his knee to provide padding for a prosthesis. This was called a flap, and they had brought in a specialist to do this. It took a multidisciplined, coordinated effort to save Sam's knee - and they did just that.

Dr. Harvey pulled us out of the waiting room to inform us that the hard part was over, and it went well. They were stitching him up and he would soon be sent to the recovery area. When Bob called Natalie, her teachers knew to let her out of class to take his call. "Hey sweetie. It went well! Sam did great. We just talked to the surgeon and he was really pleased." He gave her a few more details and then handed the phone to me.

"Are you doing okay?"

"Yeah. I'm okay."

"We'll let you know when he's out of surgery." I could hear her soft breathing on the other end of the line. My sad and brave girl. "Keep taking deep breaths, okay? "

"Okay. I will."

"I love you."

"Love you too." She put down the phone and went back to class.

11

A GLIMPSE

Whether they are asleep or awake, I have always had a compulsion to peek at my kids. My emotional well-being is dependent on their well-being. This may or may not be healthy for a parent. I think, *are they okay?* And I peek at them from around a corner to see signs of delight, if they're playing nicely, and being treated well. If so, I can also be happy and play nice.

I peeked in on them at preschool and elementary school when I had a reason to be there. I peeked at them in their church classrooms, and especially when they have friends over to the house. This necessity to sneak a peek became more obsessive after Sam was diagnosed with cancer. If Sam was unhappy, I was unhappy. But if I spotted him munching on potato chips in his hospital bed or laughing at the TV and joking with his dad, relief filled me up. My feelings followed his, which was not always good for him because his concern for me complicated his attempts to cope with his own situation.

I feared the first peek at Sam's amputation surgery. I was afraid of how I might react. I knew that he might be watching me as I looked at him. Even more so, I was afraid of what Sam would see when he had a first look at his leg.

A couple of hours post-surgery, I got a glimpse of Sam's heavily bandaged leg without a foot. For those two hours, his legs hid under layers of white hospital blankets. Bob and I stood by him in his recovery bed. My gaze was fixed mostly on his face. I warned my brain to keep my expression serene as I was exposed to the next visual. It might take me a minute to make sense of what I was seeing. I could faint or become lightheaded, or nauseous. I did my best to be ready for a moment no one can actually be prepared for.

My first view of his amputated leg happened accidentally during the transfer from his recovery bed to his hospital room bed. The nurses, skilled at this, couldn't help what happened next. The blanket shifted, and - despite my efforts to prepare - my body reacted with that autonomic response that felt like my stomach was trying to run away. My first glimpse of my son as an amputee left me mildly disoriented, as if suddenly I was living someone else's life. Sam didn't notice my reaction during the transfer. He needed a little more time to recover from the anesthesia and to settle into his new room. Then, without warning, he reached down to lift the blanket and see his new leg. I saw no signs of despair. His face was completely calm.

We were on the surgery floor, not the oncology floor, which felt a bit unfamiliar. The nurses came and went with their comforting aura and smiles. They tried to engage Sam in conversation, but Sam was still in the *I don't want to talk to anyone today* mode. He reached for the remote and turned on the TV. One nurse stood at the foot of Sam's bed, partially blocking the screen. Sam asked him, "Hey, can you please move?"

The nurse joked, "Do I make a better door than a window?"

Sam replied, "Actually, you make a better wall than a door." Sam was still Sam.

Sam's leg was amputated on a Friday. On Monday evening at 5:00pm, the surgeon came in to examine his work. It was the first time we would see Sam's amputated leg without the bandage.

The past three days had been focused on weaning him off his epidural and managing the pain, encouraging Sam to eat, and teaching him basic self-care. The layers of gauze were thick around the end of his leg, with extra padding in all the right places. The thick tight wrap created a nearly flat surface, like an elephant's foot hanging from his hip, an appendage with no apparent purpose. Sam called it his mini leg.

Dr. Harvey unwrapped his leg with a much less gingerly touch than I expected from a surgeon. I sat down by the window, afraid I might become lightheaded. To my surprise, as soon as the leg was exposed I took an almost clinical interest. I observed how my fascination with the human body could protect me and also help Sam. I rose from the window seat to cross the room and have a closer look.

The gauze was removed and discarded into a pile on Sam's bed. Dr. Harvey and Sam both leaned in to inspect the leg. The pink incision with traces of blood and evidence of the scalpel that cut through his skin looked sensitive and fragile. A long, clean swollen seam started on the inside of his leg just below the knee; then it traveled down and around the new tip of his leg, across the bottom and all the way up the outer edge, past his knee on the other side. Toward the tip, an ultra thin layer of skin about two inches in diameter was separated from the deeper skin layer creating a translucent bubble-like blister with clear fluid inside it.

"This fluid sac might get bigger and then pop in a day or two," said Dr. Harvey. "Don't worry about it, but you'll have to change the bandage right away when that happens. It will be wet and messy. Sam, you need to start straightening out your knee every day, and I want the bandage changed every day as well, ok?" He addressed Sam even though I was the one who would be changing the bandage.

"Hey, can I go home today?" Sam asked.

Bob remarked with a chuckle. "Sam, I think you're going to need a bit more time before you're ready to go home." He said it like, *isn't that cute, asking to go home just three days after his leg is amputated?*

Dr. Harvey asked Sam as if Bob and I weren't there. "Do you want to go home?"

"Oh! Yes! I do! Can I?" Sam begged.

"Well, since your drainage tube is out and you're not on a pain pump, I think you can."

"What?" Bob asked, "Doc, are you sure about that?"

"Kids heal better at home than they do in the hospital."

Sam interjected, "Mom! Can Josh come over tomorrow?"

The discharge process took most of the day. Late in the afternoon, we were packed and heading for the hospital door for the first time with our now-amputee son, crutches, a wheelchair, a bag of clothes, and a large paper bag full of medication and bandaging supplies, and, unwittingly, a hospital pillow. The crisp white pillowcase with the red inked stamp with the name of the hospital still floats around in our linen closet. Sam wheeled himself through the quiet hospital hallways in a clunky and heavy loaner wheelchair, rolling out ahead of us, pulling up the brake to check out its maneuverability and speed.

"Oh, Sam! Be careful." I winced and wondered if it was all right for me to allow him to be a bit reckless in the hospital. If a kid is going to get away with things, losing a leg does create opportunity for more lenient parenting. It was hard to say no to anything that made him smile.

We pulled up to the house just as the day began to turn dark.

Bob directed, "Sam, I'll carry you in and put you on the couch."

"No, I got it." Sam reacted. "Just hand me the crutches. I can do it."

I loved his determination, but feared the risk he was taking.

He had tried crutches once with the physical therapist. It was now nighttime. I figured he should first have a practice session at home, tomorrow at the earliest. Regardless, we handed him the crutches. Sam accepted them and carefully made his way to the front door while Bob and I hovered. In the dark. Sam moved slowly, and with some hesitation, like someone on roller skates for the first time. He skillfully mounted the first step to our front door. I darted ahead to open the door, still staying near to Sam ready to catch him if he lost his balance. But it was far from a well-coordinated entry plan.

I opened the front door wide and Sam squeezed past me. Just as he crossed the threshold to set down a foot on the entryway rug, his crutch caught on the lip of the door frame. Sam fell forward, instinctively putting his left leg out in front. His freshly amputated leg hit the ground first. Sam let out a violent scream. I dropped his bag and fell to the floor to comfort him.

"Okay, okay, okay." As I held him, I felt a hot surge of rage at no one in particular, because my son was in so much pain, and it was all so unfair and out of my control. We sat on the floor in the entry way for several minutes until Sam was able to move indoors to the couch.

I unwrapped the bandage from his leg to check for new damage, but even the clear liquid blister was still intact. I prepped his meds, prepared a snack for him and assembled a stack of pillows - including the stamped and stolen one - on his bed to offer maximum comfort for a good night's sleep. Once he was settled, I floated about the house, putting things away and starting laundry, while internally spewing a lengthy and profanity-filled rant, because I hated this fucking cancer more than I thought I was capable of hating anything.

12

SAM'S BACK

The day after Sam came home, he wanted to go to school. Our morning routine took three times as long as usual, so we arrived at school late in the morning with a clunky hospital wheelchair in tow.

I planned to stay and sit quietly in the back of the room, with Sam's consent. After a quick check in with the office ladies (aka his personal school nursing team,) he wheeled his way down the hall to his third-grade classroom. I realized the next few minutes had the potential to cause some emotional disruption to both Sam and to his classmates. These kids would likely remember, for the rest of their lives, the day Sam came to school missing a part of his leg. I wondered if they would be disturbed or afraid to be near him. More selfishly, I worried what it would do to Sam's self-esteem if his peers reacted to him like he was anything other than himself.

"Sam's here!" one boy shouted out as my son rolled in. It was group project time. The students were arranged in clusters all around the room. Some were standing, holding up scissors and construction paper; others were sitting on the floor with colorful foam cutouts. The controlled chatter throughout the room suggested the students were happily engaged. That is, until Sam arrived. Heads swiveled toward the door. Most were wide-eyed and staring.

"Hey, nice to have you back!" Sam and his teacher Mr. Axman had a banter that the other kids sometimes didn't quite catch. He added casually, "Oh hey, it looks as if you're missing something." Sam smirked and rolled himself into the classroom.

Mr. Axman had moved Sam's desk nearer to the door and away from the wall to ensure easier access. Another class walked by in the hall. One by one, the kids did a doubletake when they saw Sam. That particular class featured one of those kids with the special gift of saying what everyone else is thinking, even when it seems totally inappropriate. He spotted Sam and exclaimed, "Oh, man, that is so weird!"

The student teacher nudged him along. Sam showed no sign that he had even noticed.

Sam broke the awkward silence by getting everyone's attention, "Hey! Hey, you guys! You guys, look!" The kids' heads turned toward him and he lifted up his amputated leg so his knee touched his chin. He grabbed two imaginary handles on either side and said, "Guys, look! It's a submarine scope!" He rotated his leg at the hip, back and forth, pretending to search the seas for signs of foreign ships through this curious appendage.

The kids glanced at each other. One or two giggled. Then, several kids laughed. It was now okay to stare. Sam's mildly inappropriate humor had provided them with an invitation of sorts and reminded them that he was still Sam.

13
WOUNDS

Ten days after surgery Sam had his follow-up appointment with Dr. Harvey. The consultation was the same sort of appointment we'd had after the first surgery when he told us Sam's tumor was unusual. By now, we knew enough to worry. This time, he told us the biopsy of the tissue from the leg that remained showed that it was free from cancer cells. That was a relief. He also mentioned that they did find some live cancer cells in the lower leg, which were removed during surgery. Though it was unsettling to find out there was still some cancer in that part of his leg, it confirmed that amputation was the right choice.

Dr. Harvey unwrapped the bulky gauze to take a look at Sam's leg. I had noticed a dark spot along the incision, and a faint discolored strip of skin on the outside of his leg. It was a fleshy moist brown. As the doctor unraveled gauze and examined the wound, he paused and sighed. His expression turned cold, like the moment someone becomes angry before they've had a chance to express their disappointment in gestures or words.

"This part of his skin is necrotic." He pointed to the brown area. "It's dying."

His tone was measured and professional, but his frustration

was noticeable. I didn't know that could happen; I worried it was my fault. Maybe I cared for it wrong. Maybe I wrapped the leg too tightly. Maybe the fall in the entryway of our house killed his skin. I didn't know healing could go wrong. I didn't know large chunks of skin around an amputated leg could die.

"Sometimes chemotherapy makes it hard for the body to heal," he explained a bit more gently.

"Can I have my iPad?" Sam whispered to Bob while we listened to Dr. Harvey's explanation. Bob handed it to him and Sam slumped back against the pillow on the exam table to play Plants vs Zombies.

"So, what now? What can we do about it?" I asked. I was hoping for a medication or ointment that would bring dead skin back to life.

"I can fix this, but we'll have to wait until a few weeks out from his last chemotherapy. He'll need another surgery." He mentioned his disagreement with certain oncologists about the best time to do surgery after chemo. I had learned all about blood counts and low ANCs (absolute neutrophil count). Neutrophils are a type of white blood cell that helps the body fight infection. I knew that chemotherapy kills rapidly dividing cells, but I didn't know that it could complicate his recovery. A body needs a certain level of health and resources to heal properly. Without healing, there is death.

Over the next few weeks, a section of Sam's skin turned into a foot-long, one-inch-wide, thick, hard scab. It wasn't the kind of scab you could pick off to find a pink fleshy layer spotted with bits of blood. The scab was so bulky and deep that pulling it off would likely expose the muscle and bone normally protected by healthy skin. Sam had eight more weeks of chemo, plus the recommended extra month to allow his body to recover before they could fix the dead skin problem. A prosthetic leg could only be engineered for him once he had completely healed.

The remaining few weeks of treatment seemed to damage as

many cells in Sam's body as it could without completely destroying him. Back in September, Sam had looked healthy and strong. By April, he was skinny, bald, pale, and missing a leg. One late night in his hospital room when he was recovering from chemotherapy, and feeling awful, he asked to sleep in my spot – on a mattress that doubled as a bench beneath the window – because the hospital bed was making him even more nauseous. As I watched him fall asleep, heavily drugged with the maximum doses of anti-nausea meds he could have while chemotherapy continued to be pumped into his body, the sadness I felt for his suffering was overwhelming. This is childhood cancer.

I've always had a sensitive nature. I feel deeply, I hurt easily, and I notice the social dynamics and energy around me. My sensitivity seemed to intensify when Sam was diagnosed. Life always has its ups and downs, but after the diagnosis, the lows and highs of life resembled a seismograph. My insides yearned for stability, a respite from the flux of emotions.

One particularly painful reaction was evoked by our social circle of families with third graders. Us parents like to believe our kids are extra kind to their disabled, delayed or chronically ill peers. Especially when it's a kid with cancer. I could tell by the way the other parents of Sam's peers tilted their heads and softened their voices when they told me, "Billy made a card for Sam." "Jonny skipped recess to be with Sam in the classroom." "Matthew wanted to pray for Sam last night." It became its own category of competition: whose kid is the most caring toward the pitiable child who has cancer. Many of these kids are authentically compassionate, compelled to express kindness. Others, perhaps, need some time and maturity to cultivate their own ability to care. That can be hard on parents who wish to see early signs of empathy in their kids.

In the beginning, it seemed like the whole world expressed their care and love to Sam. It started with the special cards and public photos showcasing the community support. For example, a trip to the hospital with cookies those kids lovingly prepared with their moms. However, that compassion wasn't sustained throughout the months-long cancer journey. Nine months after he was diagnosed, Sam was still skinny and physically impaired, somehow his state of being had become normal. And quite uncool.

Several of the boys in Sam's class were especially athletic. Before cancer, at recess, athleticism served as an irresistible draw for my competitive kid. Sam was a bossy leader on the playground, which often ended up in conflict. Sam could be a sore loser and an obnoxious winner. He scowled and argued when another kid stepped out of bounds, but when a foul was called on him he insisted it was in error. Offended, he refused to let it go, making sure the cheater stood behind him in line, or had one of the worst seats at story time. Positive parenting books call it "spirited," but the occasional call from the principal's office suggested that Sam's spirit needed some refinement. It was his sense of humor, his big ideas, and his contagious energy that drew people to him, and compensated for those times when he opted to be a stinker.

The athletic kids came to school early to play basketball. They wore neon yellow Nike shoes to match their neon yellow Nike shirts and black basketball shorts with the neon yellow Nike swoosh. These were the cool kids, and their moms and dads bought those matching Nike outfits, helping them maintain a certain status. I did too, before I understood how much it hurt to be left out.

Coolness doesn't require kindness. When a kid is sporty and arrives at school wearing perfectly matched neon Nike gear, they can get away with being a jerk on the playground. It didn't take all that long for the more athletic kids to exclude Sam from their group. I spent time at the school as a volunteer – but really so I could keep an eye on him – and I watched it happen. There was whispering and pointing, scooting away, denying him a proximal space to sit with them on the floor. Sam had to locate a new place to occupy on his own, and I hope he didn't feel it the way I did.

Sam's friends drifted into other friendships. They had sleep-overs while Sam was in the hospital. New sports teams formed without him, playground dynamics evolved, and pretty soon there was one less kid on the list for afternoon play dates. Five boys, formerly friends of Sam, decided to do a school science experiment about whether their shoes affected their shooting accuracy in basketball. That must have been fun.

One Friday night, I took Sam to a school party. We walked in the door to see several boys from Sam's class all hanging out together. They gave him a sly nod, "Hey, Sam." Had they met at someone's house before the party? Which mom had rounded them up to bring them without suggesting they call Sam? I wondered how much parents could secretly relish how their boys were on the inside circle while Sam was on the outside. Maybe it was the wounds from their own childhood - feeling ostracized, unpopular, unacceptable - that made its way into what was desired at all costs for their own children.

I could see the pain behind Sam's eyes, but he tried harder and was more successful than I was in moving on. He connected with other kids, like the girls down the street who were smart and kind and never needed to fake being a friend to Sam. With another boy in his class, he partnered up for the science fair by measuring the strength of magnets, which was much more scientific than shooting hoops with different brands of shoes. But it didn't heal the wound of being left out. When Sam felt hurt, he retreated into his room with his screen. Quiet. Solemn. I am not proud of how angry I was during this time.

14
REMISSION

I look back on the time after his first year of treatment as a season of dreamy grandiosity. Grief was quiet. I was more alive and alert. I looked forward with anticipation to a more fully engaged life. I craved a greater level of depth in every experience.

I wanted to listen to people and know them more fully. To savor my food and the smell of spring. I wanted to seek beautiful places. I understood the value of laughter, and how a snuggle with one of my kids could nourish my heart. I wanted more of the things that make life rich.

I wanted Sam to live an extraordinary life. He had come through the other side of cancer with an even stronger spirit, and I felt he deserved a multitude of rewards. On his own volition and apart from the cool kids at school, Sam became quite competent on his crutches. He tested things the way toddlers test their large motor skills, trundling up and down grassy hills and ramps over and over again for the intrinsic pleasure of mastering the movement. Sam forever looked for new challenges. He found objects to launch himself over, or tight spots he had to maneuver through backwards and sideways. He gravitated toward fences and trees and boulders to climb that were out of bounds, and found himself getting away with a lot more than he had before cancer. He learned how to propel his body with a skip of his right leg to keep up with the kids on the street and their made-up games. He hung out with the friends who didn't care that he couldn't play basketball anymore.

One day he asked me to go in the backyard with him and kick the soccer ball around. After a few practice attempts at swinging his only foot at just the right time to kick the ball, he decided it would be even more funny to make a video of him flailing and falling. That idea led to him wanting his own YouTube channel and an extensive list of slapstick acts he could perform with one leg on crutches. The wheelchair even added excitement to his life, though he was somewhat disappointed at its poor handling at high speeds. While I fretted about whether or not Sam would be able to walk again, he developed tricks that enhanced his agility and made other people admire him.

Sam's smile made me happy. His spirit had changed, but in a way that made me proud. His journey from suffering to self-esteem and pride made me want to pop champagne. On those days, I could celebrate, laugh and sleep well, even though as a family our wounds were still healing.

With just one good leg, he still played with kids in the street, climbed trees and fences, engaged in Nerf gun wars, wrestled with friends, and tested the boundaries of amputated leg jokes. I could imagine him at 90 years of age, sharing stories with his great grandkids that would make them want to live just like him.

He turned ten just as he went into remission. But reentering normal everyday life after Sam finished his treatments was not easy. As we tried to move forward into fresh experiences, the previous year had a grip on us that wouldn't let us fully leave it. A month after chemotherapy was complete, Sam had surgery to remove the dead skin. We waited six more weeks for it to heal so he could be fitted for a prosthetic leg. A hole the size of a pencil eraser formed at the incision site next to his knee, an opening that plunged deep into his flesh. The doctors said it would eventually heal, but until then there was nothing Sam could do but wait. My feelings remained acute, whether it was the love I felt for Sam, or the hope I had for his future, or the longing for everything to be okay.

Still, there were instances of forward motion. One day we visited a lovely little lake, a peaceful retreat created by a local nonprofit for kids with cancer and their families and friends. On the grassy shore, Sam tossed aside his crutches and climbed into a kayak. He took to paddling quite naturally, activating some sort of instinctual ability. His friend jumped into the other kayak. They paddled out into the lily pads. With his crutches gone and his lower body hidden inside the belly of the shallow orange boat, he looked like any other healthy kid. His shoulder muscles and biceps were well-defined, strong from using crutches. A light fuzz covered his head and the color had returned to his cheeks. They decided to race. Sam leaned in with a determined gaze. He paddled smooth and fast. I hadn't seen him compete physically for almost an entire year. The moment generated a swell of joy in me. It was such a little thing but my emotional reaction was so big. It was because the sadness - all of the loss and sickness - had set me up for the flood of delight that I felt in that moment. The immense joy showed up only because we had endured so much sorrow. I never realized in those moments of sadness and grief, how each episode left a little window for profoundly beautiful moments to step inside and sweep us away. It wouldn't equal the sorrow or make up for the trauma. I react with absurdity at the suggestion. But, sorrow can sometimes create the most pleasurable moments of joy. There were many instances like this. We knew the joy of being discharged from the hospital only because he had to be admitted in the first place. The enjoyment of a trip back to my dad's cabin was magnified, only after being confined to a 50-mile radius of the hospital for ten long months. There would be more moments ahead of us, and I didn't want to miss the magnificence of each one. It left me wondering what a normal life is missing out on by being so normal. So routine. I wanted a life rich with love and emotion and connection and adventure and even darkness. But never again did I want that kind of darkness to touch my kids.

Remission gave me a chance to reflect. I knew the year had changed me, yet I wasn't completely sure how. I went back to work two days per week at the clinic and took on some volunteer shifts to assist sexual assault survivors. However, my heart wasn't in it the way it used to be. I thought if I gave it some time, my sense of purpose and satisfaction would surely return.

Over the summer, Bob surprised me by sending me to Montana on a fly-fishing trip with my friend Kirsten. I found the beauty of the rivers and the rhythm of my rod eased my grief. Kirsten then suggested I travel with her to Uganda for two weeks to serve with a nonprofit. I said yes, and the two of us spent time supporting young students rescued from extreme poverty and now in training to be leaders. I dipped my toes into these experiences, searching for renewal, and gave no time to anything related to cancer.

Our church had been through some tough times too while Sam was in treatment. The pastor, who was suddenly asked to leave, initially refused. It was quite messy, but eventually there was a change in the leadership. Like our family, our church was able to move on. As soon as my life achieved a degree of consistency, I was asked to share at the Sunday services and other programs throughout the week. I replied that I might not say what people expected to hear. I was still angry. Still sad. Still skeptical. I felt I knew what they wanted to hear, and I could not do so with authenticity. They would love to hear me speak about how their prayers and mine helped me to achieve peace. That God had met me in the darkness; He would never let me go. I could eloquently state what they wanted to hear. If I chose, I could chase the buzz of being spiritually admired.

In truth, Sam's remission wasn't nearly as beautiful as I'd hoped. I thought the end of cancer treatment would be more celebratory. But cancer held on and dampened my days outside the hospital walls. The ordeal introduced me to a profoundly deeper place within my own heart and soul. My honest internal dialog was far more aggressive than the mindset that I allowed people to see. Anger and bitterness simmered inside of me. While my friendships grew stronger through the cancer story, I worried they would become tired of my ongoing inability to express the faithful trust in God's plan. However, there are dark Scriptures too. Psalm 88 is purely an expression of vile anger toward God. It's the only Psalm that doesn't end with a lovely sort of *and yet I will praise the Lord.* Lamentations is a book in the Scriptures devoted entirely to lament - the honesty of a heart that is grieving. While gratitude is the noble, even beautiful way to respond to pain, I found comfort that the Scriptures offered seasons of groaning and a profound objection to the path of pain and sorrow. So, I figured my authenticity might still be worth sharing. Grief and joy, anger and hope, bitterness and love – and perhaps a bit of wisdom.

I said yes, and I chose to be real. I told them I was angry. I told them God was silent. Some congregants responded with warmth. They wanted to talk. They sent me cards to say at times they felt the same way. Others wanted to believe that God "cradled Sam in the palm of his hand" and would surely take care of his every need. "God's got this." "He has a plan." "He always comes through." I bristled at these assurances, and yet remained inwardly ashamed about doubting the steadfast faith of the people around me.

~

Six months after losing his leg, Sam took a first step for the second time in his life. A prosthetic leg must be a perfect fit, skillfully molded to connect with every divot and bump, while the ankle unit must be fixed with precisely the right position for each individual body. An amputated leg can't tolerate a poor fit the way a normal foot can tolerate an uncomfortable shoe. Prosthetics is both a science and an art.

For a below knee amputation (BKA), the weight bearing point of contact is just below the knee. Those bones protruding out on either side will need to bear the weight. Weight bearing on the edge of a stump would do terrible damage to underlying soft tissue; therefore the end of the leg gently rests inside the socket cup while the thicker, more solid parts of a leg take the pressure which has been biologically engineered for a foot. The socket cup must be fitted in such a way that prevents any wiggle or rub, which could lead to the skin breaking down, and cause pain.

Sam's prosthetist, Stuart, an exceptional talent, molded a cast of Sam's most wounded space. He was careful and gentle, but not overly so. It was his responsibility now to give Sam the freedom to walk again.

Our first appointment took place in a clinic that smelled like chalk. After an introductory lesson in prosthetics for beginners, Stuart covered Sam's leg with a soft, wet, meshy fabric and a paste to make it harden. He pressed into the dimples and bumps of Sam's leg. After it dried, it was removed for the next phase of production. Several days after the molding appointment, we returned for a fitting. Stuart then measured and cut a long rubbery sleeve to slip over Sam's stump for a cushion barrier between his leg and the prosthesis. He placed the rubbery sock on Sam's leg and showed him the donning technique. Sam's face flushed and his back stiffened. Tears spilled down his chin. Stuart noted his reaction and carefully removed the sleeve. He spoke quietly and told Sam they could take some time.

After a break, Sam asked Stuart to try it one more time. This time he was able to accept the rubbery sleeve. Then, Stuart slid the prosthetic leg over Sam's stump while Sam watched intently.

He pulled over a stepping stool. "Okay, Sam. I want you to stand up."

Stuart sat on a wheeled stool and was facing Sam, his hands up in case Sam needed support. Sam stood. After six months on crutches, his right thigh was noticeably thicker and stronger than his left. He stood on two legs, but listed to one side. Stuart shifted his hips just slightly to the left, so he could feel the prosthesis supporting his weight. After a few more adjustments, Stuart removed the prosthesis and asked Sam to crutch himself to a room with parallel bars. He then slid Sam's prosthesis over his stump again.

"Okay, Sam. Go ahead and take a few steps."

I stood to one side wiping the tears that were blurring this beautiful moment. I had my camera in video mode. The air in the room was completely still as Sam moved through space on two feet. For the first time, again. His eyebrows lifted as if he was surprised at his own ability. He was a different kid, bigger and stronger. I couldn't have felt prouder.

There were many more appointments to get the leg fitted perfectly. Next, Stuart would need to pair it with the proper foot. Stuart told Sam that he would break his rule and get him a more dynamic foot than was customary for a kid his age. He told Sam he expected that leg to come back looking a little beat up. Signs of wear would mean the leg was working. Sam didn't disappoint.

Sam and Stuart developed a banter of sorts that was really the surface layer of a trusting relationship. I have since learned how important it is to trust the prosthetist. No matter how many times the patient complains about the pain, a good prosthetist will have the patience and drive to reshape and perfect this non-organic body part, because kids are entitled to mobility.

As Sam became adept at walking again, his new leg swept away the obstacles to much more. He perked up to any game that had strict rules about how to maintain one's footing. Keep one foot inside the hula hoop. Tie the balloon to one ankle and don't let the other players pop it. The traditional three-legged race. Technically, he could follow the rules but at times benefit from a strategic advantage. Laughing, his peers encouraged mischievous ploys. They began to see the leg as fair game, which worked against him the day they confiscated it during a Nerf war in our house.

Sam developed a habit of disconnecting his leg whenever we sat down for a meal. The loud thunk as it hit the hardwood floor startled me over and over again.

Certain phrases became common language. "Does anyone know where my leg is?"

"Natalie, will you get my leg for me?"

"Sam, don't leave your leg in the middle of the hallway!"

Young children would ask him what happened to his leg. He occasionally delighted in telling them, "Well, I didn't eat my vegetables, so the doctor had to cut it off."

While he still wasn't sprinting like Marlon Shirley, Sam found his forward motion on a prosthesis and welcomed the creative perks of being an amputee.

15
HAWAII

In the 2012 year of remission, seven members of our family flew out of the Seattle airport at 7:00am on the first day of spring break. It was raining and 48 degrees, and Sam was wearing swim trunks. My parents don't like to stand out. They are not attention seeking or loud or flashy in any way. People noticed us: my sister and her cerebral palsy, and Sam and his amputation. The addition of his green and white flowered swim trunks only added to the number of double takes by strangers, most of whom were in REI puffy coats and jeans in the busy Seattle airport.

Sam sat in a window seat, leg disconnected and flat on the floor. He was glued to the movie player we rented for him. I wondered how he'd do with a prosthetic leg on a beach for the first time. Really, I was wondering how uncomfortable that mesh lining of the bathing trunks on his bum might feel a few more hours into the flight.

The idea of a vacation in Hawaii came about while Sam was in treatment. My parents mentioned they'd like for us all to go once he was healthy again. *Healthy again.* It was something I could distantly dream of, like breathing fresh air after spending time trapped in a smoke-filled room. *Healthy in Hawaii* sounded even better, so we jumped on the offer.

We chose spring break of his fourth-grade year to make the trip. My parents are generous and my dad also likes his space, so they rented a big house with an infinity pool on the Big island, overlooking Kealakekua Bay. Natalie and Sam had delighted in exploring the home on the online video tour. Natalie tried to claim the master bedroom upstairs with the deck and a view of the bay. We laughed but she was still secretly hoping she could spend a full week in luxury.

Sam was drawn more to the pool, and wondered what size splash he could make. Sam, was a *wouldn't it be cool if* type of kid, often generating wild ideas to make life more interesting. Most kids have a filter that tells them if they were to actually follow through, the cool idea might be more embarrassing than cool. But Sam was missing that part of the common sense filter. He looked at that beautiful pool on the website during the cold gray months in Oregon and asked, "Wouldn't it be cool if we pulled up to the house and I ran straight to the pool and did a giant cannonball?"

Great idea, but it had just one obstacle. Jumping into a pool in a fleece and jeans sounded uncomfortable, so the obvious solution was for him to travel to Hawaii in his swim trunks. I sighed and said, "Okay." This left Bob with little opportunity to oppose Sam's crazy idea. But just in case, I packed a pair of his sweatpants in my carry-on bag.

Once we landed in Hawaii, the warm air felt like a kindness meant just for us. All of us squeezed into the minivan and we drove for 40 minutes, the last ten up and down a windy road, to our fancy rental. While we figured out how to unlock the gate, Sam perked up searching for his ultimate destiny.

I grabbed my camera to record him. As soon as we pulled into the driveway, Sam leapt out of the van. Not yet agile on his prosthetic leg, he limped as quickly as he knew how around the house to the side that overlooked the bay. He headed for the pool. Squeezing the release button on his leg, he let the prosthesis smack on the concrete while he hopped the remaining few feet. The rest of us watched and giggled. He then jumped in with a loud "Woo hoo!" At last! The grand splash he'd been dreaming of. Sam's head popped out of the water and he yelled, "This feels so great!"

The rest of us stood around in our normal travel clothes with normal vacation arrival plans which never make it to the long term memory of priceless moments. Sam had created an experience, and a moment we would talk about for years to come.

Two days into our vacation, we went to a sandy beach so the kids could try body boarding. We drove to a well marketed rental shop to get some overpriced boards. While Sam took no delight in snorkeling, he was eager to go body boarding. He was mildly disappointed he wasn't actually going to surf.

My parents and sister parked their beach chairs well away from the shore. We all lathered up our pale skin with super-sized doses of sunblock. Sam snapped on his plastic water leg while I eyed the faces of other beachgoers to see if anyone was watching.

Stuart had made Sam a plastic water leg that would float if it fell off in the water. It sounded smart, but neither Sam or I knew how to properly outfit a prosthesis to fit securely on his leg in the water.

Bob took Sam and Natalie out to catch some waves while I stood at the water's edge with my camera. The waves were so close to the shore, the kids could stand in waist deep water watching for the wave to ride. The first several tries, they hopped on their boards too late and the wave rode into the shore without them.

I hoped this wouldn't be another disappointing experience like basketball. Sam had started the season with high hopes of being competitive again. However, the challenge of developing upper body skills while adapting to a completely different lower body, and playing against kids who haven't missed a beat in sports for more than a year proved to be a challenge. Sam's self-esteem took a hit. At practices he was passed over multiple times for *player of the day*, then contracted the infection in his leg, leaving him back on crutches and in a wheelchair for another six weeks. He continued to cheer on his team from his wheelchair on the sidelines. The coaches went big on the end of the season party favors and each player received a large poster of themself in action on the court. Except for Sam. He received nothing. With that experience still fresh, I wanted him to have fun and feel competent again.

The kids quickly figured out how to grab the wave as it crested. With his increasing skill and success, Sam experienced a boost of energy. He got louder and moved faster and grinned broadly. His spirit glowed.

Three waves into the fun, his leg slipped off, liner and all. Sam rolled off his board. Hopping around in the water as the waves pushed him to and fro, he yelled, "Dad! Dad! Get my leg!" Before it floated out to sea. Bob dove and fetched the leg while Sam crept back to the sand. I stood close by ready to help, and again looked to see if anyone noticed the kid who had lost his leg.

Sam had mastered the process of rolling the liner up his leg just right, but he'd never had to deal with sand. They had to then detach the slippery gel liner from inside the leg socket, wash off the sand carefully, then go through the entire process again.

I squatted down low near Sam. The day was at risk. Would he be able to continue body boarding? Or would he end up in a beach chair with his grandparents, frustrated and grumpy with a towel over his head?

Sam put his leg back on and set out for another attempt at

body boarding. Bob helped him get to the just right spot to catch a good wave. When he did, his face lit up with delight. Three more waves, and again the leg fell off. "Dad, get my leg!!" Sam's cry rose up from the sea. Those within earshot looked confused while Bob fetched the detached floating body part again.

Bob's stoic expression left me guessing how long his patience would last. There were times when Bob committed himself completely to Sam's potential for joy, no matter how much energy or perseverance was required, like the times we'd spent on Puget Sound beaches. When Sam set out to build a big sandcastle or driftwood fort, he ordered Bob around like a ship's captain in a storm. "Dad, get those rocks and bring them over here!" "Dad, dig a moat around the end of that tower!" "Dad, go get me the longest log you can find!" Bob did what he was ordered to do. The two of them came home with brave stories from the shore.

Bob was in that mode again. The limb disconnected every third wave. This became the pattern for the day. Each time his leg detached, Bob and Sam came back on the beach to put it back on. Hop, sit, detach, wash, align, roll, reposition, stand, click, ride three more waves. Bob played his part with gusto.

There was something about riding waves that ignited Sam's adventurous spirit. He got a little bit discouraged with the constant interruptions, but the fun outweighed the frustration. I wondered how much of Sam's character traits were influenced by his cancer battle. He's always been an *all in* kind of person. Maybe I'll never fully understand how much cancer added to his stubborn *go for it* approach to his life.

When we were all done, Sam came out of the water. He looked strong. With a sense of mastery, and his leg still on, he came toward me with his board under his arm. He stopped for a moment to pose for the camera as if there were 100 photographers on the beach - instead of just me - and he was a world-class surfer who'd just won a major competition. He checked my viewfinder and exclaimed, "Hey, that's a great picture! Maybe one day I could be a model for an amputee surfing magazine!"

I smiled and nodded, wondering if any such magazine existed. However, this was a dream I would let him have, even if it never came true. Little did I know.

16

TRACK

Before cancer, way back in second grade during a recreation league basketball game, Sam was taking seriously his task of guarding his opponent. She had dark eyes and a bouncy ponytail. He hovered over her with his hands up in a fierce effort to block any opportunity for her to add to her team's offense. She tried to escape his Velcro-like coverage. He chased her round and round the court in big circles. At one point, when she was attempting to gain a position under the hoop, Sam trapped her against the gym wall with his arms raised up on either side of her head. I was pretty sure that should have been a foul. I watched from the bleachers, hoping my laser focus might reach him and induce him to change his behavior, and before his opponent cried or punched him in the face.

After the game, I emailed the coach with a lighthearted apology for Sam's inappropriate game strategy. I assured him that I had addressed his tactic of pinning other kids against the wall, and that I hoped the girl's family would not request a restraining order against Sam. Coach emailed me back, "I told Sam to stick to his man like glue and he did exactly what I asked him to do." From our good-natured exchange, I understood his coach had it handled if only I could resist trying to do his job for him.

Sam was competitive. In my opinion, competitive people need to compete. Sometimes it seems like labeling a person as competitive is just a nicer way of saying, *he or she is kind of an ass.* I get that. When Sam was a little kid, a family game of Candy Land ended in one of two predictable ways. Either Sam jumped to his feet with a celebratory dance, or a lament on a Biblical scale. In the latter case, it might involve flipping over the game board and scattering the pieces far and wide, with some bitter verbiage at Natalie's expense. Sometimes, we played these games just to give Sam practice at losing. I was anxious for Sam to mature into a "good game" kind of kid.

In third grade, when Sam got cancer, he had to quit sports. And recess. Physical competition was off bounds as he watched his peers move on with another year of athletic development. Then, after his cancer treatment, he only had one leg. Bob and I had a feeling that playing the usual sports on a prosthetic leg was going to be tough. Soccer, baseball, basketball, and football were out, but since we had learned about Marlon Shirley, track seemed to be the sport that might satisfy that competitive drive and allow him to be a part of a team.

Finally, in December of his fourth grade year, I signed him up for track. Practices began in March, which seemed like a good time for him to start because it would give him seven months to adjust to his prosthesis. During this many months on crutches, he got good at using them. Crazy good. Up and down stairs, sideways through a busy hallway of kids, even backwards. And he was fast. But not running fast. Just crutches fast. Back on two legs, he would have to re-learn how to put equal weight on both feet. His brain and body had a lot of work to do, but seven months seemed like the right amount of time to prepare. Track might serve as an excellent extension to his physical therapy regimen.

In January, 2012, after just three months on his new leg, Sam developed a hot red spot on the very end of his stump. I was in Africa doing some nonprofit work with a friend. When I was in the airport in Entebbe, Uganda, waiting for my flight home, Bob called me.

"You'll never guess where I am."

"The hospital?" I said with a rush of fear.

"Yup."

"What?"

"It's not cancer." He quickly reassured me. "Sam got an infection in his leg yesterday and needed an emergency surgery. He's doing fine now. The good news is that Dr. Harvey says there's no sign of cancer there." Bob told me about the painful sequence of events leading up to the surgery. He didn't want to call me until he knew what was really going on, so he had spent the night in the waiting room alone. After an hour or so of sleep, he called me as I boarded the plane for my 22-hour journey back to Portland. I got off the plane lethargic and in need of a shower. I went straight to the hospital to see Sam.

Even the most minor surgery on an amputated leg provokes the need for a whole new socket for a prosthesis. Stuart had to start from scratch only after the surgery wound had healed completely, and all swelling was gone. Sam returned to crutches for six weeks. He finally got his new leg one week before starting track. I sent an email to the coach to let her know that Sam was an amputee. By then, his left leg had become quite weak again.

The first practice happened on a dark, rainy evening at the nearby high school. Sam's legs were covered by baggy sweatpants. He looked like everyone else.

Though not many parents remained to watch the first track practice in the damp and cold, I stayed. It was that peeking tendency of mine, and I hoped he could fit in again. But there was a long distance between watching videos of Marlon Shirley and actually competing. Sam was now confronting the hard work, at a significant disadvantage. However - both he and I knew - he had to start somewhere.

The coaches ran the kids through some warm-ups. Raincoats and sweatpants were tossed aside and speckled the track. Short distance jogs, lateral and front lunges, high knees, and butt kicks. In the rain, with all the kids all moving at different speeds, it was hard to notice that Sam wasn't actually lunging. Instead, it was more like he was taking really big steps. He was working hard to blend into the colorful chaos of athletes learning how to compete on a track team for the very first time.

The last drill was a sprint. When it was Sam's turn, he took off running right on cue. Five steps into his sprint, his weak thigh muscles gave out. He fell forward onto the rough wet surface, catching himself with both hands. He stood up, stepped away from the other sprinters, and studied his wet and dirty palms. A coach attended to him. I held my breath and kept my distance. I worried that embarrassment might make him want to quit. And it did. But after a couple of days, he went back for practice number two, and kept on going.

The meets began. He repeatedly came in last, except for the shot put. Maybe it was all in the form, because his skinny little frame didn't shout out that he was a shot put kind of athlete. However, in an early meet, Sam placed. That was a boost for him, so he decided the shot put was his event. We gave the javelin a try too. Fourth graders use soft javelins for obvious reasons. He couldn't quite master the sequence and ended up too frustrated to stick with it. Sam preferred to win easily and naturally. That was just one more thing to work on.

Throughout the track season, Sam chose events that felt as safe as possible. The workouts were good for him. He looked healthy, and was building strength, though he continued to run uncommonly slow. I wished the other parents and kids had seen him run before he had cancer. He was so fast. I wished they knew how hard it is to run without a mobile ankle joint or calf muscles. Perhaps one day he would have a running leg.

Sam's involvement in track motivated me to start running again too. When I ran, my mind would return to my loftiest aspirations for Sam's future. I had visions of him running, strong and happy, on a sleek, high tech running blade like Marlon Shirley's. This vision synched with songs on a playlist that looked a lot like Natalie's. As I pounded the streets of my neighborhood with Katy Perry's "Firework" streaming through my earbuds, I dreamed about Sam winning a race at a high school track meet one day.

Sam decided to compete in the mile run at the final track meet of the season. His only goal was to not come in last, and he wanted it desperately. We made a few trips to the practice track. Sam jogged laps to train after school, all on his own. On the day of the meet, Bob and I were there with our friend Staci. The track had covered stands for spectators, which made it feel like a big deal. Sam competed in the shot put and finished somewhere in the middle. He ran in a relay and might have been the reason the opposing team won.

I've been a regular mom watching my regular kids compete. But this was different. Sam was a childhood cancer survivor and an amputee. I wanted him to feel confident and happy and satisfied, the pay-off for all of his hard work. If he could run the entire mile, that would be enough. He was a fourth grader now, running exceptionally slow, with people in the stands watching him. I realized that could make for a really bad day. He'd had enough of those. It seemed like he was owed at least one really good day.

The mile was scheduled to be the very last event of the meet. I decided to stand near the finish line, while Bob recorded Sam's big moment from the stands. The thought crossed my mind, *what if this is the last time we see him running a mile, and Bob misses the moment?* I brushed off the fear and told myself we'd see him compete again.

There were several kids running the mile in red, light blue, and gray jerseys. The pistol popped and the runners took off. Predictably, Sam fell to the back of the pack in the first few meters. A handful of the kids were exceptionally fast; their parents must have been proud. One or two of them lapped Sam. I thought about the conversations they would have after the meet: *Johnny got first place in the mile.* They'd post it on Facebook. They'd call the grandparents on speakerphone to share the achievement. They'd celebrate on the way home with a scoop of ice cream or a burger. I was envious. I wanted Sam to have that too. But I couldn't make that happen for him. No one could do it but Sam.

One by one, kids crossed the finish line while family members cheered. A cadence of loud support came from different sections of the stands. The mile was the final event of the meet. When most of the kids crossed the finish line, people began to pack up their snacks and cushions and extra layers of clothing.

Sam was still running. I could see how he labored to lift his heavy metal leg. He kept on going, not once did he walk. I watched from the finish line while Bob and Staci in the lower stands reached out their phones to record him. As he rounded the final turn we yelled, "Way to go Sam!" I was careful to be loud but not too loud. I didn't want to embarrass him in case he didn't want anyone to notice him when he came in last.

One by one, the remaining spectators began to notice that a kid was still running. They paused and pointed and whispered to one another. I am not sure how many people knew about Sam and his cancer. They certainly didn't know the unforgiving ruthlessness of chemotherapy. They didn't know about his emergency surgery in January. Or how he didn't get his new leg until a week before the first track practice. All they could know, see or feel that day was one kid running dead last on a prosthetic leg.

When Sam rounded the last turn, the crowd stood up. They shouted and clapped and whistled. In the final stretch, every person in the stadium was cheering him on all the way to the finish line. As he jogged across it, his coach welcomed him with arms wide. Sam accepted her embrace with a proud grin.

98

17
OSCAR

Scans happened every three months. Sam's scans included an MRI of his leg and a chest CT because those are the two places where new tumors would most likely show up.

For one full year, the tests resulted in those coveted words out of the oncologist's mouth: No Evidence of Disease or NED. Cancer parents all know what NED means. We love NED. We claim it as a major accomplishment. *Three months NED!! Nine months NED!!* We boast about it the way other parents brag about scoring goals and winning races. Sometimes we credit our kids for being fierce warriors who have battled the enemy and won. We say he or she *kicked cancer's butt.* To my knowledge, there are no bumper stickers that say *Proud parent of an NED kid,* but there should be. On May 31, 2012, Sam's scans declared him one-year NED and we soaked up the happy, celebratory vibes.

The previous week, right at the end of his track season, Sam had been invited to visit the Nike World Headquarters on the very same day as his scans. Nike is only a mile from our home in Portland. We know several people who work there. This invitation came from Sam's track coach who wanted Sam to meet the famous amputee runner Oscar Pistorius.

Oscar, a Nike sponsored athlete, was scheduled to be in town just prior to the Prefontaine Classic in Eugene, Oregon. While training for his event, the 400 meter, Oscar would soon make history as the first amputee to ever compete alongside able-bodied athletes in the Olympic Games. Oscar was everywhere. Magazines, world news, celebrity news, and over-sized images on the sides of buildings in most major cities. I recorded the interviews and purchased the magazines. I let the story fuel my daydreams of Sam competing without coming in last.

Nike promoted the double amputee with sleek black Cheetah Legs, sprinting like a bullet out of its chamber. Now, a year into Sam's amputee life, I believed Oscar's popularity could help elevate Sam's sense of self and his future prospects. In interviews, Oscar spoke honorably of his disabled competitors in the Paralympics, which landed well with me. He said things like, "I hope that my presence in the Olympics will draw attention to the Paralympics." His South African accent added charm to his polite demeanor. The media called him remarkable, inspirational, and sexy. I agreed. He was proud to be an amputee and he made it look cool just when Sam needed that. The timing was incredible. I began to believe that God was surely redeeming Sam's year of agony with opportunity and good health.

For much of the past 20 months, I had carried with me a burden of anger. It was a lonely anger. I felt it most acutely in the stale hours spent in waiting rooms, driving through traffic for a late night appointment, or searching for a close parking spot in the rain while Sam on crutches waited on the curb. I felt it at home during long dreary days when Sam had nothing to do, while other kids were busy with sports or weekend trips to the coast. I felt it when Sam screamed from phantom pain after his amputation, an ache that couldn't be medicated. With one year of NED behind us, my fury was just beginning to subside. Every clear scan and every new opportunity wore away at the hard edges of my spirit. On this day at Nike, after Sam was declared NED, I could see a future for him rich with new experiences.

The outdoor track at Nike looks like a multi-laned path wrapped around a forest. There are tall fir trees and rhododendron shrubs filling in the middle. It's unique. When we arrived at the track, the folks from Nike greeted us. Sam was the amputee boy in shorts wearing a red t-shirt with a white swoosh on the front. He was coming to meet Oscar Pistorius and he was not hard to identify.

Outside lane six, we sat on a bench and watched Oscar finish up his workout. He then exchanged a few words with his coach. We were still a bit buzzed from the good news of the morning. A relapse would have crushed our spirits. But, since it was a good news day, we were full of happiness. We dressed in our best Nike apparel to celebrate Sam being cancer free after one whole year off treatment. On the day we met Oscar Pistorius at the forested track on the Nike campus, the Day family was stress free and moving on to a better tomorrow with our NED son.

To be at Nike's Headquarters can be a bit intimidating. I knew how important it is to wear Nike gear and avoid other brands at all costs when visiting the campus. There were 20 or so people along the side of the track observing and speaking quietly to one another. A couple of photographers worked the scene.

One photographer had set up a tripod on the edge of the track. Another wandered around with a camera hanging around his neck. I brought my little Canon Rebel, small enough to fit in my purse, with a lens that makes a buzzing noise when I zoom in and out. But when I saw the photographers and compared my camera to theirs, I sheepishly tucked mine away.

Oscar paid no attention to the eyeballs glued to him throughout his workout. Yet he was always photo ready. In tight running shorts and a sleeveless gray Nike shirt, his black running blades dominated his look from first to last and every angle. He had just a touch of sweat from a moderately hard workout. His final sprint around the track looked like he was intentionally giving it only 70%, no doubt part of the strategy of coaches that turn athletes into world famous Olympians.

After some conversation with his coach, Oscar turned toward us and introduced himself to Sam. He sat down on the ground in front of our bench. I introduced myself and tried to tell Oscar a funny story about my mom's friend in South Africa who played rugby with him when they were kids, and his memory of how Oscar lost a leg on the field. But I fumbled my words, forgot the friend's name, and I made no sense at all. We quickly moved on from that topic so Oscar could have a coherent chat with Sam. The little voice inside my head said *that was so dumb, just smile and nod.*

Running legs on a double amputee are designed for running but not for standing still. When Oscar had his running legs on, he shifted back and forth with little steps, the way a unicyclist moves backward and forward because they cannot stand still on one wheel. Running legs don't have heels or ankles, the components that allow us people with regular feet to stay balanced. Sitting on the track one level below us, this larger-than-life double amputee famous around the world, talked to Sam about the subject the two of them could best relate to: feet.

"What kind of foot have you got there? Can I see it?" he said in his delightful accent. Sam took off his leg to show Oscar his foot. He told Sam it was a good foot. Oscar knew the brand and the design. This offhand remark reframed prosthetics for Sam. Oscar was teaching Sam a new language. The two of them, sitting on the track talking legs and feet, were instantly an exclusive group.

Oscar then took off one of his legs and handed it to Sam. These were the famous running blades that some media critics claimed gave Oscar an unfair advantage. Sam disagreed. He knew firsthand how difficult it is to run on a prosthetic leg. It was hard to be different when that meant disabled or impaired. But Oscar knew the language of amputees and the two of them were now the same kind of different.

Oscar, scooted over to lane three, and chatted with us a bit more as he put his legs back on. He was completely focused on Sam. I noticed that Oscar wore tube socks between his prosthesis and the liner inside, just like Sam. When an amputee becomes active and the blood pumps faster, the leg shrinks a bit. The sock takes up the extra space between the athlete's leg and the prosthesis; otherwise, the prosthesis might slip off. The tube sock can be specially made, but by now we knew a regular sock would do just fine. If his leg shrunk and there was no tube sock to be found, Sam would have to quit playing, so we both made sure he was always equipped. We had those white tube socks everywhere with us. I carried one in my purse, and Sam carried one in his backpack. Socks often went through the laundry in the pockets of Sam's sweatpants. They hid in the glove compartment of the car and in his school backpack because if his leg shrunk and there was no tube sock to be found, Sam *would* have to quit playing whatever it was he was playing. Seeing Oscar's prosthetic tube socks that were just like Sam's delighted me.

Oscar invited Sam to run a lap with him. Sam, a bit hesitant, shook his head to decline the invitation to run. Perhaps he was afraid of not looking fit or running fast enough on the Nike track alongside the Olympic athlete. With a gentle nudge from Oscar, Sam finally agreed to go for a jog. The two of them took off, with Oscar chatting amiably. Pretty soon they disappeared behind the trees.

A female employee from Nike arrived to talk to me about an organization that works with athletes with physical disabilities. She very much wanted to get Sam involved, but I was having trouble paying attention as I was completely captivated by Sam running with Oscar on the Nike track with photographers all around them snapping pictures.

The two of them came back into view. Sam looked good. I was

glad I'd made sure he wore his red Nike t-shirt and black Nike shorts because, not long after their run, images of the two of them would spread like wildfire through Nike's massive network. Oscar gave Sam an in-motion hug as they arrived back where they started. The 20 or so spectators cheered. When Sam turned to me and lifted up his chin, there was a smile on his face. Affirmation. Connection. Belonging. What a beautiful moment that was.

Nine weeks after our Nike visit, Oscar ran his 400m event in the London Olympics. For the first time, a double amputee was allowed to run with able bodied athletes. That was the accomplishment. He wasn't expected to win, or even to place, so the day of the event was a bit anticlimactic. After 44 seconds, Oscar came in last, with a fraction of a second between him and the next-to-last runner. But the crowd stood and cheered him across the finish line just as we did from our television view at home.

18

RELAPSE

"It looks suspicious," Sam's surgeon said. I took the phone call in the backyard so the kids couldn't hear me. It was a late afternoon in August and the fact that he was calling to share Sam's MRI test results meant that something serious was up.

Sam came home from camp in June with a soft lump on his right foot. He thought maybe it hurt because he was hopping around so much. He hopped on a rock when he was barefoot. That must have caused the swelling. The pediatrician felt confident it was an injury. The X-ray suggested a hairline fracture. But it didn't go away. Weeks went by before an MRI was ordered, and that's when Dr. Harvey called us.

I don't know why, but for the first few months of Sam's treatment, the thought of relapse never crossed my mind. Perhaps I didn't know enough. Then one day, while looking at an image of Sam's shrinking tumor on his computer screen, Dr. Harvey said, "You don't want Ewing to come back." After that, I sunk deep into my nightmares. It was like every night someone hooked me up to an IV bag full of stress hormones. There were times when I was sincerely concerned for my own well-being, that I was standing on the edge of some mental and emotional precipice.

"It looks suspicious." The phrase could only mean: Sam's cancer was back. At age 11, he would have to face it all over again. With worse odds, and more awareness, than the first time around. I wasn't sure we could handle that. I paced the backyard patio, hopeful for any other explanation.

"Is there anything else it could be?"

"It looks VERY suspicious," he replied. This is what the doctors say before the tumor is confirmed. I started to tremble. I hung up the phone, and sat down in a patio chair. I put my face in my hands and shook.

Bob stepped outside. "What happened?"

"Dr. Harvey. He thinks it's back."

"What? No! It can't be, what *exactly* did he say?"

"He says it looks suspicious and he's going to schedule a biopsy."

We both sat for a few minutes, saying little, searching for reasons to believe it wasn't true. *Maybe he's wrong. We won't be sure until it's biopsied. There's no way to know anything until we get the results.*

Bob immediately called a family meeting in our backyard. I stared down at the concrete patio while he told the kids. His words were met with quiet stares and blank faces. The tears would come later, after their shock subsided.

There's no good time for bad news. But the devastating signs that Sam had relapsed showed up at an especially inconvenient time. We were hosting a family for dinner that night. In an hour. They had just flown in from Scotland and we had only met them once before. In fact, it was the new pastor of our church and his family. I had been on the selection committee, back when I thought we were done with cancer, and when the leaders in my church were likely more convinced that my faith was strong. Bob and I considered canceling the dinner, knowing they would understand. They had three boys, and Natalie and Sam were both looking forward to meeting them. Bob and I decided they could use the distraction. So, after some time on the couch crying into a throw pillow, I started preparing the salmon and vegetables I would serve shortly.

Bob shared the news with our guests even before they walked into the house. Within minutes, Sam had invited the boys downstairs for an introduction to his arsenal of Nerf guns. The kids hardly spoke to us all evening, but from their shouts and laughter we could tell they were having a good time. Outside on the patio, we adults talked about the church, as well as the life they had left behind in Scotland. Bob and I shared more detail about Sam's cancer. The warmth and genuineness of the conversation carried us through a pain-filled evening.

A few days later, the biopsy robbed us of our hope. Ewing sarcoma was back. We called another family meeting. Again, the only thing I can remember is Natalie and Sam's blank faces, along with the sense that my heart was suffocating.

"I know! How about we go get some gelato?" Bob suggested, after we had said all we could say. "You can get whatever you want." The shop was within walking distance, so we all agreed to head out for a dish of sugar.

I don't know what a healthy response is for an 11-year-old kid who has just relapsed with bone cancer, or his 13-year-old sister who disdains any and all forms of sadness. Their tactic was silliness. Natalie got a little bit louder and her jokes a little less sophisticated. Sam rambled about nothing in particular, but in a baby-talk sort of voice which also wasn't very funny but we were all trying to find a reason to laugh instead of cry.

On the way to the shop, regretfully, I added in my own sad avoidant strategy. I asked Sam to make a video on my phone for his grandparents with a message that he was okay. What a dumb and damaging idea that was. *Tell everyone you're ok.* He wasn't.

"Ah, hey! Wait, is it on?" He sarcastically threw up his hands. He announced, "Okay, ah, I got cancer for a second time," His voice shook and his eyes flitted in every direction except the screen of the phone where I was recording him. "I'm fine," he said, looking up at the sky. "I mean, it's not like I haven't done this before. We might as well call this an annual thing."

His eyes had tears and I noticed he was trying to suppress them. He ran away from me to catch up with Natalie. I never sent the recording to my parents, because nothing was okay.

There is a unique childhood cancer culture born out of the unfathomable reality. I had fallen into the same coping pattern that I've since seen many times among other cancer parents. We have a common language - power words and proclamations - around the bravery and strength of our kids. If we can tell the world how strong they are, perhaps the pain will be more bearable.

Childhood cancer is often quite public, with Facebook, Instagram, and CaringBridge updates. GoFundMe pages solicit help for the financial instability experienced by 90% of families coping with childhood cancer. We write about how our kids never complain. How they care more about other people than themselves. How they face each day with courage. I fell in line with this way of coping too, never really pondering how these statements might put pressure on Sam. To be amazing. Or we pretend. Like my careless attempt: *tell everyone you're ok with a video* message to the grandparents.

Sam *was* brave and strong and all those things. I have reason to be exceedingly proud of my son. But, today I also wonder if those public proclamations were unfair and unhealthy. I needed him to believe he was strong. I needed him to stay positive. If Sam could smile, I could eat and sleep. Now I wish I had given him fewer expectations, and more freedom to be angry or sad. No one should have to be that brave and strong.

Maybe the better act of bravery is to allow ourselves to be

desperately vulnerable. To simply flail. To confess our fragility, rather than pose in the armor of a warrior. Maybe the people who choose to lament with a frightening degree of intensity are the ones who manage to find an authentic peace and joy at the other end of a long, dark, disorienting tunnel.

Relapse protocol isn't as harsh as frontline therapy, but it isn't as effective either. Every three weeks, Sam would need daily infusions for five days in a row. Fresh out of surgery for a new port, he began chemotherapy again. We opted to do his first five days in the inpatient unit because we could depend on the comfort there. Nurses who had taken care of Sam before came by to see him. They pretended everything was going to be okay. As they moved past me, their loving eye contact softly communicated, "I'm sorry you're back."

Sam sank into his hospital bed, one leg propped under the white blanket, the one without a foot crossed over the top of his thigh. He sat quietly for hours, day after day, and the reflected glow of his hand-held screen lit up his face. Other than that, he slept, and requested more anti-nausea meds. He refused to look at his schoolwork, and hardly ate. "Stop!" He'd say if I tried to adjust his blanket.

When the nurses came into the room, he grunted and sighed and sometimes rolled his eyes. There was no sign of the sweetness he'd shown from his first time through. I hated every second of his sadness. I searched the hospital's video library for inspirational uplifting stories. I brought him popcorn and cookies, which had previously evoked enthusiasm; now there was none at all. *Do you want to play Uno? Can I get you a warm blanket? Do you want a new book? Can I rub your foot?* He continued to stare at his video game as if he didn't hear me.

I wanted to scold him for ignoring me. Instead, I sat down on the bench underneath the window that also served as a bed and studied the low clouds over the parking lot. But I couldn't do nothing, so I pulled out my laptop, and drafted an email. *Dear friends, I am feeling a heavy darkness today and reaching out to you to ask for help with Sam. This is pretty hard for me to write. But I know you all believe in him, and the spirit God gave him. Forgive me, I'm an emotional and desperate mom.*

I wrote to the people he respected and I asked them to stay close, to encourage him with a *you've got this* message. I wanted Sam to believe he was going to survive. I thought, if the people in his life appeared to believe it, maybe he would too.

Sam's physical therapist, Melissa, heard he relapsed and came over to pay him a visit. Sam liked Melissa a lot, and I think she had a soft spot for him too. Sam's goal when he first started PT on his prosthetic leg was "to be faster than I was before." She liked that, and the two of them became fast friends. Melissa's visit felt like the backup support I needed.

Sam put down his screen when Melissa chatted with him. I didn't see his smile, but it seemed a step in the right direction. As I walked her out down the long curved hallway down to the elevator after her visit, I had an unbearable lump in my throat. I told Melissa I was worried about Sam's spirit, and my tears spilled out with the words.

"He's older now," she said. "He understands what cancer is. He knows kids who have died." She was right. His maturity and awareness at age 11 was much different than at nine, when the disease was still a mystery. "It's okay for him to be in a dark place right now. Just don't let him stay there."

19
HOUSTON

The new tumor on the right foot emerged from Sam's first metatarsal, the big toe bone along the front arch of the foot. It touched the bone parallel to it as well. It was mostly soft, unlike his first tumor. That's when I learned that a bone cancer cell can grow in the soft tissue anywhere in the body.

Sam, now age 11, was confronting the possibility of losing his entire right foot, or maybe only the portion with the tumor. We sought other opinions. Multiple doctors agreed he should keep at least some of his remaining foot. Sam offered, "It's ok if I only keep a few toes. I could never remember what all those little piggies were supposed to do anyway. Also, I really want to have a few toes left to wiggle in the sand sometimes."

Necrosis was a new word added to my vocabulary. It means dead tumor tissue. Chemo is a known cause of necrosis. The percentage of necrosis in a tumor that is removed after a few rounds of chemotherapy can be an indicator of a patient's chance of surviving. Parents of kids with cancer want 100% necrosis. We want the tumor to be completely dead. We don't want a single living cancer cell to be discovered in the lab once the tumor has been removed because only then can we be sure the poison we've allowed the doctors to flow into our kids is actually working. Thus, the two most important questions after surgery: How much necrosis was there? Are the margins clear? The answers to those questions are available about 10 days after surgery.

On a treatment day shortly after Sam's second amputation, of a portion of his right foot, the physician's assistant stepped into our curtained-off space to examine him. Normally she'd chat about light-hearted topics, like Sam's food preferences, and whether or not he was able to watch the football game over the weekend. With her compassionate smile, she was never as intimidating as some of the doctors, even when she had to deliver bad news.

"We got the results from pathology." We stepped outside the curtain and kept our voices low while Sam played a game on his device.

"How much necrosis was there?" I asked.

She sighed, "It was zero."

I faded away for a moment. She was quiet, giving me space to process. "Zero?" I heard myself question her answer. "So, the chemo did nothing?"

"Well, I wouldn't say that. The tumor didn't grow any, so it was doing something. But it didn't kill it."

"So, what do we do now?"

"I think we need to try a different chemo. Dr. Madison can talk to you about some options. He'll come see you later this afternoon." After allowing ten minutes more to answer a few vague questions I couldn't quite formulate, she left. Meanwhile, the chemotherapy that wasn't working pumped into Sam's bloodstream.

This was about the time when my body's response to bad news started to become predictable.

I would stay away from people all day and speak as little as possible. I'd notice my heart beating and my hands shaking. I'd remind myself that I should keep taking in fluids with calories because I wasn't able to eat. I would make a panicked call to someone who'd been there too, and text a few close friends – anyone with a hopeful word. I wanted to know that I wasn't alone, but also, I wanted to be alone. I'd get through the day, maybe with an Ativan-induced nap after we got home. I'd let the kids play more video games than I thought was healthy. I'd wander around the house moving things around but accomplishing nothing in particular. I'd attempt to process conversations with Bob that contained long pauses, encouraging suggestions and asking unanswerable questions. At night, I'd slip into bed with melatonin and a glass of wine and watch an episode of Lost on my laptop until I was drowsy enough to fall asleep, for a few merciful hours of amnesia. The next morning, sometime in the early morning transition into consciousness, I'd remember: Sam has cancer.

There was another tumor.

Another amputation.

Chemotherapy isn't working.

I might lose him.

I'd start to cry before my body uncurled from its sleep position. I'd cry when I made my coffee. I'd cry when I moved to the couch, then lay back down holding my stomach and a wad of tissue for my tears. I'd cry when I pulled out my laptop and read through the listserv emails full of Ewing sarcoma parents desperate for a new and better treatment, just like me. I'd click on links to scientific articles in PubMed and read them slowly, insisting that my brain understand the science. I'd search for promising phrases in their conclusions while avoiding cautionary statements in the introduction, like: "Patients with metastatic, relapsed, or refractory tumors have a dismal prognosis due to resistance to conventional therapies." I'd remain there on the couch tearfully searching for answers, until the kids woke up.

I worried that my kids would read my face and take on my fear. I tried to keep the sadness inside myself, rather than spread it around. Flooded with grief and worry, I didn't contemplate whether or not I should let my kids see my despair; I simply hid my sorrow from them. But, reflecting on this later, I wondered if it might have been better for all of us to let them see me weather the storm, no matter how uncomfortable that might have felt in the moment. I still don't know.

My tears would subside by midmorning, usually relieved by a sudden inspiration about someone or other whom I could reach out to for help: a doctor, a researcher, a friend who works in medicine. I wouldn't wear any makeup. I'd get through the day with a peanut butter and jelly sandwich, several text messages with friends, and maybe a walk or a yoga class. Then I'd finish the day with a stream of episodes of mindless TV until I fell asleep, only to wake up crying again.

I did this for three to five days. That's about how long it took me to find hope.

Multiple parents on the listserv email group encouraged me to get second and third opinions. There were sarcoma specialists out there who had competing ideas about our next steps. Though the standard treatment was the same anywhere in the country for a newly diagnosed patient with Ewing sarcoma, the treatment after relapse is open to individual provider recommendation, as long as the FDA has approved the drugs for kids. Doctors pull from a list of potential protocols, making their best guess based on clinical trials, all of them with mixed results.

It made sense to us that we should find an oncologist who had seen a lot of Ewing sarcoma cases, and had some success stories worth paying attention to. The name of a doctor at MD Anderson Cancer Center in Houston, Texas, kept coming up in our group emails. *He thinks outside the box. He's the expert when it comes to Ewing. He saved my son's life.* We looked at the cost of flights and checked with our insurance. In a flight of desperation, with newfound hope, Bob, Sam, and I took a trip to Houston, Texas.

High up on the front of the building, there is a stunning large sign that reads MD Anderson Cancer Center, with the C-word boldly crossed out. Behind massive glass walls that magnified the intense Houston light, I imagined teams of brilliant scientists and oncologists in their white coats peering through microscopes and marveling at the dramatic results: new breakthroughs for kids like Sam. I'd heard that royal families from foreign countries around the world traveled to MD Anderson. I felt it was a privilege for my son to be seen there. Though we were hopeful, discouragement also shadowed us as we stepped through those sliding glass doors.

At our hospital back home in Oregon, I had walked the hallways, curious to know the ailments of each patient in the rooms I passed, and the severity of their case. At MD Anderson there was no guessing. No tonsillectomies, knee replacements, or back surgery. Here, everyone had cancer. There were rows of wheelchairs for patients too weak to walk to their appointments. I saw patients with hollowed out eyes, carrying emesis bags and wearing knit hats or wigs. In the lobby, a man threw up into a garbage can near the giant fish tank. The disease was everywhere, creating a community from a somewhat random collection of people.

Our first appointment with Dr. Stevens was indeed hopeful. He suggested a different protocol than what we'd been offered back home. He told us about another patient who had experienced a relapse in a situation that was similar to Sam's, and was doing very well a year later. He assured us that the protocol he prescribed was intended to be curative, and not one that would just give us more time with Sam. He suggested that Sam receive radiation at a certain dose on a certain schedule with a certain radiation oncologist whom he favored.

To access this very hopeful plan, we would need to relocate to Houston for a month.

Ten days after the consultation, Sam and I unpacked our bags in a furnished apartment in Houston just a mile away from MD Anderson.

Hope feels good. It means something is possible. It's better than a wish. A wish is something we would like to have happen even when it's just not possible, or the chances of success are so poor we might as well consider it impossible. In this world of childhood cancer, there is often a very thin and indistinct line separating our hopes from our wishes. Even the tiniest possibility of hope invited me in. I wanted to roll up my sleeves, and build the dam or fight the blazing fire! Or comb through every freaking haystack to find that damn needle. Hope says, *let's do this.*

An invitation to believe that something good could happen was the only thing that prevented me from disappearing into my despair. Life became more doable after a potentially curative treatment plan was set into motion. While a month-long medical vacation in Houston wasn't on our destination wish list, it felt that just being proactive eased our anxious hearts and even stirred up a sense of adventure.

Sometimes, when logistics come together seamlessly, as if it were all meant to happen a certain way, we allow hope to grow. This time in Houston came with an unexpected new friendship pieced together in the most random of circumstances. Back when

I wrote the Bible study curriculum, there was a church in Houston who used our study and listened to recordings of my talks for their own Women's Bible Study program. A leader in that group named Mary reached out to me because she was considering writing their own study and wanted to know how we did it. She wasn't expecting to hear that my son had been diagnosed with cancer, and I was no longer teaching or writing. Mary followed our story on CaringBridge, and prayed for Sam often. When we announced we'd be visiting Houston, Mary offered to host us. She and her husband Todd ended up being our quiet comforters, like extended family in a place we had never been. They hosted us when we flew in for the initial visit, and became instrumental in helping us find the apartment to stay in for a month. Most significantly, Todd and Mary cared for us and joined us with hopeful energy.

Tarina was a dear friend from high school, and she lived within an hour's drive of where we were staying. It had been years since we'd been together, but she also reached out and offered to have us visit. On a Saturday morning, we headed her way to spend the day with her and her youngest son, Jackson, who was 13, just two years older than Sam. It didn't take long for the boys to turn chatty, chuckling and telling stories about stupid stuff they thought was funny. I saw Sam's spunk re-emerge as if he were back home with his friends. After lunch we headed to a quiet arcade with no line for admission.

The woman at the arcade ticket counter saw the boys approaching and noticed Sam's protective boot, which he wore over his recent partial foot amputation. Sweatpants covered his prosthesis, so he looked like a kid with one normal leg and perhaps a fracture or sprain from a sporting event or a dumb idea that sounded good at the time.

"Good afternoon." The woman at the ticket counter engaged our spirited boys. "You guys look like you're ready for some fun today."

"Yeah! Hey, how fast will those race cars go?"

A quick rapport formed as she warmed to their youthful enthusiasm. "You'll just have to check it out and let me know. By the way, what did you do to your foot?"

"Well," Sam reached down for his amputated leg instead of the boot, and pulled up his pant leg. He pressed the release button, removed his prosthetic leg, and stood it up on the ticket counter in front of the nice lady. "I got cancer and they had to cut my leg off."

Sam broke into a smirk, and glanced back at Jackson, who was covering his wide-opened mouth. The lady behind the counter finally smiled, sensing the comedic nature of my son. Sam snapped his leg back on and the boys headed straight for the race cars to find out what they could do.

I started to giggle. This borderline inappropriate humor of Sam's was one of the traits I loved about him. I loved watching other people's faces in those moments when Sam's wit, or his deep thoughts, or his knowledge of things uncommon for a kid his age, would create a kind of fun chaos in the social spaces around him. Tarina and Jackson saw this side of him for the first time, and it made them smile. It was one of my favorite kinds of moments.

As we passed through the turnstile and into the arcade, I broke into the kind of laughing fit that made my eyes water and my stomach burn. The boys looked back to see me with a chuckle, then wandered off. I kept on laughing so hard that I gasped for air. I glanced at Tarina who continued to laugh with me. The two of us laughed in the quiet arcade like we were back in junior high together. I briefly regained my composure, only to lose control again, my eyes wet and blurred by the good kind of tears. Maybe Sam was just that amusing, or maybe the long-repressed laughter inside of me needed a way out. Hope served me just enough of a respite from the despair to let a little fit of laughter come rolling out. I felt ridiculously happy to be Sam's mom.

A week into our MD Anderson stay, the radiation had started to burn Sam's foot, and walking became painful. He began using one of the wheelchairs from the entrance to the hospital. After the elevators and hallways, the pediatric check-in desk and time in a waiting room with kids of all ages and all kinds of cancers, we had our turn to head to the clinic room to wait some more.

The door opened swiftly and the oncologist sat on the standard doctor's rolling stool to discuss how things were going so far, to inspect Sam's foot, and check his abdomen. I never knew why they checked his stomach; it was just something they always did. I was looking for the next dose of encouragement that moving to Houston was the right thing to do, but this time something was different. Dr. Stevens lacked the enthusiasm of our previous conversations.

When we were wrapping up the appointment, I asked Dr. Stevens a question. I would soon find out it's one of the most controversial topics in cancer care and treatment. "I was wondering, are there any diets or particular foods Sam can eat that might help prevent the cancer from coming back?" I thought it was a reasonable question, and that he might even be impressed.

I didn't see it coming.

"Not really. This cancer will probably come back, and there's really not much you can do about it." I froze while his words still lingered in the air. He then added, "Yogurt has probiotics and that's helpful. He should be eating a lot of protein, like milk." I don't remember whether I responded or not.

Nothing will work for Sam.

The cancer will probably come back.

Milk and yogurt.

His comments and his demeanor were so different from our last visit, it threw me. I expected connection and hope, but both were absent.

With that, my bad news emotional cycle was launched again, so far away from home.

Sam heard the conversation too, but he didn't respond with any visible signs of shock or distress. I wasn't sure it registered. I wanted to stay composed because in a minute Sam and I would have to journey through the extensive network of hallways for his daily dose of radiation. Whatever was protecting his emotions from the doctor's prognosis, I wanted it to continue. I wanted to protect him from the fear that had ambushed me without warning. I avoided eye contact and maneuvered his wheelchair through the busy hospital. I crossed my arms and stood behind him while we waited for the elevator, because I thought if I looked at his face I might give myself away. In the waiting room, I parked Sam in front of the TV screen. I told him I was going to go call his dad and walked away.

"Hey, how are you?" Bob answered in a peppy tone.

It took me a second. I was alone in the waiting room, just around the corner from Sam, sitting on a pastel print cushioned chair, leaning forward like my stomach hurt.

My tears broke through. "We just met with Dr. Stevens. He told me that Sam's cancer would come back."

"What? That's what he told you?"

"Yeah." I was so mad I was shaking. "I can't believe he said that."

"What *exactly* did he say?" Bob asked, like maybe I'd missed a word or phrase that could clarify. I told him the whole story. Again, our conversation was punctuated by long pauses as we searched for some hopeful phrase to hold onto. After a while we just stayed quiet. I then remembered that Bob and Natalie were to arrive here at the end of our stay. I blurted, "I think you should come here sooner."

I didn't want to have another conversation with the doctor by myself. I needed to hate him for a while longer, and let Bob do the talking. More than that, I needed to find a reason for him to be wrong. But, we also wanted to stay clear of animosity because we needed the doctors on our side. We needed him to want to fight for Sam.

Doctors are human. They don't always know how things will go, and they don't always know the right thing to say. The next morning in Houston, I drank my coffee while I cried and replayed those words: *there's nothing you can do.*

The truth is, I don't do *nothing* very well.

After Sam's radiation appointment, I drove us to the nearest Barnes and Noble to look for books about fighting cancer with nutrition. Sam headed for the youth section to scout out his next dystopian fantasy series while I settled into an aisle full of self-help books for fighting various health conditions. An hour later, we headed back to our apartment, cradling several books in the crook of my arm. Then we read.

I started with *Anti-Cancer: A New Way of Life,* by David Servin-Schreiber, a physician and neuroscientist, who discovered his own brain tumor. After treatment and some time in remission, he relapsed. He asked his oncologist if there was anything else he could do to keep his cancer from spreading, which was validating to read that a neuroscientist was asking the same questions I asked. I suddenly felt a lot less uninformed. His doctor had told him, "There's nothing else you can do. Just keep doing what you're doing."

Dr. Servan-Schreiber didn't do *nothing* very well either, so he began researching diet's impact on cancer and changing his lifestyle by turning to whole, organic, nutrient rich, cancer fighting foods. Once I read the first chapter, I found my hope. Someone much smarter than me, proficient in scientific medicine embraced a new diet and *lived*. The dread, and deep, deep pain inside me was replaced by a new inspiration.

The next several days in Houston were focused on learning what it meant to eat whole, nutrient-rich foods. I'd always wanted to be one of those super healthy people. I wanted to glow, and feel good, and be disciplined with my food. I wanted to be better than frozen pizza or chicken dinosaurs on a Friday night. I wanted to know what people were talking about when they referenced the concept that nutrition is medicine. I wanted to order the Swiss chard wrap filled with avocado, tofu, hummus, shredded beets, and carrots with extra tahini sauce.

However, until that moment, I didn't know what 50% of those ingredients were.

I devoured the books. While my brain filled up with knowledge, my spirit filled with hope. Sure, I questioned whether a diet could actually do much good. But the downside of eating healthy and being hopeful was hard to find. So I kept reading.

Sam's book choice was satisfying a need in him as well, and he repeated to me every couple of chapters: *this is such a good book!* Three days later, Sam finished his book at 7pm and he pleaded with me to go to Barnes and Noble before it closed so he could buy the second in the series. I bought another nutrition book. Instead of exploring Houston, every night the two of us would sink into the faux leather sofa in our temporary apartment to read, sharing the cheap throw blanket I bought at a nearby drugstore. Every night, Sam and I snapped shut our books and headed to bed. He didn't like sleeping on the far side of the apartment in the featureless room with the twin beds with thin brown bedspreads, so he slept next to me on the king-sized bed. I liked having him close.

"I love you, mom," He said, settled in with his head on the pillow.

He reached out to touch my arm.

"I love you too, Sam." I kissed his temple and stared at him as he drifted off to sleep.

I couldn't survive losing him.

Bob and Natalie arrived in Houston one day before our next weekly appointment with Dr. Stevens. Sam talked and talked, telling stories and performing several goofy antics for Natalie. Inside the hospital they found the ramps for racing the wheelchair down, and latex gloves for blowing up like balloons. They giggled and teased each other. I think Natalie gave Sam a much needed dose of laughter.

Since the *there's nothing you can do* appointment, I'd had a phone conversation with the doctor's medical assistant. I mentioned what he had said, and my reaction. Now, with the whole family in the exam room, the kids continued their banter while Bob and I waited for the doctor.

He entered the room and sat down on the rolling stool. "I want you to know that I'm sorry for how I worded things last week, and I'm sorry I made you cry."

He explained that it had been a rough day in the clinic. He had been dealing with some frustrating institutional issues when Sam and I came in. He told us there was still reason to be hopeful. Despite what he had said the previous week, he was prescribing a protocol that he believed could be curative. The appointment was somewhat more comforting compared to the previous one, and partially restored my trust. It didn't lessen my resolve to embrace a cancer fighting diet. However, I wasn't up for feeling foolish again in front of Dr. Stevens, so I kept it to myself.

20

ATHLETES

Four months before going to Houston, the 2012 London Olympics took place. After Sam's new foot tumor had been diagnosed, someone from Nike got hold of us. Oscar Pistorius was returning to Portland, and we were invited to go to dinner with him. He didn't know about Sam's relapse.

"Is there a restaurant Sam particularly likes?" I didn't think Five Guys Burgers was what Oscar had in mind, so we suggested dinner at the Chart House. It sits on a hill near the hospital and overlooks the Willamette River. Oscar and his two Nike handlers showed up. Oscar wore nicely fitting dark jeans with white stitching, a wide alligator skin belt, and a pink and white checked button-down shirt. Sam was in another Nike shirt and his nicest pair of jeans. He was bald again, from the chemotherapy we later learned wasn't working.

The Nike guys must have called ahead because the restaurant shut down an entire section just for us. Our neighbors Julie and Aaron joined us, too, at my request. Aaron worked for Nike, and they had been especially supportive.

Oscar didn't act like we were lucky to be in his presence. We ordered calamari and artichoke dip as hors d'oeuvres. Oscar told stories. He sat directly across from Sam and asked questions of both Sam and Natalie. We didn't talk much about cancer. He filled us in on the Olympics because we were curious. Mostly, Oscar talked about his friends and his family. He told us about a time when he and his girlfriend were trying to fix something, and he accidentally knocked himself out with a crowbar. He was a natural storyteller and he listened to our stories too. He wasn't too serious, and he wasn't too casual. He encouraged Sam to believe that life could be good as an amputee. He said the girls would like him too.

"Be confident Sam." He took a moment to drive home a message. "People will see you the way you see yourself."

After dinner, Sam asked Oscar if he would sign his leg. I handed Oscar a black Sharpie, and Sam took off his leg and handed it to him. On the back of the calf of Sam's flesh-colored prosthesis, Oscar wrote a message. Over time, the words have rubbed off. Today, I can still read a very faint: "Thank you for all the support. Stay strong. Take care, Buddy. Oscar Pistorius."

We hoped to see Oscar again one day.

One month after returning home from Houston, Oscar shot and killed his girlfriend.

Early in the morning on Valentine's Day, 2013, Bob called me from his car while driving to work at Central Precinct. I was sitting cross-legged on the hardwood floor over the heating vent, a ritual I've had on cold winter days since I was a child. With my coffee cupped in my hands, I prepared my mind and heart for another day at the hospital. Natalie and Sam were still asleep. Bob's call interrupted my moment of peace. The radio had just announced: *South African double amputee athlete Oscar Pistorius has shot and killed his girlfriend Reeva Steenkamp.* Reeva died in his home from four gunshot wounds to the head and torso.

That day was a chemo day, never enjoyable, but not typically a bad news day. No one yet knew why he did it. I wanted to defend him, but I knew that as the story emerged things could get messy.

I dreaded having to tell Sam. After hanging up the phone with Bob, I turned up the heat for a few more minutes of warm solitude and reluctantly and sadly looked up the story on my laptop.

The news of Oscar killing his girlfriend was nothing like a bad scan day, but it still hit Sam hard. Knowing Oscar had come at the right time for Sam. It was the boost his spirit needed. It also gave him something cooler to talk about than the cancer story that continued to dominate his life. But, soon the famous runner who sincerely cared about Sam would be in jail. Sam wondered if he was a good guy or a bad guy, as if the people and events in our lives ever resolve into such lucid easy-to-comprehend categories.

The same neighbor who had joined us for dinner with Oscar learned that we were about to spend a month in Houston. He pulled some strings with the Nike basketball section, and we received four passes to a Houston Rockets game at the Toyota Center. Natalie had returned back home to Portland so she wouldn't miss school. We invited our new friend Todd to come along for the fun of it.

Keith was the lead trainer, in charge of the logistics for the team. He met us at a side door of the arena two hours before the game. He was wearing a bright plaid shirt under a crisp blazer. He smiled at us like old friends as he handed us the four lanyards with guest passes.

He ushered us into the Rockets' training room with three massage tables, several therapy balls, a variety of exercise bands and bags full of tape and other sports trainer gear. There we made ourselves comfortable as the players shuffled through.

NBA trainers look like they suffer from a growth hormone deficiency compared to the players they tend to. One player was lying face down on a massage table, while a small but muscular man worked out his knotted, chiseled, overworked muscles to ready him for the game. I didn't know the names of the players. I was afraid one or another of these stunning athletes might experience an uncomfortable absence of coverage in the presence of Sam's middle-aged mom, but our new friend Keith seemed to be at ease, so I tried to act that way too.

Sam had on shorts and the same red shirt he wore when he ran with Oscar. His prosthetic leg had the skin-colored socket above a metal post down by his ankle and Oscar's signature was still visible around the back of his leg. Sam represented Nike well. A few of the friendly players, like Donatas Montiejunas, introduced themselves to Sam and posed for the standard photo op with a cancer kid. Sam looked miniature next to the 7'2" basketball star. Sam sat down on a bench and reached down to remove his leg. He asked "Hey, would you sign my leg?"

Keith grabbed a Sharpie from a desk nearby. Laughing and chatting, player after player signed Sam's leg. Then, James Harden strode into the room. His gaze avoided us all, including Sam. In a corner next to a large nylon bag full of basketball shoes, he grabbed a Theraband which he used to warm his mountainous shoulders. I was careful not to stare. Bob, Sam, and Todd continued their conversation with Keith and a semi-circle of friendly players. Harden's body language shouted out that he didn't wish to be interrupted. Once he was done, James strutted over to Sam sitting on a bench with his leg in his lap.

He pointed to Sam's leg. "Hey man, what you got there?"

"Hey. Would you sign my leg?"

"Yeah. Let me see that." James took Sam's leg and scribbled his signature with the blue sharpie.

The legendary Kevin McHale was coaching the Rockets at the time. While I knew about McHale's meteoric career with the Boston Celtics back in the 80's, Bob brought me up to date, along with the sad news that McHale's 21-year-old daughter had passed away just a few months prior. I wondered how he could still coach a team after losing a child. I pondered his pain, and the suffering of his wife and their other four adult kids, for hours.

Our seats were ten rows up from the court behind the team. Bob pointed out the team manager two seats away, looking thoroughly engaged. Even though I had announced to the family that I was preparing some changes in our diet, we all got hot dogs and soft drinks. We cheered as if we'd been lifelong fans. At half time, one of the players grabbed a T-shirt from one of the dancers. He looked into the crowd until he spotted Sam. He then launched the rolled-up shirt toward Sam. I smiled at Sam's delight.

It turned out to be a landmark game. James Harden accomplished his first ever triple double. That's when a player gets double digits in points, rebounds, and assists. It's a pretty big deal. The players and the coach instantly became a little bit drunk on their success. When we wandered down toward the court just after the game, Sam, Bob, and Todd were invited into the locker room to celebrate with the team. I was relieved to not be included.

Twenty minutes later, the boys came from the locker room grinning like kids with a bag of candy. Bob was carrying two pairs of shoes. Size twelve red and white game shoes signed by James Harden and Jeremy Lin. James Harden had gifted his first triple double game shoes to Sam. At the time I didn't quite grasp the hype, but these were the early days of the making of an NBA superstar.

"I just shook hands with Kevin McHale!" Bob's eyebrows were still stuck in the awestruck position as he greeted me in the hallway.

"Kevin McHale!" he said again as if I didn't hear him the first time. "Incredible! Sam talked to all the guys! All of them! It was surreal!"

"Oh my gosh Sam, really?" Sam wore a subtle smirk but was much less chatty than Bob and Todd.

He was still having the experience, and not yet ready to talk about it. And that was just the beginning.

21

THE DIET

Every inch of our home offered warmth after our month in Houston. Sam's foot had turned fiery from the radiation burns and he could no longer walk. The burns started slowly, first a soft pink, then a deep, hot red. It continued burning for weeks after the treatment was over. The outer layer of skin grew white and began sloughing off, exposing a raw fleshy open wound. It was hard to look at and extremely sensitive. I tended to it multiple times a day, pasting a gel-like healing ointment onto a non-stick bandage before gently wrapping his fragile, mutilated, three-toed foot.

Sam continued with the protocol recommended by Dr. Stevens, with the addition of a healthy diet overhaul. When I wasn't patching him, medicating him, feeding him, or transporting him, I spent my time researching nutrition and bookmarking an extensive list of recipes and articles. The stories about people who had succeeded in fighting their cancer with nutrition now seemed extensive. Kris Carr kept her rare sarcoma from growing with a clean, high nutrient vegan diet. I subscribed to her blog and bought her cookbook titled, "Crazy Sexy

Kitchen." Jokingly, Bob said he hoped my new program would include me cooking dinner for him in a bikini.

I read a NY Times article about a man with an incurable cancer who left the US to die on his native island in the Mediterranean. But he didn't die. The food and laughter and purpose and love that surrounded him cured him from the cancer that had been growing with his American

lifestyle. I bought magazines from Whole Foods. I watched food documentaries. I bought a juicer. I bought more books and watched numerous TED talks. I switched to all organic produce and I bought a farm share. There was so much to read, so much to cook, and a world of hope to indulge in.

Instead of choosing any particular diet - like paleo or vegan - I focused on the nutrients. I fed our family more fresh vegetables, spices with medicinal value, grains and legumes I'd never heard of. Any food with anti-cancer properties made the grocery list.

"Ok you guys, here's the idea," I said to my family before serving sticky ginger tempeh with balsamic and garlic collard greens. "I'm going to make a lot of new stuff. But each time I make a new meal, you have absolute veto power." They nodded. "If you don't like it, I won't make it again."

"Yay!" said Natalie.

Sam nodded. "Cool."

Encouraged, I went on. "I think I can make a lot of meals you'll love and that will still be healthy." My family sat at our four-person kitchen table with glasses of green juice and plates full of unfamiliar vegetables, and they eagerly gave me their critiques like a group of restaurant critics. The collard greens were a thumbs up. The sticky ginger tempeh was never to be served again.

My kids are not picky eaters. Other than tomatoes and asparagus, Natalie will eat just about anything. Bob has an aversion to spicy foods and avocados which he blames on a high school summer work project in Ecuador. He is most content with meat and potatoes, which was fine since I come from a full-on Scottish home. Sometimes when I served different food, Bob would look at me with a wrinkled brow and cocked head. I tried to convince him.

"It's a falafel."

"A falafel? What's a falafel?"

"It's Greek."

"We don't eat Greek food!"

"We are tonight! Remember, you can veto it but you have to try it." I assured him. Falafels, I later learned, are actually Middle Eastern, and I love them. To this day, they are one of those food items I make for myself, when the rest of the family is out of the house. My version got a thumbs down.

I found a new kind of stride with this cancer fight. I cooked all the time, sometimes for several hours each day, taking advantage of the unanticipated perk of not being able to work outside the home. I went to new grocery stores and filled my cart with foods from the perimeter instead of the aisles. Cooking dinner became an event instead of a reluctant task. The chops and stirs and sizzles and beeping timers were all elements of an orchestrated and well executed strategy for battling cancer. I found my purpose beyond the doctor's orders. In the kitchen I developed a rhythm and flow around cooking and moving about the grocery store or the local farmer's market. My meals were colorful, medicinally rich, disease fighting cornucopias - my personal contribution to Sam's cancer treatment.

One morning when I was changing the bandage on Sam's fleshy, raw, radiated foot, I noticed a few spots of lush new skin had appeared. It looked so interesting and lovely, like little droplets of new life vigorously multiplying in this hospitable environment. I really don't know whether he would have healed the exact same way without being so well fueled by nutrition, but when I saw those clusters of dividing skin cells flourishing on his fragile foot, it reassured me: good nutrition will help Sam heal.

With all that Sam had going on in his mid-sized body, and the availability having left my job afforded me, it was hard to find the downside of ultra-healthy eating.

Sam continued on an outpatient chemotherapy routine of five days on, then two weeks off for almost a full year. I told Dr. Madison we were eating differently. Healthier. I didn't ask for his opinion. I was surprised at his encouragement. "A healthy diet can support his immune system and maybe help get rid of some of those microscopic cancer cells floating around in his body."

I smiled on the inside and carried his simple affirmation with me for days.

Several weeks into the diet change, I noticed a difference in Sam. He seemed to bounce back faster after chemo. His skin had a brightness to it in all the right colors. Most significantly, Sam never got even a hint of a sniffle throughout the cold and flu season. When a third of his classmates missed multiple days of school, Sam continued to attend whenever he wasn't at the hospital for his treatment.

I noticed some changes in myself as well. I also didn't get sick while the people in our community struggled through the usual seasonal illnesses. Before Sam had cancer, I suffered from sinus infections every May and a chest cold every October. I could practically put those on the calendar. I saw a specialist to see if there was something wrong with my nasal cavity. After a CT scan, the doctor determined that I needed surgery to fix a deviated septum, which I opted to postpone until Sam got better. After embracing a high-nutrient, whole foods diet, I quit getting sick. No chest cold. No sinus infection. Nothing. It was a fascinating experiment and each little improvement in our health motivated me even more.

Pretty soon, food had our attention and the kids managed to

add humor to the way in which our family grew oddly clean and green.

"Wow, mom, kale chips and olives are just what every kid wants for an after-school snack."

"Mom, can you not put quite so much nutritional yeast on my popcorn this time?"

"Quit messing around Sam! You're getting quinoa in the natural buttery spread!"

At the dinner table, Natalie and Sam joked and giggled and humored me and my new obsession. But Sam drew the line when I suggested he use beet juice in the shaved ice he hoped to sell to the neighbor kids on a warm spring Sunday afternoon.

I wondered how all of these nutrient dense foods might be nourishing Sam's organs. They'd surely taken a beating from the chemotherapy. If what I observed on the outside was equally restorative on the inside, perhaps Sam's body would become more resilient to disease, including cancer.

Once I became a health nut, I started to feel that the world was working against me. Birthday parties, school parties, sleepovers, summer camp, even the childhood cancer nonprofits, offered processed snacks with other non-food ingredients designed to lure more children and sell more products.

At the hospital, friendly volunteers rolled their carts full of goldfish crackers, juice boxes, and fruit snacks through the infusion center for kids to take something appealing. When I heard them coming, I would close the curtain around Sam's bed to shut out the friendly "Hello! Would you like a snack?" I had tried asking if they had anything healthy but mushy red apples or snack bags of mini carrots were all they had to offer. I was the bad guy for declining an offering that would generate more inflammation on his small suffering body.

I got to thinking: medicine and health are quite different. Sometimes, they are even in conflict. The hospital is where we could get the medicine he needed to kill the disease or to ease the side effects, but home is where he would get the nutrition he needed to be restored back to good health.

While this new fiery conviction was rising within me, not all of our friends shared my view. One day, I took Sam to a friend's house. Before he was fully out of earshot, the other mom called out, "Can Sam have a cupcake?" I'm a courteous person who hates inconveniencing others. That meant I either had to compromise or disappoint. Sam was cooperative and ate most of the healthy dishes I made. But missing out and being different was tough on him. Sometimes I gave in, and sometimes I stuck to my guns and lived with the tension. Sometimes we argued and sometimes he pouted and I raised my voice. A nutrition-centric lifestyle challenged us, but in the long run Sam could see how the healthier choice made a difference to his body.

Similar to our experience in the hospital, I began to see the obstacles to healthy eating inside the church. I never realized how much sugar there was in church until we got healthy. My kids loved their youth group, fully stocked with red vines and sour patch candies tainted with red dye 40. Sending him off to church camp would mean sacrificing a whole week of good nutrition, where evening sugar binges offered a festival of indulgence. Kids were learning about Jesus, and the stories impacted them. But I wondered whether the sugar-induced spikes and drops in glucose would influence the emotions of a young person exploring their spiritual beliefs. Away from home, the disrupted sleep, the anxieties and insecurities kids carry are all so susceptible to their sugar intake, making it hard to distinguish a genuine spiritual response.

The conflict inside of me was growing. Both medicine and church life seemed, in some ways, in opposition to holistic health.

Long ago, maybe even hundreds of years ago, something must have gone wrong. Clearly there was illness in the ancient days. Humankind used to eat what the earth provided for us, free from modification. How can we seek spiritual wellness and keep it separate from the health of our physical bodies? And when did medicine begin to cover for good health? When and how did technology, chemistry, and consumerism modify our food so dramatically?

I suspect the ancient days of Christianity and early medicine were both intended to support healthy lives. Over time, I will argue, we've journeyed off course. On any given Sunday, I see people asking for prayer to be healed of their disease, their pain and fatigue, and the medical bills that accompany poor health. And the elder will pray for complete and total healing. After the prayer, the pastor will invite their congregants to socialize in the fellowship hall, where they will be tempted by donuts and pans full of pancakes made from a box, and syrup poured from a jumbo bottle purchased for $2.79 at the discount grocery store, along-side inexpensive synthetic sausages. Food can either nurture or get in the way of physical health and spiritual freedom.

Before I read those nutrition books, I viewed our shared celebrations with food just as everyone else did, but now my son was sick with a potentially deadly cancer. With this new lens, I wanted to convince other people to join me in a movement of change.

I scheduled a meeting with the pastor in charge of the pancake breakfasts and asked him to consider a healthier option. "I see it so clearly now. God repeatedly called his people to heal the sick, but it seems like we skip over that part. Or we limit our efforts to heal only by praying for the sick. What if we could support God's desire for healthy bodies by creating a culture of health and well-ness right here in the church?"

He asked, "How would you recommend we do that?"

"Well, what if we offered a yogurt parfait bar instead of

pancakes and sausages. We could have fruits and granolas and all kinds of healthy toppings for it. We could even include some dark chocolate chips to keep it fun and enticing."

"Well, that's a great idea, but I have a budget to manage. I think that would probably be too expensive."

I found the middle school youth pastor to be much more open to healthier options at the Wednesday night snack bar. We swapped out candy bars for fruit and nut bars. Soda was replaced with flavored sparkling water. I took dark-chocolate-dipped strawberries to any sort of small group celebration, and all of this was subtle enough to suggest a step in the right direction without offending anyone. Still, I thought to myself, one day I will teach or preach or speak or write about this and maybe a few will join me and we'll begin a spiritual wellness revolution.

Over time, as we watched Sam's disease progress, my strategy shifted. I was confident the nutrition was having a positive effect on his body and general health, but it didn't stop the cancer from growing. With each frightening scan, I re-evaluated our approach. I hired a functional nutritionist and had Sam tested for food sensitivities. We saw a Chinese medicine doctor who sent us home with a powdered tea that tasted like dirt. Sam didn't complain. I saw a Naturopath who taught me to read Sam's bloodwork beyond what the oncology team considered relevant.

His vitamin D levels were low, so I boosted them. Sam was sensitive to chicken eggs, so we switched to duck. His liver numbers crept upwards with more toxic medications, so I added milk thistle, and sprinkled our food with parsley and cilantro.

One evening I handed him a bowl and a batch of cilantro. "Sam, would you please pull the leaves from the stems for me?"

"Sure. But can I eat the stems?"

"Yes, you can," I smiled.

22

ROCKETS

Sam's friendship with the Houston Rockets continued season after season. When they came to Portland, Sam was invited to the games. And the locker room. And sometimes he left with more shoes and signed jerseys. He attended the shoot around with the team in an empty arena the day before the games. Late after one game, James Harden tweeted a photo of him with Sam and a buddy he brought with him. My phone buzzed with text messages from friends who'd seen the tweet. Sam's life was so far from ordinary. If we were to plot it out on a line graph it would show erratic ups and downs, rarely within the normal range.

When Sam was first diagnosed, I had a poignant conversation with Bob. We were still stunned at the diagnosis, wondering about the life we were about to be forced into. In a quiet moment when we had exhausted all of our information processing capabilities I said, "I really don't understand what this is going to look like, but let's do our best to live well." Even as the words came out of my mouth, I didn't know what living well could possibly mean when dealing with childhood cancer. I only had a sense that there could be opportunities to experience life in a deeper way. It could involve community, and conversations that stay with you. It could mean celebrating little things with food and music, or opening up our home to invite evenings of laughter. It would mean choosing wellness and play and doing more of the things we love whenever we had the chance. During Sam's first year of treatment, we couldn't travel, and yet I wondered if adventure could still be found within a forty-mile radius of the hospital.

Living well meant the hard stuff too, like crying when we needed to cry and being authentic with our grief and, when bearable, leaning into the intensity of our story. The road ahead of us would be frightening and hard, but with sprinkles of clear intention, it could also be remarkable.

Now we were nearly three years into Sam's life with cancer. He was becoming an adolescent with a fluctuating sense of identity and the stories made for this memoir were growing abundant. We felt deep within our bones that life could be taken away. But when it is given, we can savor it and let the solace of a full life penetrate every corner of our inner world.

Text messages and phone calls from Rockets' players came to Sam regularly, checking in to see how he was doing. Kevin McHale texted Sam too, which made Bob a little bit jealous and curious.

"Sam, have you heard from coach lately?"

"Yeah, he texted me yesterday."

"What? He did? What did he say?

"He asked how I was doing."

"Yeah? And what did you say?"

"I said I was doing fine."

"That's it? You're texting Kevin McHale and that's all you said?"

"Dad! I'm just not much of a texter."

The team went to the playoffs in 2014 and the Rockets ended up in a series with the Portland Trailblazers, which meant we could see half of the games in our hometown. The whole experience was surreal. In game three, we were the only fans celebrating in the MODA center after the Blazers lost to the Rockets in both of their home games.

Prior to the game, we lingered inside the quiet hallways near the visitor locker room. Bob, Natalie, Sam and I stood with special access passes around our necks. The players jogged in from their warm up and we managed to get a pre-game fist bump from Dwight Howard, Patrick Beverly and Donatas Motiejūnas. When James Harden came through, he caught sight of Sam.

"Hey man, I'm glad you're here!" He opened up his arms and moved toward Sam, "We need some good luck!" James gave each of us a hug and we tried to say something meaningful but brief, which ended up sounding as profound as *good luck* in five different ways.

Natalie, who is rarely at a loss for words, turned red with giggles and said "I can't believe James Harden just hugged my brother!" It was her first time meeting the team and while she'd been told all of the stories, seeing their fondness for Sam in person left her speechless with a great big grin. It was her 15th birthday.

Portland Trailblazer fans are nuts. Intimidating, highly vocal, and dressed in red, they packed the arena, and at least half of them held long red light-up wands they like to call "thunder sticks." The lights went out and the crowd lit up like fire burning around a mountain on a dark night. The energy in the arena was insane. Bob tried to temper Sam's competitive fervor so he wouldn't get beat up by a drunken emotionally immature fan who hates the Rockets.

The Rockets won in overtime. We spent another hour after the game in the visitor training room. Dwight Howard asked Natalie about her boyfriend and told her, "You make sure he treats you well. And if he doesn't, you let me know."

Patrick Beverly told Sam repeatedly, "You be good to your mom." He was my favorite.

After game five in Houston, it was 3 - 2 in favor of the Blazers, but the Rockets had the chance to keep themselves in the series. Immediately after we watched the game in Houston, Sam got a call from their lead trainer. "Hey Sam, looks like we'll see you on Thursday!"

In the car on the way to game six, Sam said, "You know, cancer is really hard, but there's a lot of good stuff that happens when you have cancer."

Any Blazer fan who followed the 2014 series still remembers how game six ended. It was 98 - 96 Houston. The ball went out of bounds with .9 seconds left on the clock. It was obvious to the fans sitting around us that we were there to see the Rockets win again, which would leave game seven to decide who would move on to the second round. The game was paused and the crowd waited for that final fraction of a second left to play. The Rockets were about to win.

Sam turned to the people behind us, who were rather good natured about the whole thing. He reached out his hand and offered, "Hey, good game." Then to the next guy, "Good game."

"Sam, hang on." Bob cautioned him. "This isn't over yet." Sam put a pause on his rather polite engagement.

In that fraction of a second, Damian Lillard crossed the court unguarded to receive the pass. He pivoted and tossed it up for a three point shot just as the buzzer went off, and the ball went in. That arena blew up. The Blazers won the series by one point for the first time in 14 years.

Sam didn't go to the locker room that night and I wished that all of his life experiences outside the hospital could be wins instead of losses. But I saw how he handled himself with this disappointment. It was just a game, and although he was discouraged, he treated it that way. If gratitude really does help to lower stress, I had a therapeutic dose from watching Sam enjoy the honor of being a part of this incredible experience.

The following season, the Rockets went to the playoffs again, and Bob decided that he and Sam would travel to one game in each series. In Los Angeles, they were comped a room in the same hotel as the team. They had breakfast with them and rode on their bus to the arena. They had VIP passes to special rooms with buffets and big sofas. At one of these games, they were invited to the shoot around with the team the day before, where players stayed loose with casual dribbles and shots and light-hearted banter. The media was outside closed doors to the gym for a period of time, with the promise that they could enter, film, and interview when the team was ready. When the doors opened, Sam was out on the floor shooting hoops too. He was at ease enough to use James' signature "stirring the pot" gesture in a timely moment, which made Dwight Howard laugh and call it out. Until that day, there hadn't been any effort by us or by the team to make Sam into a media story. But within a few moments of the cameras being in the gym, they noticed the kid with the prosthetic leg and started asking questions, which then became a story.

The Rockets won their round of the Western Conference finals. Sam wasn't at the game, but shortly after it ended, I got a text from Kevin McHale's wife telling me to watch the press conference.

Coach McHale started by saying this, "Before I get started here, there's a little guy, his name is Sammy Day. He lives up in Portland. He came down here for treatment many different times, the little guy is a fighter. And he's the biggest Houston fan. Sammy, this one's for you, bud."

It was strange how far we'd drifted from normalcy. We always knew these experiences were extraordinary. But there came a comfortability with the extraordinary and a gratitude for how we lived inside them. These were moments to savor before the destructive side of cancer depleted the reservoirs of delight. For Sam, these experiences were never something to boast about among his peers. Sam was a kid who craved a great experience, which we welcomed with restful breaths between heavy days. A gracious opportunity to live well.

23
BECOMING A SURFER

Sarah Reinertsen, a petite, energetic athlete who had lost her leg as a child, oozed with encouragement and warmth. In 2005, she became the world's first female amputee to complete the Ironman World Championship. She's also a spokesperson for the Challenged Athletes Foundation (CAF), a nonprofit offering adaptive sports equipment and community to athletes with physical disabilities.

Shortly after a portion of Sam's foot was amputated, he was invited back to the Nike campus to meet with Sarah and a few top executives from CAF. After an hour of chit chat and video stories about their inspiring mission, Sam was asked to come to San Diego to participate in four days of adaptive sport activities along with other disabled youth from around the country.

Our first trip to a CAF event was in the fall of 2013 when Sam was 12 years old. CAF booked us a hotel room on a beach in La Jolla, along with a dozen or so other kids with missing limbs. The first clinic of the weekend: surfing. Since the Oregon coast is an hour away from where we live, and the ocean water is so cold you need a two-inch thick wetsuit most of the year, I couldn't see surfing in our future. I considered skipping the clinic. But Sam wanted to give it a try. He mentioned that he'd dreamed of becoming a surfer in a few deep-in-thought episodes ever since he tried bodyboarding in Hawaii.

The clinic was a short walk from the hotel. We could tell we were getting close by the different body types. Next to the red CAF tent, we saw above-knee amputees, double amputees, and triple amputees: strong young men and women getting ready to surf. Their high tech black and gray prosthetic legs made amputations look cool. Kids scurried around greeting old friends. Those missing both legs above the knee bounced around on their running blades as if they were born to move that way. Others, like Sam, lingered near their parents, intrigued by the other bodies who looked different yet similar. Here, amputation was the norm. Sam's chemo at the time hadn't caused him to lose his hair. Unless we told his story, in this crowd he was just another kid.

We checked Sam in. It was his first time, so a volunteer helped him navigate the wetsuit. Getting a tight neoprene wetsuit on without two legs to stand on is no simple task. Sam took off his leg and rested it on the grass. Once he got it on, we helped Sam roll the wetsuit leg up over his knee so he could slide his stump into the socket of his plastic leg. Then we rolled the suit down over the prosthesis, wiggling and twisting it until everything felt tight and secure. I searched Sam's face for any signs of embarrassment at this very public challenge but was relieved to see that he was flushed with excitement and smiling.

The kids gathered on the beach for a brief introduction to surfing. They laid down in the sand to acquire some basic moves, including the most critical one of all, the *shaka*: fisted hand with an extended pinky and thumb, a classic gesture of stoke. Then, the kids moved cautiously into the waves with their designated surf coaches. Prosthetics and wheelchairs were left behind. Some parents stood at the edge of the water holding their kid's legs to make sure the sand didn't get into the grooves and pockets of this essential equipment.

Sam lay prone on his red foam longboard, gripping the sides to stabilize himself. His instructor guided him out past the first set of waves. They floated out in the calm ocean water for a few minutes, watching the waves come in. His coach eventually maneuvered Sam around until his board was aimed back toward the beach. They waited. At just the right moment his instructor pushed him gently into the shallow wave. Sam lifted his upper body so he was on all fours, then lifted up his hands and balanced on his knees for a ride back to the shoreline.

As he fell off his board and popped up onto his feet he shouted, "Woo-hoo!"

Bob and I watched Sam steady himself with one hand as his board stopped on the sand. He punched his fist in the air and called out, "That was awesome!!!" He was taken out again and again, riding soft waves until he could do it standing up. A good smooth ride ended with the shout out, "Mom, did you get that on video!?" Of course I did.

Those waves seemed to wash away the residual yuck that comes with cancer and replace it with the buzz of a new challenge. For three days prior, Sam, nauseous and lethargic, had been hooked up to multiple bags of chemotherapy toxins. Now, the waves had washed away the residue of pain and fear and replaced it with the buzz of a new challenge.

The surf clinic launched a full weekend of sports, camaraderie, and learning, including an amputee running clinic, swim lessons with paralympic coaches, and role models who opened doors to countless other opportunities. Sam met a muscular young Ewing survivor, about 19 years old, who'd lost his leg above the knee. He excelled on his high school water polo team. His dad told us stories of watching the look of surprise among spectators when he exited the pool revealing he only had one leg working beneath the surface of the water. Sam thought that maybe he could play water polo too.

Our weekend with CAF was the most inclusive and motivating group experience that I had ever witnessed or experienced. But maybe it was the darkness we were emerging from - that oppressive loneliness, and sense of loss - that made the joyful bonding of this community so transformative. Not just Sam – but Bob and I too - were riding high, feeling the surfer's stoke.

Sunday was the annual San Diego Triathlon Challenge, CAF's biggest fundraiser of the year. The first wave of 50 or so participants in pink swim caps for the open water one-mile swim were all challenged athletes. We watched from the cliff above La Jolla Shores Cove, mesmerized by this sea of possibility. Throughout the day, our eyes were fixated on the finish line as athletes of all ages crossed in their racing wheelchairs or wearing their running prosthesis. We wandered around the vendor tents and talked to folks we'd met throughout the weekend. Inside the VIP tent, we felt like honored guests.

I hoped Sam was as motivated as I was to establish some new fitness goals. In my head, I was a future distance runner in a CAF tank top and Sam was a swift young swimmer with an inspirational story to tell.

At the awards banquet on our third night, that year's notable athletes were recognized: paralympic medalists, Ironman competitors, and a Rising Star award for a young athlete who showed special promise. I dreamed of Sam one day on that same stage. I was pretty sure he was having the same thought. This vision could come true, inside a community where he belonged, if only he could beat cancer.

24
WONDERING

Sam preferred the bed at the end of the row for his outpatient infusions. That spot had a window, and only one side of us had another patient. With a curtain dividing the bed spaces, we could hear the child and their parent, from the crinkle of their snack packages to whining and excessively verbal parenting styles.

Chemotherapy infusions happened for five days in a row, then Sam had two weeks off to go to school and recover. These days started at 9am and lasted from anywhere in the 3 - 5pm window, depending on who was our nurse. We spent the entirety of our days in the small infusion space walled off by privacy curtains.

On this day, we had Betsy. She appeared to be picking up the pace a bit since we last had her. During the last week of chemo, I'd noticed a pattern of longer days when we had Betsy and shorter days when we had Amanda, so I'd finally said something to Betsy about trying to move things a little bit faster. Of course, I waited until I was thoroughly cranky before saying something, which I am certain came through in my tone of voice. I'm pretty sure there were notes about me in Sam's chart by now.

Sam pulled the swivel-arm TV in front of his face with his

head under two stacked pillows. His prosthetic leg lay on the floor, and his liner and sock were off to the side of his bed. He would only need it for a trip to the bathroom. Settling in for the day, Sam would nap from the drowsiness induced by his anti-nausea medications. I would sit near him all day, and perhaps curl up at the foot of his bed for my own afternoon cat nap.

Sam and I repeated the same daily routine from morning till night on infusion days. Every minute of our day was now an auto-mated movement pattern and we were in sync from home to the hospital bed the way fish move through the water together. We'd load into the car, Sam with his cup of Chinese herbal tea, and me with my second cup of coffee. Sam would adjust the volume of the radio for the morning NPR topic. We'd find a parking spot, then navigate the complicated hospital hallways to our destina-tion, the outpatient clinic waiting room. He took a seat while I checked us in.

The nurse assistant opened the automatic double doors to call us into the small room to measure his height and weight.

"Samuel Robert Day. Six-Twenty-Three-Oh-One." He'd say to her as she checked the ID tag in her hand before securing it around his wrist.

He'd step on the scale, then stand tall against the wall to measure his height, always glancing back to see the number for himself. Next was the outpatient infusion space, where we usually ended up in the bed next to the window, saying hello to a nurse or two along the way.

Living in such routine synchrony, we must have felt each other's presence in a way we never consciously acknowledged. Maybe his heart rate, or his blood pressure, or his breath would change according to how near I was to him. Maybe he was affected by how anxious I was, or whether I was sad or hopeful, or irritated about Betsy moving too slow. Maybe he was more at ease, or less at ease, depending on my proximity to him.

While Sam watched TV or slept his way through infusion

days, I searched the internet for stories of cancer survivors, nutritional guidance, and scientific papers with potential new therapies. I was on a listserv email group of families whose kids had Ewing sarcoma. Before the relapse, I avoided the group because I didn't want to know about the kids who had relapsed - those whose doctors had told them there were no more curative options. Those stories triggered a sick feeling in my stomach that would stay with me for the rest of the day. But after Sam's relapse, I became curious, as I felt I had become one of the parents who fit the desperate situation category. A small core group of individuals were the most engaged. Some of them were quite direct, lodging pointed questions like *Why would your child start that drug if he has disease in his lung? Or, You should get a second opinion immediately. Or, take him off of that protocol. It doesn't work.*

I read and responded with caution, creating boundaries for myself by not asking questions specifically about Sam's situation. If I were to open the door to feedback, I could spiral over the hint that I'd made a foolish choice about his care. I protected myself from the idea that Sam didn't have a chance at survival. The last thing I wanted was pessimistic predictions directly related to Sam. I was, however, sucked into the dialogue about other kids because of the remote possibility that someone would know about a new and promising protocol. I built a wall to encircle my hope.

Now, several years since he's been gone, I can wonder more freely about what Sam might have been feeling and thinking about his own mortality. I can wonder how the intensity of my care and the compulsion to protect Sam could have also shielded us from some other rich experience. I wonder when he thought it was likely that he would not survive. I wonder how much of his intention in life was pretending that there could be a cure for him, and that I could find it. I wonder if he protected my hope simply because I needed him to.

I've seen young adults accept their pending mortality with a kind of grace that seems to require a strength I cannot compre-hend. They are the most profoundly deep and beautiful humans I have ever observed. At the time, I felt the most noble and powerful actions were to dedicate myself entirely to the pursuit of saving Sam. If I lost him, I thought, I would know that I did everything I possibly could to save him. As I look back, I wonder if maybe the most noble and brave thing would have been to accept the inevitable, and allow death to bring our whole family into a more profound experience of life. What would have happened if I'd let myself accept that my son was going to die? I wonder whether I could have been able to expand my own heart and soul, instead of protecting it for as long as possible. I have not decided which is better. I'm most comfortable continuing to wonder.

I am proud of how my family chose to live well and say yes to as much adventure as we could pack in. But, I wonder whether Sam could have lived a more extraordinary life if he'd felt free from the need to help protect his mom's heart. Extraordinary people have the most expansive hearts. And yet, most of us are not extraordinary. We are simply regular people navigating extraordinary heartbreak.

25
THE VACCINE

In the beginning of Sam's crusade against cancer, I didn't know what to do with fear, except try not to feel it. With deep breaths, intentional focus, and prayer, I worked at trying not to be afraid.

I failed.

Fear serves a purpose, and now that I have known the fear of losing a child, I understand why it was included in humanity's original design. It's a highly functional emotion when someone's life is at risk. That flood of cortisol that I tried not to feel was actually a fully loaded energy resource for my body to fight or to run like hell from whatever it is threatening my life or the lives of my family. That's why people call protective moms *Mamma Bears*. Female bears will kill whatever endangers their babies. There is no hesitation spurred by societal norms and courteous behaviors. When a cub is in danger, momma bears feel the same rush of angry energy I felt every time I entered a cancer clinic with Sam. I've come to believe that fear is actually a divine early warning system, summoning the courage to do whatever is necessary to save precious lives. Imagine how many people would be dead if they hadn't first been afraid.

The trouble is, when this life-saving alarm sounds in the middle of a doctor's appointment, there's nowhere to send that army of energized neurotransmitters looking for a fight. In the cold rooms of the Children's hospital, I could only grip the edge of that hard plastic chair listening to the details about the threat that was slowly invading Sam's body, and the inadequate list of options we had from Sam's calmer-than-a-tree-sloth oncologist. That fight-or-flight fear had nowhere to run; instead it would battle inside my adrenal system, and wreak havoc on my mind.

In March, 2014, at a time when the likelihood of Sam relapsing again was high, I arrived at the appointment in which I would receive the results of his scan with a battle plan to put my high-octane fear-energy to work.

"It's not good news," his doctor said. "There are some spots in his lungs." He told me the location and size of the tumors. There were three of them. They were small. He reminded me, when Sam was first diagnosed, he had three tiny spots which had been dismissed as nothing to worry about. The three spots were too small to determine whether they were cancer, and since all humans are likely to have a few non-cancer spots on their lungs from residual illness, or a random lint or smoke inhalation, Sam was originally declared non-metastatic.

On this particular March afternoon, three new spots had appeared in the exact same places as the ones previously noted in his medical file. The spots, cancerous from the start, disappeared when chemotherapy made its way through his body. Now, instead of a 75% chance of survival, he had only a 20% chance. That meant that, from the very start, he'd had poor odds, and we didn't even know it. Since the relapse in his foot, Bob and I had learned how to deal with a bad prognosis. We knew what fear felt like, and what it was meant to do. Passively awaiting advice from the experts was counter to the hot impulse of my body to make war against the disease.

"I know what I want to do." My voice was unexpectedly

assertive. "There is a phase one clinical trial in Dallas. It's a vaccine. They would take Sam's tumor and re-engineer it to recognize his cancer as disease, then he gets a shot once a month for as many doses as they are able to make." I told him about a girl I knew, from the listserv emails. Carley had been on the vaccine and was cancer-free for 18 months. She became part of the vaccine trial after a relapse, despite an exceptionally poor prognosis. I didn't allow much room for discussion, though no one in the room was challenging my plan, or my fired-up instinct to protect.

Dr. Madison said he would look into it. I suspect he didn't have anything better. I immediately stepped out of the examination room to call Carley's mom, Laura.

It's a distressing moment when a parent first becomes aware that no pediatric sarcoma specialist is fully informed of every clinical trial or innovative treatment. I wasn't a busy doctor - I had only one patient to concern myself with - so I designated myself Dr. Madison's personal Ewing sarcoma research assistant. Over the past several months, I had spent long hours glaring at my computer screen, educating myself on the research around new approaches, drugs in development, and potential nutritional therapies. Over time, I introduced Dr. Madison to cutting-edge scientists, sent him peer-reviewed papers to keep his reading list current, and provided him with the contact information for the medical investigators engaged in the upcoming trials, to make his inquiries into Sam's treatment a cinch.

It was now three years since Sam's original diagnosis. When Sam developed that tumor in his foot, I began looking into what new and amazing cures might be right around the corner. I saw stories on various national and world news outlets about groundbreaking breakthroughs in cancer research: immunotherapies and targeted therapies. It was "the beginning of the end of chemotherapy" and the tantalizing suggestion that all cancers could be abolished in the next few decades. Hope swirled, but when I dove deeper and deeper into websites like Pubmed and the National Cancer Institute, I soon learned that pediatric cancer research was at the bottom of the list. Though bald-headed children with sweet smiles and sparkly eyes appeared prominently in every cancer research marketing campaign (other than a few obvious adult cancers), when it came to the research, kids with cancer were a low priority. I learned that the National Cancer Institute allocates only four percent of its research budget to all forms of childhood cancer. Turns out, the 65-and-older age group had much more reason to hope for a cure than my 11-year-old with a type of cancer that had not seen a new drug in over 30 years.

One experimental drug, developed for bladder cancer and still undergoing trials, was of interest to Big Pharma, and it could also work for Ewing sarcoma. Carley had no side effects. No nausea. No hair loss. No long days in the hospital. And her cancer was gone. When Laura answered the phone, my voice was quivery. Leaning against a wall in the back of the cream-colored clinic hallway, away from the kids and their families, I asked her, "How big does a tumor need to be to get a vaccine?"

"Oh Lorna." She knew what this meant, she knew my fear, she knew I was going into battle and that she would be there with me. "Two centimeters in diameter. However, sometimes if there are multiple tumors, they can take several smaller ones and still get a good vaccine."

The FANG vaccine uses the tissue of the tumor to re-engineer T-cells. Those are the cells in our immune system that are responsible for recognizing disease early, and attacking it so the illness is not able to take hold. Cancer cells tend to trick T-cells into disregarding them. The cancer then has free rein to multiply. The FANG vaccine was designed to use the patient's tumor cells to teach the T-cells to recognize the cancer so they can launch an attack. It's specially designed for the individual patient and targeted at their disease. Like many other vaccines, it's delivered in a series of shots. This was my weapon of choice, should Sam's cancer reappear. Also, it gave me something productive to do with my fear.

I hung up the phone with Laura. Before leaving that hallway, I phoned the doctor running the trial in Dallas and left a message. Bob and Sam left the examination room to find me, and we walked through those hospital hallways quietly, with our eyes on the floor, down in the elevator and past the Starbucks in the lobby, to our car on the top level of the parking lot. A well-worn path.

Just as we got to the car, my phone rang.

"Dr. Gordon, thank you for calling me back." I paced the parking lot and explained the situation. I asked if Sam was eligible for the vaccine. It felt right. This was what my fear wanted me to do. Screw the deep breathing and prayers, I was in momma bear mode, with enough executive function to execute a plan.

Dr. Gordon told me that he would need Sam's recent images and a summary of his history before he could give me an answer. I told him, "Okay, I'll get you everything as soon as I possibly can."

26

PUZZLEMANIA

Before cancer, waiting was a bothersome disruption to the next interesting task. Once cancer hit, waiting tested my sanity. Anyone who's been through it knows what I am talking about. Waiting for that first doctor's appointment when we suspected something was wrong. Waiting to consult on the very first X-rays. Later, waiting for the results from an MRI or CT scan. The worst kind of waiting came after the bad news, and a plan was yet to be determined, while all reasonable approaches had already been exhausted. The anxiety around waiting was at times so intense that I still feel it when I am near certain hallways and hospital spaces.

After the news of Sam's lung tumors, we had that kind of wait. Even though I was prepared with information and contacts for a groundbreaking new immunotherapy clinical trial in Dallas, it was possible Sam would not qualify because his tumors - three of them - were so small they might not provide enough tumor tissue to create the vaccine. If only we had known about the trial when Sam relapsed with one soft tumor in his foot. He would have been the perfect candidate.

We would find out in a week or so. End-of-the-week waiting is the worst because it means facing down the weekend. On Thursday, I called the film library at the hospital - something I had learned to do instead of waiting for his oncologist - and ordered discs of the images to be mailed to Dallas. We FedEx'd them on Friday morning - which meant Saturday, Sunday and maybe Monday too - would be waiting days. I was nauseous with worry. So, I came up with a plan to help us through the wait.

My friends say they appreciate how I usually know what I need, and then voice the request. They are more than willing to help. Early in the cancer journey, I realized one-on-one conversation was a challenge for me except on the rare occasion with the right person at the right time. Even with close friends, going out for coffee was oftentimes too much. Their only aim was to comfort me, distract me, and let me cry, but even that would require my fullest participation, and I wasn't always up for that. However, too much alone time could send me into a downward spiral. I began to ask my friends to meet with me in pairs, or in threes, or more. If just being present was the most I could do, the rest of the group could carry the conversation. I was surrounded by those I cared about, but with permission to tune out their talk and just rest if that was what I needed. So, when the weekend of waiting came up, I decided to create space for our whole family to be with friends without necessarily needing to be fully engaged.

When you invite others over for a meal, or even a snack or tea, conversation is expected. But I knew that the simple pressure to converse could push me toward isolation, which also wasn't helpful. I concluded that maybe puzzles might be the solution. You don't have to talk when you're doing a puzzle with other people. It's socially appropriate to work on a puzzle with others in total silence. Add background music, the absence of conversation delightfully fills the space. I created a list of friends the whole family tended to enjoy and sent them this email.

Hi friends.

As you can imagine, life can get pretty sad in the Day household right now. In an effort to boost Sam's spirits through the weekend we have created "Puzzlemania." (Actually, he thinks I'm pretty nerdy when I say that so I'll try to come up with another name).

Natalie seems to be doing well but she is also supported and lifted up by the people who love her. We don't want her to get lost in all this.

We brought out the folding table and moved around the furniture to work on some puzzles. We want to have an open door (off and on) through Monday and if you would like to come by any time, there will be puzzles to do, music to enjoy, maybe a basketball game on or the Paralympics. Just text me if you want to come by. We won't be here all the time so just check in ahead and see if we're up for it. This way I'm not trying to set up times for this and that, working around everybody else's schedule.

Keep in mind that I am the only introvert in the family and may be a little low energy with my own social interaction. It's all about Sam and Natalie.

– Lorna

Our friends showed up. They trickled in, a few at a time, all weekend long. Pandora played my favorite coffee shop music from Mumford and Sons, Passenger, The Luminaires, and the like. Our small living room was rearranged to accommodate a large folding table. The new orange armchairs were pushed over toward the bay window, and extra folding chairs brought round from the neighbors were positioned around the table, with a 1000-piece puzzle of a cottage with an English garden. On the coffee table, we had a colorful, busy puzzle of a cartoon with mobs of people at a county fair. Though none of my friends do puzzles on a regular basis, pretty soon we began to establish mini-rituals around organizing the pieces, mastering little color sections, and celebrating the satisfaction of completing one part of the picture.

Some people quietly put together whole sections before someone noticed, exclaiming, "Wow, look at you!" Others, like

Sam, celebrated every piece in its place as if he was winning a championship competition. "Boom! Nailed it! Oh yeah, who's the master? I am a master puzzler!" Then there was Bob, who seemed to believe he had an inexplicable and impressive puzzle intuition. Each time he dropped in a piece, he tapped the table three times with his middle finger, in a sort of mystical jigsaw puzzle incantation. Of course, his belief in his own secret powers was blown when he noticed Sarah beside him who quietly placed several more pieces while he tapped.

Bob is the most talkative person in the family, so he took the time to explain our situation to those who came by, including the appearance of three new tumors, the possible options for Sam, an ideal treatment scenario, and the alternatives. "We might need to try another shot in the dark chemotherapy regimen... We really hope Sam can get this vaccine... We could be flying to Texas next week..." I interjected whenever he got the details wrong.

Of our family, Natalie is the least interested in puzzles. But she loves our friends, so she came and went from her room, depending on who was in the house and the topic of the conversation. Natalie usually wanted to know the broad outlines of Sam's treatment, not the details. Like, was it good news or bad news? Would we be traveling to another city for a second opinion? Would Sam need to go back on chemotherapy? Again? Beyond that, she chose to play the part of Sam's goofy older sister, confiding in select adult friends when she needed extra encouragement or a prayer.

I spent the weekend roaming between puzzles, tidying up, napping, and cooking in our adjacent kitchen. I made a huge stack of veggie black bean enchiladas. Bob reminded our guests over and over again, "You know, there's no meat in these," adding with a smirk, "I'm just sayin'."

After two days of puzzlemania, I felt grateful for how friendship, music, and a puzzle can calm the anxiety of waiting. While my hands kept busy, my mind turned inward, buffeted between fear and hope. Instead of opposites, I reflected, fear and hope might be more like twin emotions. Both of them equipped me with fuel for the fight; hope just feels better.

Like a soft warm blanket and some homemade broth can get you through the flu, I was thankful for the meditative power of working on a puzzle with friends.

27
HOPE

The spots in Sam's lungs were too small to make a vaccine. We could wait and let them grow, or choose another treatment from a list of discouraging options. His doctors cautioned that after a second relapse, none of the existing protocols for Ewing could save him, though they might prolong his life. The only hope for a lasting cure was something new. Every day, new immunotherapy and targeted therapy treatments protocols were being introduced into the treatment of adult cancers. I believed then and still believe, kids should have that option too.

After extensive outreach to other Ewing parents, consults with other sarcoma specialists, and an intense study of the most recent research publications, the FANG vaccine was the only treatment I could identify that was both potentially curative and available. Three other targeted drugs specifically designed for Ewing sarcoma were in the testing phase, with clinical trials only a year or more away. Down the road, it seemed a targeted drug, paired with a vaccine, might potentially replace the current cocktail of chemotherapies that Sam and so many other young people with Ewing were forced to endure.

At this point, during our clinic appointments, Sam's oncologist had taken on a more resigned tone. "Unfortunately, I don't see any new clinical trials that look promising right now. I don't really know what to suggest."

"What about the anti-PD1 drugs? I know they're not available yet but what about pursuing it on compassionate use? I know of a couple of other kids with Ewing who are just starting on it."

"Yeah, that's something we could try. There's just no data yet that can give us an idea as to whether it might work. I can start that paperwork if that's what you'd like to do."

We were sent home to pray that a new drug – designed to treat adult cancers only – would somehow be approved in time for Sam.

During this time, I often sat on our living room sofa with nothing in front of me but a cup of coffee. The crowded, fragmented thoughts in my head whirled around chaotically. Musings about prayer and faith, as well as the hurt in my heart, presented questions I couldn't suppress. I thought about the concept of miracles and healing, and what it means to be truly resilient. I remembered the things people had said to me over and over again, and my private inner recoil at these suggestions. I wondered if these proclamations were grounded in the Scriptures, or simply interpretations that made them feel more at home in their beliefs.

God's got this.

He knows what's best for Sam.

God has a plan. You just need to trust Him.

I dissected the cliches I'd heard over and over again, wondering if I'd ever find the words to describe why my heart was rejecting them. Disparate thoughts and questions wandered through my mind in disarray, until gradually a new thought emerged to maintain my focus. I'd examine it for a while, turning it upside down and hypothesize it with multiple circumstances. I'd meditate on this one thought and consider its opposition to a more commonly accepted notion.

I truly believe everything happens for a reason. But what if that unexplained causality is the reason the world is NOT how it's supposed to be?

All you need is God. Actually, God told Adam that it's not good for him to be alone. So, maybe we also need other people.

God is in control. He's got this. But wait - before Jesus died, he placed the responsibility of making the world better squarely on the shoulders of his friends. He told them to do the things that he'd been doing - even greater things. So, what if the most hopeful outcomes are less about our prayer, and more about how we engage?

I found a certain solace in asking these questions. This process didn't provide easy answers, but it helped me make sense of life, given the reality of my experiences. For example, well-meaning people kept telling me to have faith. *God would never give Sam more than he can handle.* But, thinking about all the pain that he suffered, and what was ahead, that didn't seem logical. Sam didn't have a choice but to endure his suffering.

Asking myself the tough questions was better than mindlessly repeating platitudes I didn't really believe, but I was still seeking a bit of wisdom that I could anchor myself to, something that could get me through the day.

In the dizziness of this dilemma, I thought about hope. I wondered if I still had a reason to be hopeful. I approached the idea with caution, and could see how a loving parent might slip into a naïve, or false hope. The expectation of a miracle. *Don't get your hopes up.* This culturally-embedded realism sounded loudly in my head. *Don't be foolish* - the unspoken warning I received from doctors who have a responsibility to make sure we are fully coping with the situation before us. The truth was, without hopeful research or a God-granted miracle, Sam would die from this cancer.

Yet, I wondered, what would happen to me if I made the choice to stay hopeful? Rather than surrendering, if I one day lost

Sam, would it actually hurt me more because I had allowed myself to hope? One thing I knew for sure, every day that I had hope was 100 times more tolerable than a day without hope. Glassy-eyed, I pondered the influence of hope, quietly in the living room of my empty house, staring at the wooden bowl of smooth Puget Sound stones I'd collected for the top of my coffee table.

This was a moment when something inside of me shifted.

It was a conversation with God; simultaneously, it was a negotiation within my own being. I refused to be naïve, yet I had to wonder if Bob, Natalie, me, and especially Sam, could sustain any degree of joy if we decided that hope was no longer an option. Not a false hope; instead, a hope rooted in possibility. A rebellious, resilient hope, the kind that gets me out of bed in the morning and through the bleakest day. At night, it's the kind of hope that allows me to laugh and sing and snuggle with my kids. A hope that never fully removes the fear, or the sorrow, but instead allows one lit candle to illuminate the evening gloom. Because, with no warmth or light, not even a single hour of happiness can exist. So, I chose hope.

We decided to let the tumors grow until they could be removed in order to create a vaccine. It was a rational decision, the kind that could lead a rational person into insanity. A weekend of waiting turned into two months of waiting, until another chest CT showed growth, including a couple of new nodules. At last, it was time to go to Dallas for the surgery.

Sam had had eight surgeries by the time we flew to Dallas for the partial thoracotomy. While he couldn't grasp how this next surgery - or *any* surgery - could be more painful than his amputations, he was becoming a pro at the pre-surgery process.

"Mom, see how long I can stay awake when they give me the

anesthesia." It had become a kind of wager with himself. When part of his foot was amputated, he bet Bob that he could last 30 seconds before going to sleep. "Ten bucks?"

"Sam, I bet you'll be out in no more than 30 seconds."

"Deal. I get ten bucks if I can stay awake for more than 30 seconds after they start the anesthesia. Have my ten bucks ready when I wake up." Sam's anesthesiologist was in on it. Since we couldn't be in the surgery, he set up a stopwatch on his phone. He emerged to announce that Sam was out of surgery, and that all went well.

He then pulled out his phone to show us the timer. 42 seconds. He added, when Sam briefly woke up after his surgery, he immediately asked, "How long did I make it?" The doctor smirked as he told him the time. Sam cried out, "In your face, dad!" He then went limp and fell back asleep.

Lung surgeries are extremely painful. While we knew this going into it, the story I am about to share contains details of a few of the most difficult moments Sam has had to endure.

The surgeon removed seven small tumors from Sam's left lung. Though the operation was successful, it involved several steps that later contributed to a painful recovery, like spreading the ribs apart, pulling lung tissue outside of the ribs, manipulating the tissue with their fingers, and installing a rigid drainage tube in between the ribs so that the fluid could drain out. When Sam was wheeled into the recovery room, he was fairly comfortable at first. They had used an epidural around his chest, which lessened the pain for a time.

The nurses bantered with Sam. "You have beautiful eyes, Sam," one of them said while checking his vitals.

"I know," he replied. "I also have perfect hair, and a perfect chin. But my leg's not too good."

Sam was soon transported to a room. With a tube protruding out from the inside of his ribcage to a bag of fluid draining out of him, the pain and nausea began to grow more intense. I hit the button to call the nurse. She was slow, and when at last she arrived she announced that they didn't have his preferred anti-nausea medication ready, Zofran. Sam moaned, begging for help with the pain. I didn't think the epidural was working but the anesthesiologist told us Sam did a very good job.

Following this, hours of poor pain management. Sam's heart rate escalated. He vomited. Then he shouted and said things I wouldn't want anyone else to know about. He begged to be put out again. The head nurse came into the room while he was screaming. She suggested he get out of bed and move around. Maybe then they could take the tube out. Today, when I cry about all that Sam had to endure, those few days in Texas come to mind as the pinnacle of his trauma and suffering. He was two weeks shy of 12 years old.

There was a moment when the nurse finally came in with Zofran - in a pill form. "I think he's just going to throw that up." I suggested, attempting to be polite and defer to the professional. She replied, "Well, let's just give it a try." Sam swallowed the pill with some water. Within two minutes, he threw it up. His weak, pale body writhed over a bin set up to catch the bile from his empty stomach.

Something very primal came over me then. "Shit!" Sighing, I stood beside Sam's bed and closed my eyes for a moment. Then I looked at that nurse and directed, "Here's what you need to do. Sam needs five milligrams of IV Zofran and an extra bolus of fluids. Nothing by mouth. If he doesn't get sick for the next 30 minutes, then we will give him some crackers and sips of water. If he keeps the crackers down, you can give him his antibiotic and I will try to get some more food in him. I want Zofran scheduled for every four hours until tomorrow morning, and his pain meds should be given an hour after the Zofran is in his system. We'll worry about the constipation tomorrow." The nurse left the room to get the IV Zofran ordered. Sam lay back on his pillow with his eyes closed, paler than I've ever seen him.

Through the night, Sam was finally able to rest. In the morning, he was comfortable again. The skin under his eyes was dark. His shirtless body showed all of his bones. But he could sit up, and I could see a faint sparkle in his eyes again. Finally, he started moving. He got out of bed and took a slow walk around the unit. He ate. The tubes were removed. Our relief settled over us like a warm blanket.

In the morning when Sam was to be discharged, Dr. Gordon came for a visit and to tell us some good news. There was enough tumor tissue to make six vaccines. For the trial, he needed four. We were then sent home to recover. In a month, we'd be back for his first dose, a literal shot in the arm with a one-of-a-kind vaccine manufactured just for Sam.

28

SUMMER CAMP

Back in 2012, when Sam was in remission, he was invited by the hospital social worker to go to a camp for kids with cancer and their siblings: Camp Ukandu. I was a bit reluctant to send Sam to camp at age ten. I don't think I'm an overprotective parent, but since Sam was the kind of kid who knew the school principal somewhat better than the rest of his classmates, I had reason to be concerned. I wasn't sure a whole week at camp would be life-giving for him or the people in charge of him. But, the social worker kept pressing us. Reluctantly, Sam agreed to go.

Prior to camp, I took the opportunity to prepare his leaders as best I could by writing a letter of sorts, with a long list of suggestions for handling any misbehavior. I filled out the form in elaborate detail, including an attachment with extra tips and additional guidance. I dropped it off at the office headquarters so that I could personally interview the camp manager to make sure I wasn't sending him to a wonderfully fresh and inexperienced staffer who would want to retire at the end of a week with Sam.

When it came time to deliver him into the hands of some cheerful young counselors, I had packed his bags exactly according to the checklist, including the three self-addressed stamped envelopes. All week I kept my phone nearby in case we needed to come get him. We heard nothing. I checked the mail each day the instant the postal truck drove off, hoping for one of those self-addressed stamped envelopes with a note in Sam's terrible handwriting. After seven days with no word, Bob and I drove out to pick him up. I could feel the anxiety building in anticipation of a kid who was angry because things didn't go his way, and the frazzled camp counselor who had to manage him.

I couldn't have been more wrong.

His camp counselors thought Sam was hilarious. He loved all the games. He either followed the rules, or got away with breaking them, with his charm, and by turning things up a notch on the fun meter. This was a place where rules could be broken in order to squeeze a bit more fun out of the week. Not only did he make sure that everyone was included, he had some pretty deep things to say about life.

Sam wore a leather circle on a cord around his neck with an imprinted word: *Pretzel*. This was his camp name, because of how his body could contort into awkward positions that made the other kids squirm. He volunteered to demonstrate this whenever possible. As we walked him out of camp, at least a dozen people old and young called out, "Bye, Pretzel! See ya next year!"

On the drive home, Sam told us story after story about camp. There was Tutu Tuesday, a song called Cows with Guns, and a cabin leader who woke them up in the morning with a guitar singing Johnny Cash's *Ring of Fire*. He told us how when he climbed the rock wall, his leg fell off halfway up. He bragged about how awesome he was at gaga ball, and that Natalie *had* to come with him next year.

He described the final campfire, more serious than all the other nights. Counselors and kids remembered the campers who'd died since the previous summer. They wrote their camp names on paper bags, each one with a battery-operated candle inside. The final gathering recognized the common thread amongst these campers. Sam struggled with the reality of it all and left the campfire in a mess of emotion. Afterwards, Sam had a difficult time processing, until he got a visit from a therapy dog named Vegas. I sensed that at camp he had engaged in a much needed emotional release he may not have known he was holding in.

To me, his face, though physically tired, seemed more serene. Away from healthy unimpaired peers with cool haircuts, unscarred bodies, and afternoons filled with sports and gaming, something had moved his spirit to joy. Camp had been saturated with the grief and loss that goes hand-in-hand with childhood cancer. However, with other children living similar lives, the daily experience of their shared frustrations and triumphs created a sanctuary where Sam could fully indulge in the gift of life again, and possibly more profoundly than he ever had before. It was because he had known such sorrow, that this joy was so piercingly present, and I thought what a profound human reaction to connection in the presence of so many kids with cancer.

Back at home, I unpacked his bags and found those three self-addressed stamped envelopes, crumpled, and untouched. Also, five pairs of clean underwear.

The following year, the year of his lung surgery, his 12th birthday would take place at camp. Sam told Natalie as his birthday present, he wanted her to go with him. She reluctantly agreed.

I filled out Sam's form again, and this time it looked a bit different.

Why does Sam want to go to camp? I wrote *because he loves it.*

They asked what he was most nervous about. I wrote *he's not nervous.*

They asked what to do if Sam became homesick. I wrote *he won't get homesick.*

He fit in at camp, better than any other familiar place, including the principal's office.

This time, camp was just two weeks after his lung surgery in Dallas and he was almost 13. After a good long chat with his medical team, I sent him off with boxes of pain medication. At the end of the week he was tired but so much stronger, singing his heart out to the new camp favorite, *Ghost Chickens In The Sky*. He was no longer in need of the pain medication. His camp counselors said he was becoming a leader. He noticed and welcomed in the new kids, reached out to others who had trouble fitting in, and organized the cabin skit inclusive of even the most awkward or impaired kids.

After a week of camp, something changed between Sam and Natalie, something new in their relationship. I may never know all that happened between the two of them, but camp gave them a safe place to open up and enter each other's hearts just a little bit more. The two became known for their lively spirits and humorous antics. Sam and Natalie appeared in dozens of photos shared with us by other parents. With big smiles, like the best of friends.

Though the anxiety meter had needled down a few degrees since the surgery, the next step in the vaccine was more waiting. This time, for the news that six doses had been cleared. We knew there was a possibility that the vaccine might become contaminated with bacteria, either from within the patient's body, or from inside the lab during its production. It was a glitch they were still trying to remedy. Three weeks post-surgery, Dr. Gordon called to inform us that Sam's vaccine, though not completely ready, was looking really good. We relaxed. For a time there was a routine sense of ease and joy inside our home.

A few days later, I needed to call the hospital in Dallas for some unrelated reason. I can't remember what it was. I spoke on the phone to a receptionist who was not on Sam's medical team.

As she was looking up Sam's file, she mentioned a note that Sam's vaccine had an issue with contamination.

"What? No, Dr. Gordon told us last week that it wasn't contaminated." I was in my bedroom. I ceased multi-tasking and stood still. "That can't be true. We're flying out for his first dose next week."

"Well," she let out a breath, "all I know is what it says here."

An angry edge broke through in my voice. "Can you please have Dr. Gordon call me as soon as possible? Or at least check in with him about what's going on?"

It was one of those moments that got imprinted in my memory: exactly where I was standing and what absurdly mundane task was occupying me when I heard the news. Thirty minutes later she called me back to confirm the notes were correct. Sam's vaccine was contaminated.

29
BRIAN WILLIAMS

After bad news, I got an urge to find a family pick-me-up. Something to keep us distracted while we figured out what to do next. As the years went on and we'd had experiences with NBA basketball teams and Olympic athletes, I became bold about the possibilities we could indulge in. Once we heard about the vaccine being contaminated, I wondered what might be possible.

Around this time, one of the youth leaders at church asked me what Sam's favorite TV show was, to get an idea of what kids were watching these days. "Sam loves NBC Nightly News with Brian Williams," I replied with a smirk. He could soak up information, form an opinion, and articulate as well as any rising news correspondent, in between the commercials for the home maintenance accessories and life-extending drugs for the elderly.

Sam was a social studies teacher's dream. He craved a vibrant class debate, though he found that his peers didn't quite have the knowledge or attention span for developing a strong position on World War II's influence on our current global economy. Natalie, a freshman in high school at the time, occasionally complained about a boring discussion in her World History class. Sam's eyes drilled into hers as he organized the thoughts inside his head and offered her several talking points. Once, he suggested she drop in some facts about the fall of the Soviet Union, another time he developed a parallel theory between a contemporary issue and the conditions that lead to the Civil War. He was disappointed by Natalie's lack of enthusiasm. The conversation usually ended with Sam tossing his head back with an exasperated, "I can't wait for high school!"

Natalie and her friends learned the hard way not to ask a question about world events when Sam was around. Visiting Disneyland with another family, Natalie's friend Josie casually asked, "What *is* going on in Ukraine anyway?" With rapid strides, Sam caught up with her. Step by step he explained the political current state of affairs in Ukraine, its politics and past, as well as what should be done about it. He didn't realize that when Natalie's 15-year-old friend asked a question about something in the news that day on her way to the next amusement ride, she wanted the Cliff's Notes version. In a playful panic, Natalie ran back to me, waving her arms, demanding that I rescue her friend from Sam's lengthy commentary. "Mom! Josie asked Sam about Ukraine!"

After the crushing news about Sam's vaccine, our whole family slipped into another fog of fear and sadness. Sam's oncologist recommended a new round of chemotherapy, one that could not cure him but only slow down the progress of the disease. Sam returned to the now familiar routine of infusions, nausea, hair loss. As well as the heartache that went with it.

I went to Facebook in the hope of finding someone who could ask Brian Williams, the anchor for NBC Nightly News, if he would be willing to meet a 13-year-old fan with cancer. It worked. The father of a child with Ewing offered to reach out to someone at NBC.

Soon after that, I got an email address from our friend with contact information for a TV personality at ESPN. "Oh yeah?" Bob asked. "Who's the contact?" I pulled up the email. "Kenny Mayne? Or something?"

"What? You got Kenny Mayne's contact information?" Bob exclaimed.

I didn't watch the network much, so I didn't know he was a high-profile ESPN anchor.

Bob asked like a kid begging his mom for a sleepover. "Can I reach out to him?" Bob emailed Kenny, who could not have been more gracious and helpful. He connected us with Brian's assistant and just like that, plans were in motion. We were going to New York!

Since Sam had begun his new chemotherapy regimen, we had to schedule the trip in between treatments, but only if his white blood cell counts remained strong. We kept the news a secret from Sam until everything was in place.

During this time, some of my friends joined me in planning our first grassroots cancer research fundraiser. We were raising money to support the development of one of those targeted drugs for Ewing, which was projected to be available in clinical trials in about a year. Asking people for money wasn't exactly within my comfort zone, yet the need for more effective cancer treatment for Sam and other kids compelled me to do what I could. The hope inside my heart reminded me: if enough people cared, one day this goal would be achieved. A team of dedicated friends pulled together an elegant outdoor banquet at a nearby golf course, with a silent auction and some special music. We called it the Sam Day Soirée.

We decided to surprise Sam with the news of our trip to NYC at the Soirée. Our guests gathered round the pretty tables set up underneath a white tent on the edge of a golf course. There was a sense of uplift and hope as people dressed in their lovely summer best, connected with one another. Everyone there had at least one thing in common: a compassionate urge to do something mean-ingful for Sam. This made us a community.

It was a hot day - 95 degrees - but the air turned pleasantly cooler as the sun set. Sam looked smart in a blue button-down shirt and tan slacks held up by a leather belt cinched tight around his skinny waist. He was bald again from the chemotherapy. Sam had an aversion to any serious conversation around cancer, and he wanted nothing to do with the formal program for the event. During the hour or so of presentations, his plan was to take off in a golf cart (with adult supervision) and ride to a house where some of his friends were hanging out. We insisted that he stay for the first few minutes, reassuring him there would be no tearful stories told by his mom, not while he was still there. Sam reluc-tantly agreed.

Bob welcomed everyone and thanked them for coming, and somehow he did this in a way that makes people laugh until they cry. He informed the audience of Sam's love for world news and his admiration of Brian Williams, setting the stage for the surprise announcement.

The large screen lit up with high-def video of Brian behind his shiny blue news desk. "Hey everybody, Brian Williams here from NBC Nightly news headquarters in New York. I've asked to talk to you because I have a special message for Sam." Sam's eyes grew big and his jaw dropped.

"Hey Sam, we can't wait to meet you when you visit us here at NBC Studios," Brian bantered.

"What!!??" Sam blurted out with his hands on his head, a once-in-a-lifetime moment that I managed to capture on video. He punched the air with both fists.

"New York City!" Brian went on, "You, your sister Natalie, your mom, and your dad. Oh Sam, this is happening. We'll see you here."

Our guests applauded and cheered, and those around the edges of the lawn rose up in their chairs to catch a glimpse of

Sam. I continued to record with my phone, as his ecstatic grin faded and his hand met his eyes to catch happy tears. Unknowingly, Sam had provided the perfect illustration of my keynote for that night: Sometimes, when sorrow enters our lives, it creates an opportunity for joy.

Less than a month later, a town car greeted us at the airport, graciously provided by our hosts from the show. Our driver held up a sign with our name, which elevated our sense of self-importance. Once again, some generous friends of a friend who happened to own a penthouse with a balcony about a half mile from NBC Studios invited us to stay with them. It was just blocks from the United Nations, and the Waldorf Astoria where President Obama and other dignitaries had stayed the day before. The noise and delicious smells and bright lights of Manhattan overwhelmed our senses long into the night.

The afternoon of Wednesday, October 1, was reserved for our visit to the TV studio, and Sam's leg was sore from all the walking. He limped along slowly, while I watched for signs of the greater kind of pain that could ruin his special day. While we strolled those three blocks toward NBC Studios, Sam sheepishly and sadly confessed his belief about his date to meet Brian Williams. "The only reason this stuff happens to me is because I got cancer." That thought had occurred to me, too. I told him, "Sam, I think there is some truth to that." He walked with his head down. Finally, he looked up and said, "Kids with cancer get to do cool stuff because they also have to do such awful stuff."

I remembered Sam's first few chemotherapy treatments and my fear that the brutality of his treatment would cause irreparable damage to his spirit. But now, after three years of what felt like pre-meditated child abuse, Sam's crazy, curious, well-informed good humor had somehow remained vibrant. He was more compassionate, more wise, and more loving.

"That may be true," I replied, "but people are really drawn to *you*, not just because you have cancer. They're drawn to you, because you have been able to maintain your spirit in the midst of cancer. People are amazed by you, despite everything you've been through." He offered me no sign that he was buying it, though that was better than an outright rejection of the idea. I went on. "I think that your opportunities are more about how you live your life than the cancer itself." I could tell he was thinking about it.

We showed up at the studio ground floor at 4:10pm, where we checked in and met Craig, our friendly and professional tour guide. Craig led us through offices and hallways loaded with photos of iconic actors from the best NBC TV shows. We stood behind a thick glass wall above the Saturday Night Live set and attempted to describe the history of the groundbreaking show to Natalie and Sam. Then, we walked through the Today Show set, surprised at how the camera can make a small space feel larger when projected on a TV screen.

After our tour, we landed in the newsroom. The wall-size screens behind Brian's desk displayed world maps in shades of vibrant blue, with twinkling lights in the populated areas. Cameras, mounted on tripods, surrounded the large production room. One more hung down from the ceiling. The space was magnificent and airy compared to the Today Show. This was not a studio made for comedy sketches, celebrity gossip, or the latest fashion trends. This was the place where international secrets spent their final minutes of anonymity before being fully exposed to the world of the well informed.

While we waited for Brian, the cameraman asked if we'd like to get some photos of Sam sitting in Brian's chair. Sam wandered over to the glowing plexiglass desk and sat down. Under the bright lights of the studio, with the NBC peacock on the wall below him, Sam looked sharp in his pinstriped button-down shirt and brand new jeans. His eyes were happy. I loved it when Sam was happy. The cameraman flipped some switches and suddenly he was displayed on the wall sized screens. Sam seized the opportunity to strike a few sophisticated and distinguished power poses.

A moment later, Brian walked into the newsroom and asked playfully, "Hey, was someone in my chair?" Sam was about to answer when Brian quickly offered him his hand. "Bro, how are you? It's good to meet you." Brian pointed toward the desk. "You looked good! I was in my office. We have a dedicated camera watching this chair in case of intruders. Instead, I see a very handsome young man sitting in my chair." "Well," Sam reasoned, "it's a really nice chair."

As I watched this exchange, I grinned until my cheeks hurt.

Brian and Sam wandered back to the *really nice chair* to pose for some photos which the folks at the studio promised to share with us.

The two chatted for about 15 minutes. Brian was exceptionally charming, and funny too. I only wish they'd had a bit more time together. Since Brian graciously carried the conversation, he was unaware of Sam's ability to engage grown professionals in discussion about world leaders and recent foreign policy news. He missed the delight of Sam's wit that could make his teachers, doctors, and nurses laugh more than his peers. The time was too short for Brian to experience that moment I was craving, of realizing this kid is an intriguing kind of unique. However, that day Sam wasn't concerned with impressing anyone. He was just buzzed to meet his idol.

Monitoring the time closely, the cameraman then asked Bob, Natalie, and me to join Sam and Brian at the desk for a few more snaps. I must say, I now understand the magic of studio lighting, not just for celebrities, but for average, middle-aged women like me.

After photos, we said goodbye to Brian. We were escorted to the control room to watch the show unfold. The small room was dark, with three rows of wall screens. About a half dozen employees worked the computers underneath the screens. Toward the back of the control room, a woman in a red power suit - with a strong yet welcoming demeanor - appeared to be in charge. I'd never been briefed on control room etiquette, but we had the sense we should keep quiet and stay seated against the back wall while the eight or so employees set up for 30 minutes of live, high pressure synchrony. The show was about to begin. In the exact center of the room, one employee waved and shouted, "Go go go!" Rocking back and forth on the balls of his feet, like a maestro conducting a live performance.

Another employee, on a headset, was talking to a reporter standing in front of the Center for Disease Control in Atlanta, Georgia. The reporter was about to give an update on the Ebola threat. In another city, a doctor stood by, ready to deliver a one-minute explanation about how the disease spread. In West Africa, yet another correspondent was standing by to weigh in on the potential impacts of the fatal epidemic. The doctor spoke longer than the time allotted, so the report from West Africa was cancelled, which meant that Brian had to spontaneously invent an extra 30 seconds of commentary. The show then went to a commercial.

I was mesmerized. The woman in the red suit, focused but calm, reassured us they'd clean up the footage before it aired on the west coast. The final segment of the show was about to air, usually the feel-good type of story Sam liked best. For two minutes, we'd see the logo and hear the outtake music and everyone in the room would be breathing easy. We didn't know it, but we were in for a surprise.

"Who's that sitting in my chair?" Brian said to the camera as he came back on air. On the screen was a bright photo of Sam with his shiny bald head. "It's none other than Sam Day!" Brian announced to the nation and the world. "Sam is raising money to cure the very rare Ewing sarcoma!" After a brief summary of Sam's challenge and achievements, and one or two appreciative comments, Brian closed the segment by saying, "Well, Sam, our money's on you!"

In the back of the room, the four of us gasped and giggled while we tried to comprehend what had just happened. Later, I realized the significance of that experience. Sam had arrived at this moment as a result of his passion for history and world affairs. Now he had become part of that larger story. Not just because of his ordeal, but because of the strength of his spirit. It was an uplifting moment, and one that was pure Sam.

The woman in the red suit turned to him and remarked, "Don't worry. That only went out to about ten million people."

30
THE FDA

Throughout our adventures, fun and fear existed inside of me. The New York trip coincided with another week of waiting for some critical news from Texas.

Shortly before the trip, I got a call from the scientific developer of the vaccine trial. He had determined that Sam's vaccine was contaminated with his own streptococcus bacteria, a germ which many of us can carry in a dormant state, and very likely harmless to Sam. Instead of storing the unused vaccine in a refrigerator, he could cite a long list of logical, scientific, and ethical reasons for offering to Sam this personalized drug made from his own tumor cells. He had written to the FDA to ask for an exception.

The FDA said yes. Sam could have his contaminated vaccine. Sam was the sole patient to receive this exemption, so the investigators planned to document every suspicious symptom no matter how mild. Therefore, we were asked to remain in Dallas for a few days following the first dose so his medical team could monitor him. We booked the flight and waited hopefully.

~

Before heading to Dallas, we squeezed in a return trip to San Diego for another four days of sport with the Challenged Athletes Foundation. Bob was unable to make it, so this time Sam and I went alone. After his first year, Sam dreamed of swimming the mile in the triathlon at the weekend's close. He'd worked up to a half a mile at the local athletic club, but with the intermittent chemotherapies, surgeries, and travel, he hadn't had the where-withal to build up his endurance. But, he knew he could surf.

He had new swim trunks and a sun-resistant shirt. This time, Sam greeted the kids he'd met the year before. Younger kids yelled, "Hey, there's Sam!" This time, he was bald, and parents gently asked me "How is he doing?" With anxious expressions, I watched them whisper to one another. In a hopeful tone, I delivered my standard report on cancer nutrition. I talked about evolving treatments for Ewing, and mentioned how Sam was about to take part in an immunotherapy trial which had already demonstrated remarkable efficacy in a handful of patients. I cultivated an atmosphere of can-do optimism around me because I needed to be surrounded by hope.

Sam was introduced to his surf coach, an amiable blond fellow in his 50's named Liam. Liam had no experience surfing with people with disabilities, but he was a pro at the sport and an enthusiastic affirming presence. The two of them headed out into the waves. I watched from the shore, chatting with parents I'd met the previous year.

After catching a few small blips close to the shore, Sam and Liam made their way farther out beyond the swelling waves. They floated and studied the sea. Liam led Sam to a rising wall of water. He guided Sam toward the right wave at the right moments. Sam managed to stand up on one partial foot and his plastic leg, reaching his left hand down to steady the board. Meanwhile, water photographers with flippers on their feet swam around him, capturing his wide grin and a shaka.

"Wow, look at Sam!" I heard other parents shout, and I was so proud. Again, Sam and Liam patiently floated and studied the sea. Some people are nervous in deep water, but Sam and Liam are both seekers of that mesmerizing sense of happiness with the water and the waves. For them it was that feeling where you lose track of time and of everything happening around you because you are so immersed in an activity that challenges your body and mind in exactly the right way. Though one year younger he rode the waves yelling "This is Awesome!" this year I saw in his eyes a slightly more mature and deeply felt *this is awesome*. While he and Liam took every last minute of opportunity to surf, Sam's spirit was also nurtured by beauty, friendship and sport.

I watched from the beach, allowing myself to be hopeful. I thought: *the vaccine could work. Maybe Sam could become a great adaptive surfer.* I thought that perhaps he would survive and live well. I thought it was okay to dream that way.

The surf clinic was over, but Sam and Liam kept cuing up for an even-better wave. Finally, a staffer yelled that it was time for them to come in. Out of the water they emerged with smiles and high fives, while a photographer captured their stoke. Liam, along with another instructor named Sean, hoisted Sam onto their shoulders. The three posed with shakas. This sparkling image of resilience and joy and hope would be used for years to come by the CAF marketing team.

When Sam made his way up to the beach among the observers, he reappeared with a new identity. He wasn't just the kid who lost his leg to cancer; he was a surfer.

Of all the kids on the water that day, Sam was the only one fighting for his life. Others had lost their legs to cancer too, but none of them was currently living with a life-threatening disease. He was different among a sea of kids who were different. But in every other way, he belonged. His grin was contagious. His stoke, iconic.

I learned later that Liam was a surfer with influence. He had a hand in all-things-surfing around the world. Since that day, he has often described how surfing with Sam changed his life. If a bald kid with cancer and one leg and half a foot could discover his zest for life on a board, Liam felt surfing needed to become available to others, no matter what their age, health, or economic status.

Though I didn't know it at the time, that afternoon sparked on-going conversations between CAF and the International Surfing Association to broaden and widen their missions. The first ever international adaptive surfing competition was held in La Jolla, California, in September, 2015. A whole new wave, inspired by Sam.

After another shout out for prayers from our community of supporters, Sam, Bob, and I flew to Dallas for Sam's first dose of the vaccine. We went a day early because one of the stars from the Houston Rockets was now playing for the Dallas Mavericks. Sam's NBA connections earned us access to games around the country. After the game, Chandler Parsons gave Sam another pair of signed shoes which we somehow found room for in our suitcases.

We arrived at the clinic in good spirits. A nurse took us to a small room and set Sam up on the usual paper covered bench. She told us to wait for the doctor and the vaccine. Within ten minutes, Dr. Gordon burst through the door with a nervous energy. "Okay, I'm very sorry, there's a problem." We sat speechless as we waited for the doctor to explain. "The bacteria has interfered with the final processing of Sam's vaccine. I am very sorry, but he cannot have it today."

Once, when I was a kid, I had the wind knocked out of me. This feeling after bad news felt similar, and it was becoming familiar to me now. Though I wasn't literally gasping for air, there was a sudden suffocating grip in my chest.

"I think we can fix it, but we've never had to do this before." He explained to us how the lab would need to run the vaccine through an additional sterilizing process. It would take 7 - 10 days. That meant another week or more of waiting, this time in Dallas. We decided to fly home for the week. The hospital reimbursed us for the flights.

On CaringBridge, I told our friends NOT to pray. I had noticed people in the church celebrating the power of prayer when the things they wanted to happen came true. But I was beginning to experience a physiological aversion to prayer, a mild but persistent stress response developing from those moments of crisis when I had asked our family, friends, and supporters to pray. On nearly every occasion, it was followed by more bad news. I counted 11 times that we'd asked people to pray, with a devastating outcome. It was like saying a prayer for safe travels when every time I left the house I was injured by some freak accident the minute I stepped outside.

I wanted freedom from this chronic challenge to my faith. So, I invited people to put something good and kind into the world as a representation of their compassion for Sam. I realized, I would rather sit in wonder about God's involvement in this tragedy of childhood cancer than try to convince myself that, with enough prayer and faith, He would take care of my son. I needed a new kind of experience. At the risk of prompting my church friends to sign me up for spiritual counseling - or organize an inquest - I gently requested an alternative to asking God for things to go right. I suggested: *Be quiet. Listen. Watch.* I suggested they turn their compassion for Sam into something good for the world. It allowed me the respite I needed from pretending I trusted God to do what we want Him to do.

The quality control process was ironed out, and Sam received three doses of the vaccine before he had another set of scans with mixed results. Mixed results were better than poor results. Several tumors were shrinking, but two were still growing. For his fourth dose of the vaccine, his doctors recommended a procedure that would freeze the tumors called cryoablation. There was evidence to suggest this could kill the growing disease while activating what was called the abscopal effect, and possibly stimulate the immune system to work even better with his next dose of the vaccine. Extra time was needed for our next trip to Dallas.

After pressing every button on his hospital bed to determine its mechanical capabilities, Sam settled in with his screen, listening through his red Houston Rockets headphones. Three doctors entered. One of them was Dr. Gordon. They greeted Sam with the usual cheerful small talk.

"Good morning, Sam," One of them remarked. "Are you ready for surgery?"

"I guess so. Hey, can you tell me when you're going to start the medicine to make me sleep? I want to see how long I can last."

He chuckled. "Sure, that's no problem."

"Wow, those are some nice headphones," another doctor commented.

"Sam, tell him where you got those!" I wanted these doctors to know how much the Houston Rockets loved my son.

"Oh, James Harden gave me these," Sam said with a quick glance toward their gaze.

After the brief chat with Sam, the three doctors asked me to step out to view the scans we had sent in two days earlier to provide them with a clearer picture of the spots they were intending to freeze.

I followed them down the hall, through some doors, around a corner, and down another long hallway. I chatted to the radiation doctor about Sam and his relationships with NBA athletes while he appeared interested and impressed, my mind quietly wondering if they had bad news for me. It was kind of like being in the elevator with someone you don't really know. There wasn't enough time for a real conversation, but not talking at all felt awkward so I pulled out some comments about Sam which, I'm sure had undertones of a proud mom hoping they would see how special he was and then be motivated to work extra hard to get rid of his cancer.

The hallway floors were carpeted in blue. It looked like no one had ever walked on them before. I felt a slight dizziness. I tried to stay focused on Dr. Gordon, who was leading the way. With no windows or other humans in sight, we wandered deep into the hospital. The quiet hallways felt far away from Sam. I reassured myself that it was standard procedure, the final review of the protocols before getting started. By now, the twin emotions of hope and fear were my constant companions. They kept me alert, and ready for action, while at the same time I could act calm and normal.

Clinical research is quite sacrificial. But as a parent of a child with a fatal disease and no other options, I approached the clinical trial as a portal to hope. Perhaps it was part of some astonishing plan that God had in mind for Sam. Bordering on the miraculous. This could be our great story. We'd be the next cancer related spot on a daytime TV talk show, the special child who'd been chosen to overcome the odds, offering hope to hundreds of other cancer families. But phase one clinical trials are set up more for sacrifices, not miracles. I was being led like a lamb to the slaughter.

One of the doctors gestured me into the tiny dark room with a large computer monitor on a standing desk. With the clutter of random chairs and scattered briefcases, I knew it wasn't a room designed for patients or family members. I scanned their faces for any hint of worry.

Dr. Gordon is brilliant and compassionate, and he gives hugs. Dr. Armani was from India. New to us, had been selected to do the procedure. Over the phone, he had been thoughtful and patient in answering all of my questions. He had quickly gained my trust. Dr. Davis, the anesthesiologist, was the first black doctor we'd ever had. He was responsive and kind in an understated way. The diversity of this team was uncommon in our medical experience so far, and I had warm feelings about all three.

"Let's walk you through this from the beginning," Dr. Armani began. I paid close attention, wondering why they were telling me what I already know. We compared the spots from Sam's September scans to those in January, noting the cloudy tumor-free regions after his recent radiation treatments, as well as the two spots they intended to address today.

"Now, here is the scan from last week," Dr. Armani pulled up a slide and ran a little arrow over three white spots on the opposite side of Sam's lungs. "Unfortunately, these three spots have grown quite a bit in just the last month. Before, they were stable, like the others. But, now they just seem to keep growing." My body didn't move, but a surge of fear traveled upward until it singed my cheeks. My eyes drilled into the three white spots in the center of the scan of my son's lung. The rest of the room went dark.

The three doctors stood by me. They didn't offer me a hug, or a single word of comfort, but their loving presence kept me upright as I stood there wishing for Bob, who was 2000 miles away.

Dr. Armani continued to explain to me why the current plan was no longer an option. "We had hoped to knock down the disease by treating the two spots, but now there seems to be more, and the calculation of risk versus benefit has changed."

As gently as he could, Dr. Gordon asked "Lorna, do you still want to go ahead with the procedure, to take care of one spot? Or do you want to go off the trial and do something else?"

Off the trial? Was this really happening? My immediate reaction was *NO! We're not coming off the trial!* I nudged my brain to use its reasoning skills, instead of fight or flight. *Keep breathing.* I told myself. *Survivors stay calm and keep breathing. There must be another way.* Yet I knew, we all knew, if this didn't work there were very few options left for Sam. "Can I sit down?" I was feeling nauseous and lightheaded. Dr. Gordon quickly removed the briefcase from an office chair. I sat down in the chair and held my head in my hands.

I thought about walking into the room where Sam sat in his hospital gown, hungry, but pleasantly distracted by his handheld screen. I thought about telling him he's not having the procedure or the vaccine. It was like telling him that we no longer had hope. I could hardly bear to do that.

"I want to go ahead with the procedure and the vaccine," I announced. "I'm not going to tell Sam anything until later today. I'll wait until he's feeling better." The three doctors nodded, affirming my decision, reiterating that there was still hope for the vaccine to kick in, maybe with another round of radiation. I clung to their measured optimism. It seemed valid. Legitimate. Educated.

They led me back to Sam's room. I composed my face with a lighthearted expression, knowing that he would be watching me carefully for any signs of bad news. The medical team quickly set up the anesthesia. I didn't have to maintain a brave face for long. Sam reached out for a hug. I kissed him on the head as they wheeled him down the hallway toward the operating room.

A nurse led me back to the blue and green waiting room, too bright and harsh. I walked to the farthest corner, away from other families and their children. The second-floor balcony overlooked the entrance to the children's hospital, with two tall windows that let in the bright Texas sunshine. When I tried to eat a bite of the protein bar hidden in my backpack, my stomach clenched. I wasn't crying yet. Instead, a tremble emerged from deep inside my gut as the thought hit me again, *I might lose him.*

I called Bob. "I have some bad news." This wasn't supposed to be that kind of trip. We had plans to see another Mavericks game, visit some friends in Fort Worth, with a few days of relaxation at the Ronald McDonald house so Sam's lung could heal before flying home.

I told Bob the whole story. In disbelief, we remained silent for several minutes. Then, the tears started and wouldn't stop. I located a box of tissues in the waiting room. Over the next hour and a half, the doctors stopped in to update me on the surgery, reiterating that they still had some hope. My tears kept flowing until my face became red and puffy. I texted Bob, ate a few bites, and tried to fix myself up before I would need to greet Sam.

Over the next 24 hours, time moved slowly. After recovery, the doctors moved Sam into the very same inpatient room he had stayed in after his lung surgery several months prior. The memories of Sam's pain and trauma undid me. As soon as Sam was asleep again, I fell apart. My frantic mind searched for solutions, miracle remedies that kept vanishing in a swirl.

Dr. Gordon recommended that Sam have another scan in one month. He felt it might be worthwhile to see if things turned a corner. I found comfort in knowing we had four more weeks to gather information and consult with doctors across the country in anticipation of coming off the trial. I found help and support from the new friends I'd met raising funds for cancer research. I vacillated between taking care of Sam, and collapsing in a flood of tears.

Outwardly, Sam didn't react much to the discovery of three small spots on his left lung. He was more concerned about the possibility of another chest tube. Since that wasn't needed, he was relieved. Though it worried him to see me cry, he tended to let me carry the heaviest burdens, and I preferred it that way.

Finally, it was time to check out of the inpatient room, and head over to the research clinic so that Sam could receive his next dose of vaccine. We were packed up and ready when Dr. Gordon suddenly appeared. He asked me to sit down. Sam could tell this was something he didn't want to hear, so he left us to scout around in the hallway.

Dr. Gordon said, "I am sorry Lorna, but the independent reviewer has pulled Sam from the trial. I cannot give him any more vaccines." It didn't matter how appalled I was or how much we'd already been through or the power wielded by an independent reviewer with the FDA who'd never met us. Hopefulness can turn to despair in an instant. That was the end of the vaccine.

Days later when Sam had healed, we flew home from Dallas on an evening flight. I looked out the window, drawn to the soft pink light caught in the clouds. A wish entered my mind, *I want to be someplace beautiful.* Like feeling thirsty or needing sleep, I wanted to rest for hours and weeks in a serene place that could restore me. High up in the sky, with the sun glowing, I imagined resting near a calm river in a quiet canyon. I thought, maybe there is a place of beauty that could hold me for a bit. I felt a wish to be free from this ordeal, to find a new resting place.

31
I AM SAM

Sam continued attending middle school whenever he felt well. His English teacher tasked the students with writing a poem. The evening before his assignment was due, Sam opened up his homework binder at the kitchen table with a frustrated sigh. His assignment was to write a poem titled "I am Sam." He pulled out a piece of college ruled paper with his verses written in pencil. Much of his page had gray smudgy eraser marks with thick pencil leaded words. I could see his frustration on his page of erratic scribbles. He told me it was terrible and asked if I could help.

I read through what he had and my heart took notice of what he was trying to say. Ninety percent of his intention was there on the page. It only needed some organization. I drew lines to mark how he should divide the verses. He took a clean sheet of paper and started to re-write it in a different order.

I AM SAM

I am from waiting in cold sterile rooms
for the doctor to arrive
with words of sadness or joy.

I am from hoping that this time it worked
That all of the cancer is gone.

I am from sadness and mourning
Of those who I once played side by side with.
I am from never taking anything for granted
And knowing that everything is precious.

I am from laying in a bed
Watching tears roll down my mom's face
As I am rolled away to surgery.

I am from overcoming obstacles that, at first,
Seemed impossible.

I am from falling on my newly amputated leg
Because I do not know how to use crutches.

I am from summer camps
Where the different feel normal
And all of our sadness is shared.

I am from coming home in tears
To the caring arms of my mom
Because I was not picked at the game at school.

I am from love and compassion
From friends and family helping me through hard times.

I am from email groups
Where traveling across the country for a risky surgery is common
And despair is often.

I am from caring with all my heart for the ones I love.
I am from running a mile at track just weeks after surgery.
I am from pushing through pain and nausea just to go to school.

I am a cancer survivor.
I am Sam.

32
DECREASED
METASTATIC DISEASE

A promising new treatment, one of those targeted drugs in development, achieved a timely breakthrough. It could be the next hopeful option for saving Sam's life. In the meantime, we needed to keep Sam's disease at bay until it became available.

Along the way, I had become connected to a couple of rather intelligent physicians, and a Yale professor and philanthropist, who all had kids with Ewing sarcoma. They spoke my language of hope. We were all monitoring the development of the new drugs for our kids, and funding them when the money was needed. Some of these parents were wealthy and could contribute funds to the research out of their own resources. I relied on the generosity of our community at the Sam Day Soirée to do whatever they could to advance this critical research.

Pazopanib was a relatively new drug, originally used to treat advanced renal cell carcinoma. We considered it as a drug that could keep Sam's cancer stable for a while, knowing it would not be a curative option for him. It had begun to show some efficacy with sarcomas. We consulted with doctors, who warned us that the side effects would most likely be difficult for Sam to tolerate.

And, that it probably wouldn't work. But with few other options - and none of them very promising - we decided to give it a try.

I learned how to keep the side effects manageable with herbs, lymphatic massage, exercise and good hydration. Guided by multiple professionals, I kept track of his liver enzymes with each new blood draw, as liver toxicity was a serious concern.

Up until that moment, I had considered the ketogenic diet too extreme. But with the chance of Sam surviving long enough to access this new clinical trial, the ketogenic diet started to look more appealing.

I have a friend, Melanie, who is a PhD researcher in nutrition with expertise on pediatric metabolic disorders and fatty-acid oxidation. I still don't fully understand what this means, but my friend is one of the smartest people I know. I trust her. She told me she had read enough about the ketogenic diet to become curious about its impact on cancer. She grasped the scientific rationale but cautioned me, "We still don't have enough research to confirm how effective it could be, but I've read a few pretty incredible case studies."

The ketogenic diet is intended to switch a person's fuel supply from glucose to fats. Our cells use carbohydrates, which break down to glucose for fuel. Cancer cells do the same but to a frenzied extreme. It's why we hear people say that sugar feeds cancer. Normal cells in our body, including our brain cells, can also use ketones, derived from fat. Cancer cells can't use ketones, so the shift from glucose to ketones leaves cancer cells starving while the rest of the body thrives.

A ketogenic diet is sugar free. It's high in good fat like avocado, coconut oil, macadamia nuts, and fattier meats. It requires a moderate protein intake, while it's very low in carbohydrates.

Leafy green vegetables are important, but root vegetables contain too much glucose. I've never heard a doctor speak about the ketogenic diet with any particular expertise. I've heard them express their disapproval. I've seen them roll their eyes, speak sarcastically about it with peers, and discourage patients by telling them it's very difficult to maintain. I would have preferred to hear *I don't know much about that but will do some research.* I would have reconsidered if they had provided some rationale with evidence of potential harm. I would be generously respectful of doctors who were curious about things they don't know much about.

In the end, Melanie and I talked it over and decided on a modified ketogenic diet, which could still have the metabolic effect without the nutritional risks posed by an extreme ketogenic diet. I bought the books, and the blood-glucose monitor and the keto strips to test Sam for ketone levels. I promised him meals with bacon and ground beef and continued providing all of the vegetables and spices he'd learned to appreciate. I monitored his bloodwork and paid attention to his energy.

After two months into this patchwork of a treatment plan, Sam had scans. Pazopanib had another odd side effect in that it turned his hair completely white. Since the previous chemo-therapy had made him bald again, Sam now had a white fuzzy glow on his head. He liked it. For the first time in three years, Dr. Madison walked into the clinic room with a big smile on his face. The report from his chest CT read, "decreased metastatic disease." Not only were all of his lung tumors shrinking, they were shrinking dramatically.

Dr. Madison added, "I don't really understand all that you are doing, but keep doing it. It's working."

Sam took a photo of the printed report and shared it with friends. Bob and I cried. We rushed home to get Natalie and we all went out for ice cream, which was not on the ketogenic diet. As I stood in line at the ice cream place, I noticed how my peace eased into and flowed throughout my body. I said to Bob, "This feeling is so unfamiliar. I just can't believe it." For the next three months, we could breathe easy. Sam lived his days almost as if he didn't have cancer. It was a blissful, beautiful time.

33

THE PARTY AND
THE SURF BOARD

I had a secret I wasn't supposed to share with Sam. He was going to be given a surfboard, at a party in a fancy house on the beach in La Jolla. But that's all I knew. It happened on a September evening in San Diego for the very first International Adaptive Surfing competition. The event drew people from all around the world with amputations, spinal cord injuries, and other physical impairments. The event was treated like any other surf competition with corporate sponsors, sports commentators, vendor tents, and a beach speckled with spectators. It was history in the making, and Sam was an honored guest.

I've known enough of these athletes to understand that their drive to compete in sports of all kinds is so much greater than their desire to be an inspiration. But sitting on a beach watching people from around the world with physical disabilities compete in a surf competition for the first time ever, is enough to be imprinted on the mind and heart.

After the Decreased Metastatic Disease report, Sam looked healthy and he felt great, as long as he stayed hydrated and ate well. His hair was growing in white because the drug he was taking removed his pigment, but he thought it made him look like a California surfer so he embraced it.

The party that night was within walking distance from our waterfront hotel, so we walked the boardwalk, me in my flip flops and black sleeveless dress and Sam in some cool surf shorts and a gray I Am Sam shirt. This was our best interpretation of "So Cal Casual."

When we arrived, I realized *So Cal Casual* was a lot more fancy than I envisioned. The heels and eyelashes and impressively artful fingernails left us feeling a bit out of our Pacific Northwestern element. The house opened up to an outdoor patio, complete with a full bar and an ice sculpture in the shape of a wave, surrounded by jumbo shrimp. Photographers wandered the space and the waves crashed along the beach just a few yards away from the party.

"Sam this is crazy!" I whispered to him with a smirk.

"Hey look, there's Travis!" Sam pointed to our friend from CAF and we attached ourselves to him while I grabbed a glass of wine from the server.

After some hors d'oeuvres and social chatter, The CAF Board President used a microphone to gather people's attention and we all wandered to a spot where we could see his presentation. He welcomed the guests, and then invited Sam to join him.

"Sam, what's your goal down the line?"

"Well, I'd love to compete at this event in a couple of years from now." He said, still buzzed from the day on the beach. The guests all cheered and treated Sam like he was the celebrity in the room.

Mike Coots was called up to present the special surprise. Mike is an amputee surfer from Hawaii whose leg was bit off by a shark when he was 18. An avid photographer, Mike took a career in shark conservation and now spends his time studying and protecting sharks, capturing the most stunning underwater images only feet away from them. Of all Sam's surfing coaches and mentors, Mike was the one who was also an amputee, and his life was remarkable.

From just around the corner Mike picked up a bright green Rusty branded surfboard with artwork specially created by California artist Andy Davis. The board had been personally shaped by Rusty Preisendorfer, a legend in the surfboard design industry. Sam's eyes grew wide, his grin was contagious, and the house full of guests applauded while Sam and Mike stood on either side of the surfboard. The house was alive with that California stoke, a great setup for auctioning off some items that could only be available at a party on the beach like this. They raised $80,000 to help sustain the adaptive surfing movement.

All of a sudden, Sam took a new, confident stride through the party. I asked him if he wanted to stay a while and he answered me, "Yeah! These people love me! I'm gonna have some more shrimp too!"

We spoke with spouses from the band members of Switchfoot, and a darling young woman who asked to get a photo with Sam. She was into nutrition too, and we talked about the future of nutrition in medicine. I finally asked her, "OK, I think you are someone I should know. How do I know you?"

She smiled and said, "I'm Tenley from the Bachelor." Later that night she posted a photo of her and Sam on Instagram.

As the party simmered down, Sam and I picked up the surfboard and carefully walked it out of the house. It was one of those long boards, much easier to transport if we each carried an end. We moved in unison with the board tucked under our arms, me in front and Sam in back, and together, we walked along the darkened beach all the way back to our hotel room, giggling as we went.

34
BIOLOGY 211

After three months of delightful relief from the hardships of cancer, another scan continued to show his tumors shrinking, though not quite as dramatically as at first. Sam had remained on a modified ketogenic diet, exercising and feeling great. Now into winter, the days were darker and the kids' lives were full of school and activities and friendships. It was during those times when the crisis subsided, that grief hit me the hardest. A year before, while undergoing treatment after his first relapse, Sam said to me, "Mom, you do really well when there is a crisis. But when things get slow, that's when you kinda fall apart." Until I heard him say those words, I wasn't aware that he was paying such close attention.

Sam was right. When his condition worsened or a crisis arose, I became a momma bear, focused on doing whatever I could to protect his life and make it as tolerable as possible. But with long-term cancer, there are seasons within seasons. Seasons of crisis brought out the fight in me, while short-lived episodes of stability allowed me to breathe easier.

A season of peace - a tumor removed, a clear scan, a multi-month treatment plan - allowed me to drop my 24-7 cortisol-inflicted hyper alertness, at least for a little while. Sam could go to school, youth group, and play practices. He could eat normal meals with us and travel more than 30 minutes away from the hospital.

The tension in my body relaxed every time I heard him laugh. I slept better. I cried less. I was happy for my son. Logically, these periods of rest should have given me time to restore. But in these times of quiet stability, my attention shifted to my own starving spirit. When Sam was suffering, I needed to be there for him completely. When he was doing better, as hopeful as I tried to be, I was afraid to make commitments because I didn't want to let others down when more bad news arrived.

Meanwhile, Bob was moving up in the bureau. He'd been promoted to Commander of Central Precinct in 2011, overseeing the downtown core of Portland. He'd led the precinct through the sit-in Occupy movement, managing large unscheduled marches, and a growing city of tents in a downtown park. He stayed in close communication with the Mayor and other city leaders, and his performance was noticed and affirmed. In 2015, he was promoted to Assistant Chief in charge of operations - the management of all patrol officers throughout Portland.

Bob was good at his job. He could walk through the streets engaging with all sorts of Portlanders like a glad-handing politician, or lunch with business leaders and city council members with a collaborative relationship, regardless of whether or not they agreed on the city's next steps through a crisis. There were stories, like visiting a homeless man very near to dying, arranging for him to get medical care and a bed to sleep in, or strategically detouring a mob of lively protesters headed to block the freeway. He often called to let me know he was working late to make sure he wasn't needed for anything. I couldn't justify telling him to skip the 7:00pm roll call just because I resented his worklife success.

There was talk of Bob being promoted to the highest level. I was uncomfortable with that potential. Law enforcement work in Portland can be challenging. Portland is a complex environment with diversity of views and values, rooted in activism and community involvement. The views about how police officers should do their job is also quite diverse. I have always wished our community valued the high level of policing they receive. And at the same time, I recognize that, in the eyes of some Portlanders, the Portland Police Bureau has not always been seen as just and fair. The ongoing tension is picked up by the media, exposing all of our officers to public scrutiny, and seeping into neighborhoods and schools. I didn't want Bob to become the Chief of Police, not ever. Especially not when my kids were in school, subject to the outspoken opinions of their peers. And, I didn't want to be the chief's wife. That being said, Bob was masterful at his job, and I wanted the chance to be masterful at something too.

What a privilege it is to do the work we are uniquely designed to do. It is one of life's greatest and most underappreciated pleasures. Call it natural giftedness, or divine design, there is something intrinsically satisfying about doing work perfectly aligned with someone's natural abilities, temperament, and values. I can see this in the Scriptures, starting in the Book of Genesis. "Then the Lord God took the man and put him in the Garden of Eden to work it and take care of it." (Genesis 2:15). It is a concept I continue to embrace, though I have rarely heard it taught. While there was no greater purpose than caring for my son through cancer, I still longed for the freedom to work - to do something well, and to live into the identity of a skilled professional. Though the sacrifice was entirely my choice - and one I felt secure in - my relentless focus on Sam's cancer made me ache for a different kind of purpose.

One afternoon, as I managed the laundry and the kids, I guess my negative energy was especially loud. All day I'd been holding back a well of tears and it seemed as if anger was the only reliable response. Bob was doing yardwork in the backyard, and I needed to ask him a question.

He considered yard work his therapy. With his work gloves on, he rested his hands on the yard debris bin full of cut grass and tree twigs. He told me, "I'm probably going to have to go in to work tonight." Two policemen had been shot at during the previous night shift, and he wanted to go in and speak with the officers in charge. Some bitter phrases came to mind, but I kept quiet. I loathed the idea of spending another night dealing with persistent negotiations over homework and screen time with the kids. I had no life left in me, and certainly no energy for showing up well for my kids.

"Okay." I steadied myself and asked, "Do you want dinner before you go?"

"No, I can grab something while I'm down there tonight."

"Okay." I started to walk back toward the house.

"Lorna." Bob called me back. I turned around but without making eye contact, "I'd really like it if you could try not to be so resentful."

My throat tightened. Wiping away one tear, I nodded my head and went inside.

At the kitchen sink, I stared out the window at the light caught in the pale green leaves of a mature Japanese maple. I felt a longing to be dead. It didn't feel like a dark wish, or even a negative desire, it just felt light and peaceful. Freedom from the endless list of mundane tasks. Freedom from crying through my mornings and Ativan afternoons. Freedom from carrying fear. A freedom from difficult one-on-one conversations. As if the idea of dying served as a momentary stand-in for an elusive something that I longed for but couldn't have. It was like wishing to be on a warm sunny beach. I wasn't thinking of taking my own life, but it worried me a little, the pleasure I felt while imagining I was dead.

I resented Bob telling me not to be resentful. It was better than feeling defeated. Some more popular Christian self-help books, many of them by women, suggest that no matter what the circumstances, we should focus on our blessings. A woman's role is to serve her family in the home. Perhaps that's what gives some women their sense of purpose, and I am quite respectful of that desire, but it wasn't mine. I wanted my resentment. Letting go of it would mean I was surrendering to a role that my spirit was so adamantly rejecting. Rather than asking me to accommodate myself to a more circumscribed life, I wanted Bob to see that I was trapped, and needed help. Or at least to partake in my discomfort.

While it seemed my only two choices were to continue being resentful, or embrace this way of life, neither option would work. Some deep reflection led me to a third option. I had some choices to make around how I could continue to exist in this life. I felt a powerful pull to discover something meaningful. So, with a little creative brainstorming, I found rays of light peeking into my dark world suggesting there might be a way to step outside again.

I found an article on the therapeutic benefits of writing. I started to put my thoughts and feelings down on paper. I then discovered a memoir writing class at a local community college just one evening per week. It was a non-credit class, so I didn't have to worry about letting anyone down or ending up with a bad grade if I suddenly had to drop out.

For eight weeks, three times a week, I enjoyed an active engagement for my mind. It was a new scene with fascinating people who had no firsthand experience of childhood cancer, and that was refreshing. Opening up my laptop to the new folder with class assignments and personalized feedback was like discovering a secret spice in the kitchen cabinet. Removed from the shelf, and sprinkled on the right food combinations, it introduced a pantry of new flavors, savory and sweet, filling our home with a wonderful aroma. In between the crises, writing became my gift to myself.

Nutrition engaged me in similar ways. I was now an expert in fighting cancer with food, or at least fueling a body to withstand the toxic treatments and recover from them more quickly. As we headed into Sam's third set of scans under the diet/Pazopanib protocol, I told myself that if the results were still positive, I would look into the possibility of a master's in nutrition from the National University of Natural Medicine in Portland.

On Wednesday, when the house was empty, I called the university to inquire about applying. The polite lady on the phone told me that I had been out of school for so long I would need to take an advanced biology class before applying. In front of our wood stove, I sat with my computer on the carpet reviewing the local community college academic schedule to see when I could fit a biology class in before applying in the spring. Cedar snuggled up against me. I was in my exercise clothes, intending to take him out for a run.

The information came at me like a slow-moving train that I somehow needed to board without a ticket. Applications to the fall master's program were due in April, which meant I needed to complete a biology class immediately if I wanted to apply within the year. The class schedule at the local community college listed my required prerequisite, Biology 211, and it started that day.

In an hour.

The first session of Biology 211 consisted of a two-hour lecture, followed by a one-hour break, followed by a three-hour lab.

I processed the logistics and wondered whether a normal level-headed person would make a last minute decision to enroll in a science class. The next three months of my life should be quiet, considering the good scan results. Sam felt good. It was winter and I needed something to do. The only obstacle was the 45 minutes in front of me, so my deprived sense of adventure said go.

Shit, I thought, *this is crazy. I'm too old.* I didn't have a notebook or a backpack. Or a parking permit. *I haven't showered or taken out the dog. Sorry, Cedar.*

I raced upstairs to change out of my running tights and called Bob's phone. It immediately went to voicemail. "Hey, so, remember how I mentioned that I might look into the possibility of going back to school? Well, um, I'm going to take a class at PCC. But it starts in 40 minutes. It costs about $500. I'll be home around 5:30 so dinner will be late tonight. Okay. Bye!"

The Portland Community College campus is less than five miles from home. I parked illegally in the permit-only parking lot hoping I wouldn't get a ticket, and hustled onto the campus, searching for one of those big maps with a sticker on it that says, "You are here." I made it to the lecture, not just on time, but a few minutes early.

Inside the classroom, tables faced each other in groups of four. I chose a seat near the front of the room. At the teacher-only table, the instructor sat quietly with her arms folded, regarding each student as they entered, all in their late teens and early twenties - except for me. This would have been intimidating on my best day; in terms of personal hygiene and fashion, this was one of my worst.

Summoning up my likeable self, I strolled up to the front desk and explained to the teacher how desperate I was to get into the class. She stopped me, and told me in no uncertain terms that it wasn't up to her. I'd have to find out later if there was room in the lab, which was taught by someone else.

The lecture began. Without smiling, she shared her resume and the rules of the class. Phones must be turned off and put away. We were to have open book online quizzes every week. We should expect a comprehensive and challenging final exam. We were responsible for purchasing the appropriate Scantron forms.

I triple checked my cellphone to make sure it was on silent.

I soon realized how important it was that I didn't skip the first class. It was a biology class, but since chemistry is the building block of all living things (which I put together in my first hour of class), it began there. Lesson One included *atoms, molecules, positive and negative charges* and *covalent bonds.* The first lecture was supposed to be a review. It might have been for others, but not for me. I took notes furiously. It felt a little bit like learning the names of various conditions, chemotherapies and complications they caused. I hoped my brain, jolted into action by the adrenaline, was up for it.

The lecture concluded and I got up quickly to scout out the lab. Next, I wandered around the science building until I found a spot to sit down, facing a wall of windows so I could eat the granola bar and apple I'd grabbed from the house. I was sure everyone around me wondered what that older greasy woman with no one to talk to was doing at the community college.

I showed up early to plead my case with the lab instructor. Like the first teacher, he was rather cold to me at first. He told me I could stay, but since the roster was already at capacity, he asked me not to take a seat on any of the tall lab stools beside the wooden tables. Instead, he pointed at a worn-out office chair. When I sat, it jogged down to its lowest setting, and made a loud *clunk,* drawing the entire room's attention to the middle-aged woman hunkering against the back wall.

Lucky for me, two students didn't show up. At age 45, I was a college student again, and I loved it. I took copious class notes and later rewrote them to imprint them on my brain. I read every word of every assignment, and I quizzed myself with the end-of-chapter reviews.

I visited the instructor who'd delivered our lectures during her office hours whenever I didn't understand something. Her response to me warmed; she seemed to like teaching someone who really, really wanted to learn. In no time at all I'm pretty sure I became her favorite student.

I told her about Sam, so she could explain to me how a particular concept might relate to cancer, or the treatment of disease.

"What about cancer metabolism?"

"What does a fusion protein look like?"

"How does an enzyme cause tumor growth?"

I wanted to be able to call on her for help in the future to help me grasp the implications of the scientific data in cancer research. For twelve weeks, Biology 211 consumed me, and I loved it.

Parenting a chronically ill child carried many layers of challenge. Fear and stress around Sam's well-being, depression-inducing episodes that followed bad news, and painfully slow periods of wondering if the current protocol might work. It had been five years since Sam was diagnosed and the life I was crafting for myself disappeared, as if I had fallen asleep and now lived in a perpetual bad dream.

Long before cancer, I found my purpose in the midst of other people's suffering, drawn to that place where the human spirit is most in need of light. My calling seemed clear. At age 40, I was beginning to transition away from my domestic home and church bubble, toward a career with so much opportunity to engage and grow. Five years had now passed since Sam was first diagnosed. Biology 211 was the first step in a return path to my life's journey.

I noticed that I was more relaxed at home. I delighted in being unavailable for periods of time. My attitude toward Bob softened, not because of anything he was doing, but because the class - and all that I was learning - had reawakened my sense of purpose. I smiled warmly at others and engaged with them more. I stopped wishing I were dead. I studied hard, hoping for an A. I got a B+.

The day after my final exam, Sam had another scan. The tumors were bigger and fluid was beginning to build up around his lungs. And, just like that, I slipped back into the version of myself who deals with crisis.

<h1 style="text-align:center">35</h1>

LEFT SIDE OF THE ROPE LINE

I asked the naturopath about marijuana for Sam. This was 2016, in the early days of legalized access to cannabis. The naturopath wasn't licensed to issue cards, so he sent me to the MD in the office next door.

"Hi, my son is 14 and he has cancer. I'm wondering about getting him a medical marijuana card." He gave me some pamphlets and an application like I was applying for a Target rewards card. "Bring that back and we can submit it for approval. I don't expect an issue."

"So," I lingered in front of his desk, folding and unfolding my crisp new pamphlets. "My husband is a police officer." Actually, as an Assistant Chief, Bob was becoming more visible, depending on the chaos in the city at the time. Nervously, I pressed on. "Should I be concerned about my son's use of medical cannabis if my husband is in law enforcement?"

"Uh uh. Everything about this is totally legal now."

"Okay, I guess I'll talk to him."

I felt like I was deceiving Bob by asking about medical marijuana. In Oregon, recreational marijuana was legalized in 2014, and medical marijuana was passed through a ballot initiative six years before that. Even so, I knew how unsettling the topic would be for Bob.

But the more I read, the more I believed medical marijuana could bring Sam relief from the cancer treatments and potentially help fight the cancer too. I mused for days over the dreaded conversation, searching the internet for the most credible information I could find on benefits of cannabis for kids with cancer. I sought peer-reviewed papers and testimonials from other straightlaced citizens. Honestly, I wanted someone exactly like Bob to post a video of themselves proclaiming the miracle of marijuana as a cure and a blessing for the whole family. That's really what I wanted.

"Here is my application." I handed my signed application to the MD next door, who said, "Expect Sam's card in the mail in about two weeks." His words energized my brain like a little hit of dopamine.

Among law-abiding, substance-free, *nothing stronger than Advil* civil servants like Bob, the taboo of cannabis use comes from seeing the negative ramifications of drug use.

In the '90's, as a young officer on the streets, Bob made arrests for possession of large and small amounts. His stereotyped image of a marijuana user: a young man in baggy jeans, stealing cheap beer from the local convenience stores, lying to him about minor breaches in the law as obvious as the shotgun sticking out of his front pocket, and clearly hiding underneath the length of his pant leg. "These aren't even my pants!" insisted one of Bob's streetcorner desperados. It wasn't exactly the picture of the kind of young adulthood he dreamt about for his kids.

However, I was beginning to see from another angle. Marijuana had potential for fighting disease and easing the impact of cancer. Its recreational use and abuse had very likely hindered serious research to validate it as a helpful medicine. But Sam's disease was advancing, and he was nearly out of options. If medical marijuana eased his pain, it might buy us some time. It gave me a reason to be hopeful.

At a restaurant with Bob, I chose a booth for more privacy. I ordered a chardonnay. I wondered if he could tell I was nervous. I'd rehearsed all the various ways I could bring up the topic. No matter how I introduced it, I was sure his reaction would lead to an uncomfortable meal.

Here we go. "I think we should try cannabis with Sam." My words hung in the air and trembled as I focused on the flames of the votive candle on our table. I rattled through the information I'd read online, including multiple references with enough scientific lingo to show him that smart people believed that cannabis could fight cancer.

When Bob is serious, he gets this eyebrow furrow. I keep telling him he needs to be aware of this when he's interviewed on TV because it makes him look angry, or at least very irritated. Right off, I got the unfriendly eyebrow furrow. As expected, Bob remarked, "I'd have a lot of concerns about giving Sam marijuana."

"I've been worried about bringing it up, for about a month now. However, I've read enough to believe it's something we should consider."

"You've been thinking about this for a month?" He suddenly became thoughtful. "What would it look like?"

"I can get Sam a medical marijuana card from a doctor in Sam's Naturopath's office. I've already talked to him about it." I told him about some leads I was following, such as an organization that manufactures super clean products for children with serious health conditions. Our niece in California could drive a selection of these products up here for Sam to try.

"That's illegal." Bob quickly shut down the idea of transporting products over state lines. He said he might consider local use if Sam received the proper medical authorization, but first he would need "to talk to some people with the City Attorney's Office." He wanted to be absolutely certain that every move we made was above board and legal. I expected this. I was more surprised that he was this open to trying.

"Can you do that this week?"

"I'll reach out to Joe tomorrow and see if I can get a phone call with him."

I was relieved. As Sam's tumors grew and his options shrank, I had discovered something that would ease his pain and keep our spirits alive. It wasn't a cure, but it was something we could do, freeing us to live our days with at least some small degree of hope. And happily, it was no longer a secret.

The next day, Bob phoned the City Attorney's office, confirming that giving medical marijuana for Sam with a legitimate card posed no risk for Bob's work. He still wanted me to handle it.

So, I did just that.

Southeast of the Willamette, the wide and sparkling river that divides Portland, is a vibrant marketplace of integrative medicine clinics, yoga studios, and other non-westernized healing practices. The marijuana dispensary on Hawthorne Boulevard had a sign with a big green cross. I got a tingly feeling imagining the bohemian experts inside, with their unkempt hair and sophisticated glasses, expounding the medicinal benefits of marijuana on the endocannabinoid system. No doubt, this would be the place to find the not-yet FDA-approved treatment that might control Sam's cancer until cutting-edge research came up with the so-called magic bullet that would save him. Turns out that was a little naïve.

Inside the front door of the dispensary was a check-in desk

with a guy behind a plexiglass barrier, like the ticket counter at a movie theater. He handed me a clipboard to sign in. I was nervous, like the first time I went through customs in a foreign country. The very picture of a suburban mom, I wondered if I should have worn my black T-shirt and that leather choker I had made last summer.

Anyway, they buzzed me in.

The air was heavy with the sweet smell of weed. In front of me, on a grey carpet, there was a rope separating the white display cases on either side of the big room. A makeshift sign directed customers to one side or the other. Recreational marijuana to the right, medical marijuana to the left. I was the only one on the left side of the rope. The eight or so people on the recreational side were chatting, laughing, and storytelling. I envied them for their lighthearted banter.

On the left, inside the display cases, there were bottles, syringes, and lotions, and packages wrapped up like fancy chocolates. No one was behind the counter, so I shuffled back and forth studying the products carefully. Soon enough, a young woman with thick messy hair tied up on the crown of her head came over to help me.

"Hi. I was told to ask for Matt. Is he available to chat with me?"

"Um, I think I know who that is but he's not here today."

"Okay, well, I'm looking for a product for my son. He has cancer. We haven't tried this before. I don't want him to get high, but I want whatever I can find that could help fight the cancer. So, I'm wondering if you could recommend something for him?"

Right away I sensed she wasn't the medical expert who could woo me with the remarkable results of the products on the left side of the rope line. Instead, she responded as if I'd asked her what color lip gloss looks best with my skin tone. She reached into the pretty display case and grabbed two small dark bottles. One had a blue label, and one had a gold label. "I'd recommend either of these two. This one has a 1:1 ratio of CBD and THC. This one has a lower ratio. It's not like no THC, but it's super low so he wouldn't even feel it."

I felt perplexed, but I didn't want to leave empty handed, so I said, "I'll take the one with the lowest THC, please. How much should I give him?"

"Oh, two or three drops a day would be good."

I followed her to the register, and she asked me if I wanted to throw in a gummy or two. "No, thank you, not today," I said coolly, as if I did this often.

"That's $88.00." I handed her my credit card. "Oh, we only take cash."

The pretending was over.

"Shoot." I said, refusing to meet her eye.

"There's a bank machine over there if you need it," she said, smiling at me sweetly.

I paid for my product and headed out the door with a feeling of *Oh my gosh, I'm glad that's over*, and I held tightly to a small brown paper bag from a shop on Hawthorne.

I'm pretty sure I would have never stepped foot in a cannabis dispensary if I wasn't trying to save my son's life. But some challenges are compelling enough to make us endure the uncomfortable, embarrassed feelings, with hope as our only escort.

At home, I held up the brown paper bag with the tincture inside. "Sam, I got you something for you to try."

"Oooh! Is it marijuana?" He said with wide eyes. At 14, Sam was a pretty intuitive kid. I think he knew if I was willing to venture into the world of recreational drugs, there were not many other options left. He must have known my desperation was rising to the surface again, but the way he joked about it he didn't appear concerned. Rather, he seemed eager to try something new. I played along. "It's not supposed to make you high."

"Awww," Sam said with exaggerated disappointment.

I took a few drops, just to be sure. I'd never done this with any prescription medication, though a few of them are more addictive than marijuana. I felt nothing.

The drops were easy for Sam to take. They didn't taste bad or make him feel sick. We started a routine of daily drops added to his multitude of supplements throughout the day. Soon, the marijuana tincture was just one more thing he had to take.

After my first cannabis purchase, I quickly grew comfortable in a dispensary. I always went to the same one. I got cash out of the machine in the corner first and then asked for the bottle of the low THC tincture with the yellow label. I continued to say no thank you when they offered a couple of packaged chocolates or gummy samples.

And then came scans. His tumors had continued to grow.

Discouraged but still determined, I scheduled a meeting with a trained expert on cannabis and cancer. She was based in California, the place with the best information and products. A phone consultation would cost me $225.00. We talked for an hour. She told me that to have any impact on the growth or symptoms of cancer, Sam needed high doses of CBD and high doses of THC. I reacted with concern, until she told me about a form of THC without psychoactive effects, called THCa. She told me that it's the heating process that activates the psychoactive effect. However, for medical use, it can be formulated at a lower heat, without that unwanted side effect.

The problem was, it wasn't available in Oregon. We found it in California, made especially for kids with severe medical problems. However, there was this *married to a cop* thing that prevented me from driving south and over the state border to get the safest version of THC and CBD for my 14-year-old son hoping to survive cancer. I was frustrated, and I let it show. The consultant offered up another option: I could cook it myself.

She said she would do some research for me on the best places to get pesticide- and mold- free cannabis in Oregon, and we concluded the call. Even though it was legal, and there were medical dispensaries everywhere, weed was still not well-regulated. She promised to provide me with contact info for the cleanest product in the state, along with instructions about how to prepare it. Within 24 hours, I had the name and address of a dispensary. "Be sure to get a lab report." She instructed. "You need a lab-tested flower."

The new dispensary was like a mid-century modern organic herbal medicine museum with beautiful walnut cabinet display cases and proper lighting to make everything look appealing. It wasn't like the other ones, with the handmade signs separating the medicinal users from the recreational customers. Each product was packaged with elegance.

I was attracted to the pretty bottles and jars, but I had my instructions. The well-informed young man behind the counter shared his recommendations and told me that getting the lab report wouldn't be a problem. He disappeared into a back room and came out with two small green jars. One was called "OG Kush' and another one was "Dog Shit Cherry Pie." I smirked, thinking about Bob's reaction when I told him the name of the marijuana I'd be giving our son.

I spent the day purchasing my supplies. I ordered the little dark dropper bottles from Amazon. I bought a hotplate, olive oil, a thermometer, and some cheesecloth at Fred Meyer. I moved about my day, alone but not lonely, hopeful at this new resource. As always, it felt good to have a plan.

Dog Shit Cherry Pie got its name because it is especially pungent. Since I had to cook it over low heat for two hours, I needed to set up an outdoor kitchen (you could call it a lab) to avoid making the entire house smell of marijuana. I put the dried flower into a coffee grinder until it was a fine powder. Then I combined it with some olive oil and heated it in a pot over my hotplate. The solution needed to cook at 140°F for two hours. On the covered patio outside the back door of our basement, I cooked and stirred for two hours, checking the thermometer every few minutes. The wooden fence outlining our backyard kept curious neighbors from peering in to see what was in the smoking pot. However, I was sure the scent wafted for at least half a block.

Once the solution was adequately heated, I let it cool and strained it through the cheesecloth. I bought a cute little metal funnel to pour it into the dropper bottle. Then I did the whole thing again for the OG Kush version, Sam's daytime dose. The final result: two pretty dark bottles with non-psychoactive, cancer fighting THC.

I had learned something new. I felt happy, and more worldly and sophisticated. I felt like maybe I should start wearing different clothes with bookish glasses to reflect my edgy new lifestyle, because now I knew much more about the medicinal properties of marijuana than my friends.

Bob came home while I was still cooking. He looked shocked. In my excitement, I guess I hadn't kept him up to date on my plans.

"What the hell?" He exclaimed, stepping into the backyard patio that I had turned into a marijuana kitchen. He shook his head and rubbed his forehead.

I smiled and giggled a little bit.

The bottles were stored in the fridge. A sheet on the door kept track of Sam's schedule. We needed to start him off with a low dose, incrementally increasing it to a high dose. I didn't want to screw it up. A while back, I remembered that Natalie had received a label maker for Christmas. I asked her to make me two labels: one for the nighttime dose and one for daytime.

She went to work and came back ten minutes later.

Apologetically, she said, "I didn't know how to spell marijuana." She handed me the labels: *Daytime weed, and Nitetime weed.*

36
SCOTLAND

I am 100% Scottish.

At least, I'd like to think so. My mom and her parents are from Scotland, and my dad and his parents are from Scotland. I have a family tree of my dad's side of the family hanging on the wall in our house, detailing our Scottish heritage through the generations. Now, with the emergence of commercial genetic testing kits available online, most people realize they're actually a mix. Though I appreciate the complexity in all things, I still like to think of myself as a 100% Scottish.

My parents have lived in the States for 55 years now. My dad managed to hold on to his Hebridean accent, a few Gaelic phrases, and a robust knowledge of Scottish history. He took up the violin as a boy. He's now an accomplished Scottish fiddler, and a master of the Hebridean sound. My mom, born and raised in the working-class city of Glasgow, managed the books for the local Scottish Country Dance Society in Seattle. She regularly attends events with folks who have become her people, dancing jigs and reels. Still, her accent is most pronounced when she's on the phone with her twin sister in England, or her older sister still in Glasgow.

Our ancestral home is the captivating Isle of Tiree. When the clouds lift, there are four colors on the island. The earth is a brilliant green blanket. The sea and sky are deep blue. White homes, with wooly sheep in the background, speckle the island. An occasional old red phone booth sits along the lane. Tiree boasts 600 people and 5000 sheep. There are no trees, traffic lights, or drive-through conveniences to be found.

While busloads of tourists travel the adjacent Isles of Mull and Iona, Tiree remains unbothered, like the introvert in the family who hides away with a good book while the party gets more crowded and louder downstairs. In the summertime, the ocean waters are still bitterly cold, but the brilliant white seashell sand and a bold blue sea against the vast green fields are soul stirring to me. I've been to Tiree many times. There, I embrace a sense of belonging and pride, knowing this is the land of my family's past and present.

In 2013, Scotland was heading into a vote on the referendum to determine whether they would break free from the United Kingdom or remain in a full partnership. Sam followed the story through his preferred international news sources. While he was at it, he took a deep dive into Wikipedia to learn about the history of Scotland. He was curious to know whether we had any connection to royalty, sword wielding, or kilt wearing legends like William Wallace.

And whisky. Whisky is the most likely connection to the MacKinnon clan. Sam discovered that our ancestors had obtained the recipe for the now popular honey-spiced whisky known as Drambuie on the Isle of Skye, as a thank you for providing sanctuary to a rebel prince after the 1746 Battle of Culloden. The MacKinnons were then kicked off Skye, and today my dad's family considers the neighboring Isle of Tiree their generational home. Dad spent his youngest years there with his grandparents because it was a safer place to be than the mainland during WWII. Once the war was over, he lived with his parents in

Glasgow so he could get an education, and also to avoid the harsh winters on the island. But summers were always spent on Tiree.

One evening, after a world news report on a monumental upcoming election, Sam gave voice to his own pent-up passion for the Scots' freedom. "Dad! I need you to help me apply for my Scottish citizenship card!"

"Sam, what are you talking about?"

"I need to be able to vote on the referendum!"

"What? You want to vote for Scottish freedom?"

"Dad! We need to be free!!"

"Sam! You are free! You live here, in Oregon! This is a free country!"

We had planned on taking a family trip when Sam was 13, four years into his struggle against cancer. To make the trip work Sam and Natalie would have to miss a week of Ukandu. By this time, Sam had become a leader, an over-the-top engager, a competitor, a magnetic comedian. Not just another kid with cancer. We had our tickets booked with Delta and my parents were going to join us. But, by early spring the vaccine trial went awry, and the trip was cancelled. Camp became the saving grace that softened his distress at missing out on our trip to Scotland. Delta gave us a refund.

Fast forward to the spring of 2016, after my Biology 211 class. Sam was now 14, and experiencing a shortness of breath. He developed a few small tumors that were irritating the space between his lungs, resulting in a buildup of fluid. An hour after returning home from the oncologist, Bob found me standing by the sink with my pain-saturated heart, weary and glassy-eyed.

"I can't believe I'm suggesting this, but I think you and Sam should go to Scotland." Bob said with one elbow leaning on the high white counter in our kitchen. "This doesn't mean I think Sam is going to die. But we do know his next treatment is probably going to be more difficult. I think you should go while he's still on Pazopanib."

Live like you're dying. It was a hashtag and a title to Caring-bridge updates, and a magnet on our fridge. Living well was what we did. The saying offered hope. Though it encouraged us to cherish every moment, it also helped me to believe that Sam might survive. I wanted to keep it that way. Now Bob seemed to be asking me to consider that he might not.

He said with a gentle voice, "I've looked at the schedule and I just don't see how we could make it happen with all four of us. Junior year is too important for Natalie to miss, and I can't see leaving my position so soon after becoming the AC."

I looked away to suppress my tears. "OK. Let me think it through."

I believe in the mantra of going for it. I believe in adventure, with a reasonable amount of risk. And, despite all the things one can't control, I believed in the imperative to live well. As beautiful as that sounds, we still have schedules to manage and we can't live well in multiple places at the same time. Sam had other life-affirming commitments, like Camp Ukandu, and an adaptive surf camp he was set on attending in July. If we were going to Scotland it had to be in May, and thus we would have to sacrifice the company of Bob and Natalie.

As usual, Bob was the designated informer. We sat Sam down at the kitchen table. "Sam, this is kind of a hard conversation, but I think that you and mom should go to Scotland."

Sam listened without comment, his eyes darting back and forth.

Bob added, "Natalie and I can't go with you."

"What? No!" Sam reacted. "I want you and Natalie to come too!"

"Listen," Bob stopped him. "Since you have so many summer plans, we think you and mom and Gran and Poppa should take a trip to Scotland before the summer." Bob continued. "We tried to go last year but it didn't work out. And this summer is filling up so quickly, we think it's important to make it happen."

"I really want you and Natalie to come," he said. The bad news robbed him of any real pleasure in the news. I wished we could turn it into the perfect vacation, like New York. This one would require a big compromise, yet I hoped it would still be worth the effort.

Then Bob voiced what until now had remained unspoken. "Sam, we're not recommending this because we think you are going to die." He looked right at Sam, who looked down and started to cry. "What we don't know is how long you'll be on the next treatment, and whether you'll be able to take a break to make this trip."

Sam rested his head on his hand, elbow propped by the kitchen table. After a long pause, he said, "I do really want to go to Scotland." He stood up, kissed me on the cheek, and gave Bob a hug. "I love you, mom. I love you, dad."

Reexamining the pieces of Sam's story - his pain, the social roadblocks, the obstacles to his education, his insane schedule of medical appointments and treatments, and the cancer invading his youthful lungs, we could only hope this long-postponed trip would provide a deeply meaningful distraction from an unbearable reality.

The tissue around Sam's lungs was filling up with fluid, requiring a procedure called thoracentesis. It's simple: a mild sedation, a puncture into the fluid filled cavity, and a tube inserted to drain that fluid. The hope was that with the fluid drained, an additional drug could be added to his regimen to shrink the tumors, which would then eliminate the cause of the buildup of fluid. It was painful for Sam and it didn't work.

Within a week, as the date for our Scotland adventure date drew nearer, Sam was having trouble breathing. The next option was to have a procedure called a pleurodesis. In addition to draining the fluid, the surgeon would coat the newly drained cavity with a talc, which would cause the outer surface of the lung to adhere to the inside of the chest cavity. That way, fluid had no place to settle, and Sam could keep breathing normally. We were warned that the healing process could be painful.

I spent Mother's Day in the hospital with Sam while he recovered.

~

On our way to Scotland, I called Bob from the gate. "He doesn't look good. I feel sick to my stomach."

Bob said the things I needed him to say. "Dr. Madison said it was fine. He wouldn't let Sam go to Scotland if he didn't really believe it was fine." With a lump in my throat I listened to Bob's confident reassurances.

Upon our arrival in Glasgow, we pulled into the narrow driveway of my Aunt Audrey's little white brick and mortar home in Sandy Hills. I'd been there so many times and I knew the neighborhood well. Turning into her street zipped open a deep satchel of memories I spread out before Sam.

"Sam, see those two tall buildings up the street? On the 17th floor Gran would wave to us when we walked from Aunt Audrey's house to go see her." I indulged in recollections of visiting my grandmother, who died during my month-long visit when I was 23. The street is narrow, the sidewalks are wide and smooth and the short walk up to her apartment building felt quiet and safe even as a child. Even the smells in Scotland are different from Portland or Seattle. No matter how similar the US and Britain are, the differences are what I love to remember. These childhood memories were potent for me, but not for Sam. He somehow managed to produce a smile and a lifted eyebrow as he listened politely, but he really needed some sleep.

Sam and I got out of the car and approached the front door of Aunt Audrey and Uncle Bobby's quaint home with roses under the windows on both sides of the front door. The house is bright and clean. Aunt Audrey was standing outside before we even got out of the car. Her glasses were hanging from the same style of beaded strap I remembered from years ago. She has small eyes that are also bright and cheery. With a familiar smile, she gently cupped Sam's cheeks as she looked him in the eye and said with great delight, "Oh look, you're in Scotland!" Sam smiled a genuine smile.

Sam and I were directed upstairs to the spare room with twin beds. Audrey appeared two minutes later with gifts. My extended family had been loving him from a distance for some time. Sam had a whole gaggle of young fans down there who've been following his story from the start. A hooded sweatshirt had been sent over from my cousin's family in England. Then, Audrey handed Sam a new wallet. Her manner left no room for protest or discussion. He opened the wallet to find several pound notes inside. "That's for your trip to Tiree in case you find something you like and want to buy it, ok?"

Sam smiled big. "Oh wow! Thank you so much!"

Audrey put her hand on Sam's head and told him to get some rest. After she left the room, Sam whispered with more eagerness than I'd seen in him for many days, "She's so wonderful!"

After a heavy nap, it was finally morning time in Portland. I texted Bob. Apparently, he had been sick with worry since the plane took off. As soon as we were in the air, he panicked. He suddenly worried that he had it wrong, that the entire venture was a mistake. When I finally reached him to tell him we were fine, he relaxed and then went straight to Natalie. He told her, "I heard from mom. They're at Aunt Audrey's now and they're doing fine."

"Oh, I know," Natalie said.

"What do you mean, you know?"

"Sam and I have been Snapchatting since they landed in London."

Bob opened his mouth to say something, but instead just sighed.

The ferry to Tiree is a white needle-nosed ship built for transporting cars and people to the small islands off the West coast of Scotland. The sea can get rough during the three-hour journey. I've been a victim of the nausea-inducing waves before, so I will forever refuse the sausage and toast breakfast on the boat ride out. That day, however, the weather was beautiful. For several miles, the sea, sheltered by land on either side, was calm.

I left Sam and my parents to have a moment next to the water, to allow my mind and heart to come out of hiding after 36 hours of travel and worry. Approaching the coast of Tiree, the calm waters become more intense. Light is abundant. Even on a cloudy day, the sea reflects and multiplies the light, as if to amplify that gift.

My dad tells stories. Many of them start with "When I was a wee boy." He introduced his relatives and neighbors with the word "the" in front of their names: The Auntie Maggie, The Old Uncle Hugh, The Auntie Nan who ran the post office. Even though I'd never actually lived there, I still managed a few stories of my own. Sam's favorite was from when I was 23 and travelled alone on my bike and then stayed with The Auntie Maggie, often wandering through the rolling green fields groomed by those 5000 sheep who inhabit the island.

Sheep are such funny creatures. Eating and chattering all day long, they live in a state of nervousness. In the massive green, I would walk quietly toward the sheep, all by myself until dozens of white wooly faces looked up to stare at me. There was a certain distance they would tolerate. Suddenly, in their herd-like manner, they would pivot to casually wander away. One time, I got the urge to run toward them. They panicked and fled, like a school of fish. It was as if someone had yelled: "Everybody run!" I did this often. I stopped, and waited for them to settle. I'd creep up again, wondering how close I could get before they sprinted, diverted by the site of fuzzy round bums bouncing along in unison.

When I told this story to Sam, he chuckled. This activity of mine may have been a bit unkind to the Tiree sheep, but I loved the sound of his laugh.

My dad was our tour guide. There's basically one road on the island, with no traffic signals. My dad talks as he drives, his accent already thicker than it is back home. "There's the house where Donald The Plumber lived." or "My aunties used to send me to clean manure out of the cow shed. Then I'd have to haul the coal inside the stable to keep it dry for the winter." I was enthralled by my dad's stories as we passed by the green carpet stretching out on one side of the road, and the white sandy beaches on the other. Though it's exceptionally cold and windy on Tiree, it's one of the sunniest places in Scotland.

"Oh look, he's a relation of mine. I'm gonna stop and say hello." My dad turned into a driveway leading up to a lone white house, and a gentleman in a bright blue sweater with a mustard gold knit hat watched us draw near. My dad hopped out of the car to speak to him and my mom followed along. On Tiree, "A relation of mine" does not necessarily mean *The Cousin Roddy;* it could mean my dad's mother's auntie's grandson from Balephetrish.

Sam, still sitting in the backseat of the car, noticed some sheep grazing nearby. His eyebrows lifted. "Can we chase them?"

"Well, you know," I smirked, "there's a strategy for chasing sheep."

Sam and I got out of the car. Strolling toward the sheep, he kept his hands in his pockets. His slight frame was swimming in the new hooded sweatshirt Aunt Audrey gave him. It hung down past his behind. His jeans needed a belt to keep them up.

The air was only breezy with that lovely smell of the sea, blended with the smell of cow manure. Sam was so frail I doubted he could chase them for more than a few steps. But maybe this activity would get him to move around a bit more. I wanted to see him strong again. I was always looking for ways to get him to use his muscles.

I immediately started taking photos of Sam and the sheep with the beach just beyond. It wasn't long before he wanted to sit down again, so we settled down on the big stones half-covered with grass and looked out at the ocean until my parents finished up their chat and got back to the car to continue our tour.

Finally, we arrived at The Lodge. It was not especially lovely, but it was quiet and the food was wonderful. Sam roamed the halls and the empty restaurant looking at his phone in search of wifi service so he could participate in the group text with his friends back home.

Behind the Lodge, there is a cemetery where my grandparents and other family members are buried. We could see it from the window of the inn. There are only a few names ever used on Tiree. Duncan, Hugh, John, Hector, Cathie, Anne, and Mary are some of the repeats. The family names are about as redundant: MacKinnon, Lamont, Campbell and Kennedy. I come from all of them. Beyond that cemetery is a smaller group of headstones dating back to the 18th century. The headstones are rough and fallen over. We were both intrigued and curious about who in that old cemetery we were related to.

After some gravestone exploring, we noticed some more sheep nearby. Sam and I gave each other a look. We walked slowly toward them. The closest one looked up at us. We halted. Twenty sheep lifted their heads. Sam froze for a moment, then leaped. The sheep that was closest turned to his fellows, then the whole herd took off running.

Sam laughed with his mouth wide open. I managed to catch a photo of seven fluffy sheep butts angled like motorcycles rounding a bend at the racetrack in unison through the green pasture.

He got it. Sam got to experience with me the fun of chasing sheep on the Isle of Tiree. Just us, no one else is around. He laughed and he moved faster than I'd seen him in weeks. He needed that, and I did too.

~

Over the past few years, my dad had gotten to know the Island doctor, who had also become a Tiree historian. Doctor John Holliday. He and his wife invited us over for dinner. I was nervous about going because on this vacation Sam was still not his most charming self. He still carried some anger for so many valid reasons.

I tried cheering him up while we discussed whether he was really up for visiting people he didn't know, but he just sighed and looked away. Finally, I snapped. "Sam! Make a decision. Are you going to sit in this room for the whole trip? Or are you going to make an effort to enjoy being on freakin' Tiree for the first time in your life?"

I could see his eyes turn watery and red. "I'm just mad. I want Dad and Natalie to be here. I can't text my friends. I probably won't even be able to eat anything they have anyway."

A tear dropped onto his pant leg.

"Sam, I get it." I laid my hand on his back. "I don't know if tonight will be interesting or boring. But I think we should go and give it our best." Sam turned over on his side and flopped his head down onto the pillow.

When the time came, my dad drove us to the other side of the island for dinner with the Hollidays. Their home backed up against a hill, which served as a shelter for the greenhouse where they grew their own produce. John greeted us in his warm, soft-spoken way.

His wife Clare invited us. Their home smelled delightful. The entryway was a small mudroom with boots and oilskin jackets and hats hanging from hooks on the wall above the rustic wooden bench. A second door into the living space helped keep the cold out. Inside, simple book shelves and tables revealing their natural grain were everywhere.

I felt as if I belonged there. I should own an oilskin jacket and a pair of wellies on the Isle of Tiree. I should be spending winters unpampered, working on the upkeep of the land and finding my delight in the simplicity of good books and cups of tea. Thinking deep thoughts and enjoying the remote island life. Managing the coal burning stove. Preparing simple meals with lamb and potatoes grown on the island and butter made from the neighbor's cows. And, definitely driving a rugged blue Land Rover.

It was a romantic fantasy I've always had about the Isle of Tiree. If I ever had the chance, most likely I would discover I wasn't cut out for life on the Hebrides. However, if generations of my family lived on Tiree before I was born, then I can still claim that a part of my soul also belongs on Tiree. I hoped Sam could feel just a bit of the connection that I felt.

Our dinner was simple and clean but rich with flavor. There was a leg of lamb, a beet and lentil dish, and a butter lettuce salad with cold cooked asparagus, capers and bits of smoked salmon. We were offered wine, which was not only delicious, but served as a lovely antidote for the worry I'd been feeling about this evening and multiple other realistic worries.

Sam was quiet. I was quiet. Conversation moved along while Sam ate without speaking. Then John brought up the topic of American Politics.

"Your elections are drawing a lot of worldwide attention these days." May, 2016 was just six months before the presidential election of Donald Trump. Characteristically, Sam was following every detail from numerous news media and political journals.

John asked Sam, "What do you think about all this?"

"Well," Sam rejoined, "the Democrats have a few things working against them right now." Holding his knife and fork the way I had taught him, he still managed to gesture. "People don't trust Hillary Clinton, and Bernie Sanders is too much of a threat to independence for conservatives." Now everyone's eyes were on Sam. He went on. "Plus, they are spending too much money on the military right now because we really don't need the military as much as we did a few years ago. Even the military says they don't want the money"

"And what about Donald Trump?"

"I don't understand why people want Donald Trump to be president because he really favors the rich people, and not the working class, but so many of them think he's going to give them the opportunity to be rich like he is." He continued in this manner, just like the time Natalie's friend Josie asked him what was going on in Ukraine, but this time the adults in the room were riveted.

Sam, who has fought for more freedom and less control since he was in preschool, could relate to at least one element of Trump's agenda. "I definitely think that the government should allow for more local control and less Federal influence, which the Republicans are in favor of." In second grade he let his teacher know how unfair it was that he had to wait until he was 18 to vote. From that time, he staunchly believed those we elected should use their influence to serve one and all. He continued, "I don't think Donald Trump is going to care that much about the people who are voting for him. I think he will only care about the rich people just like him." Sam went on answering questions and offering his perspectives. The conversation elevated every pleasant sensory detail in that simple Tiree home: the food, the wine, the laughter and insight.

I focused on the faces of the other adults in the room, so attentive to Sam. His opinions were balanced and informed, with a fair consideration of both political parties and the needs of all Americans. That space behind my sternum filled with a fluttery happiness. He was engaged. He ate well. He made people think and laugh. There are few experiences more delightful than watching other adults become mesmerized by the unexpected insight of my son.

The remainder of our trip to Scotland consisted of more visits with family, historic castles, and city tours. Aunt Audrey filled his belly with traditional Scottish delights, like black pudding and haggis. Haggis is a savory pudding containing sheep's pluck, in other words, the heart, liver, and lungs mixed in with herbs and spices and barley. "Aunt Audrey, can I please have some more?" This delighted her to no end.

Throughout our travels we always shared a room, with my parents never far away. In a way, we became a bit more like travelling companions than mother and child.

Sam had bought a leather-bound navy-blue journal from the University of Glasgow Bookstore. He wrote in it as we settled into our hotel room at night. He drew diagrams and made notes. On our last evening in the hotel in Glasgow while he was working away at that journal, I noticed that *deep in thought* look on his face.

"Mom, what are the names of some of those areas that we visited on Tiree?"

"Well, there's Balephuil, Balemartine, and Scarinish." I listed a few more while he jotted them down with his tongue sticking out like he does when he writes.

"Okay, what about the houses? Ternfell, and what were the other ones called?"

"Ardlui and Braeside."

"Got it, thanks." He continued writing. I watched him long enough to take pleasure in the moment before asking, "What are you working on?"

"Well, I'm creating a board game. It's like a battlefield strategy game and it's set in Scotland."

"Wow. That's cool. Tell me more."

"So, there are different levels of weaponry. Like, Level One has one catapult and five swords. Level two has two catapults, five swords, and three Royal Guardians." He continued explaining his idea for a 11th century strategic Scottish war game. I wasn't able to follow, but I knew that excited look on his face and it gave me peace.

"Mom, I know you're not really tracking this, but is it ok if I keep telling you about it?"

"Absolutely. And I'll do my best to understand it."

Sam went on to explain the game while I watched him talk. I loved how much he loved telling me about it.

Sam ended our trip to Scotland with more color in his face, more meat on his bones, and more dreams in his head than when he boarded that plane in Seattle. That was enough.

37
SURF CAMP

Sam walked toward the beach behind me with hands in his sweatshirt pocket and a hood pulled over his head, as moody as the dim morning cloud cover. His black carbon fiber prosthetic leg was exposed below his blue beach shorts. I walked ahead of him and resisted another glance back to look for signs of light in his face. I hoped someone at surf camp could bring back his smile.

A thin layer of golden sand covered the parking lot, and spilled from the towels and surf boards of thousands of beach-goers before us. We'd come to expect the misty overcast mornings in San Diego. By noon the sunlight would warm us again, but the damp gray air hung above as we walked from our rental car toward the beach.

Early morning surfers, the really obsessive ones, were rinsing off after their sunrise time on the water. Before heading to their day jobs in office buildings and corporate headquarters, they managed to satisfy their craving for the waves. Others, perhaps, worked at the surf shack down the street, making barely enough to afford decent gear and a small apartment just east of I-5. Surfing had an addictive quality, which I could see emerging in

Sam. But we could only manage about three trips from Oregon each year, which was hardly enough time to foster an adolescent addiction to those California waves. Every time we came, though, he discussed the possibility of going to college nearby, or maybe a summer gig near the beach if he opted for an international college experience.

Parked along our path sat a detached cargo trailer, branded with photos of young surfers grinning into the camera, each of them missing an arm, a leg, or the ability to use them. I knew those faces. The cancer survivor with a magical singing voice, the girl adopted from Vietnam with a power-personality, the boy with spina bifida who frequented the skate park in his custom-made trick wheelchair. Just past the trailer, I turned back to see the other side. A life-sized image of Sam occupied premium marketing space. I took a reflexive deep inhale and planted my feet to take it in. Riding a low wave on a red foam surfboard, sporting a bright yellow rash guard, he engaged the camera with a shaka and mouth-wide-open smile. His head was shiny and bald in the sun. In the background behind him was a fleet of other kids on surfboards. Literally, it was a billboard sign reminder of why we were there.

"Sam, look." I broke our silence and pointed to the trailer.

"Huh." He grunted and peeked out from under his hoodie to see what I was looking at. "Nice." he reacted with an ounce more positivity than I'd seen since early the day before.

Surf camp came shortly after a collision of events our whole family was having trouble working through. Across the country, another person of color was shot by the police, and the shooting sparked protests and emotional outcry on social media. Then, five police officers in Dallas were killed at one of those protests. I married Bob long before police work became such a harshly judged profession, back when he rode a horse and spent his days chatting with animal lovers in the city square and checking on with folks he suspected were off their meds. Almost 25 years later, the horses were gone, and the community conflict was rising. We were a police family with a new kind of unease around how we ought to feel or think or talk about law enforcement's role in racism. I didn't understand.

At home, police bureau leadership was facing its own scrutiny over concerns about the Police Chief's truthfulness. A new chief was appointed, and he decided to transfer Bob and the other four assistant chiefs to lower ranks in other parts of the bureau - a demotion without cause. I still find it difficult to reconcile the decisions that were made during that time. It was quite public, and Bob was unable to defend his integrity before an investigation was completed many months later. His salary was significantly cut. At this time in our lives, the move took an especially hard toll on Bob's well-being.

Sam had always been interested in understanding opposite sides of a political or social argument, but the controversy over Black people being mistreated by the police overwhelmed his ability to do so. Online, someone in his peer group made a verbal attack on the police through social media. Sam replied in defense of the police and sounded both angry and protective. Very quickly he removed his comments and posted an apology. The controversy, and his own place in it, left him feeling distressed. And while these social conflicts became heated, the heaviest burden Sam carried was the understanding that his cancer was growing in his lungs, taking over the tissue meant to help him breathe. A storm was simmering inside the mind and heart of my magnificent boy.

I felt inadequate to manage the emotional impact of these stories, stifled by my own internal chaos. Maybe some other mom could have put a smile on Sam's face. Maybe some other mom would have the wisdom to walk him through the inner conflict he carried. Maybe another mom would have the intelligence to wade through hundreds of scientific studies to uncover a drug combination that would save his life. Sometimes I did these things well, and many times I executed poorly. But the one thing I could do better than any other mom could, was love him, and get him to the places and the people who would feed his spirit.

We soon located the blue tent for the Challenged Athletes Foundation. Two of the program managers buzzed around with final set-up tasks. Sam checked in with Travis, whose thigh high prosthetic leg could be mistaken for a prop for Optimus Prime. Lauren, the youth program director, dropped the folding chairs she was carrying to give me a long, tight hug.

Our emails over the previous few weeks revealed some of Sam's new medical issues and she knew how serious they were. I wiped away a couple of tears with my sweatshirt sleeve. "Sometimes I think we're not going to make it, because of all the stuff he has going on. But you know, we just keep showing up."

"I'm so glad you guys are here. We have a lot of cool stuff planned."

"I know everyone is happy to see him. But I also think they're just surprised he's alive."

"I know, I know." She understood like few others could. "He's such a great kid. I wish you guys didn't have to go through this."

A few years earlier, Lauren's brother, Robert, battled Ewing sarcoma, and survived. He lost even more of his leg than Sam did. Now Robert played water polo and had a lovely girlfriend. If, like Robert, Sam could one day become cancer-free, he might find the same sort of happiness in his own life. It was better to live hopeful than in despair.

An hour was spent getting kids into wetsuits and navigating their varying shaped limbs through rubbery sleeves. The age range was wide. A seven-year-old little person appeared to be the youngest. He was confident he could catch the waves without any help. A handful of teenagers managed an awkward hello.

I'd learned, over the past few years, that a sign of a real surfer is their ability to change into a wetsuit quickly under a towel even in a public place, as easily as brushing their teeth, and Sam was an aspiring young surfer in every way. Getting help from his mom invited almost as much embarrassment as dropping the beach towel at a particularly vulnerable moment.

A few yards up the beach, he let me hold the towel up for him. I looked at the ground and spoke as little as possible. Once his body was sufficiently covered, he sat down in the sand and peeled the wetsuit leg up over his knee, making space for his plastic water leg to attach. He was careful not to get any grains of sand stuck in between his skin and the tight-fitting liner, while I resisted the urge to help. He rolled the rubbery leg over his prosthesis, to keep it from sliding off and floating out to sea like it did in Hawaii five years earlier when he was the only amputee on the beach.

As we walked back to the group, person after person greeted Sam by name. A few were in wheelchairs equipped with thick beach tire wheels for navigating packed sand and shallow water. Of all of the inaccessible places one might choose to explore, the beach ranked just below the mountains. But surfers need to surf, regardless of their bodily impairments, so they make their way to the shore with rugged wheels on constructed paths, or roll out rugs designed to minimize the potential for a spin out. They modify the design of their boards when needed, and always surf with friends. They are real surfers in every kind of body.

"Sunblock! Guys, don't forget to put on your sunblock!" Alex, an instructor with a perpetual smile, walked through the group with a tube of thick goop with an SPF of maybe 400. As Sam lathered his face above the wetsuit collar, I could see he was missing sections of his neck and ears.

"Sam, do you want me to help you get the back of your neck?" I asked.

"No! I got it." He said, turning away from me.

He didn't, but I let it go. A sunburn wasn't life-threatening. I walked back for a cup of coffee from the CAF tent. I sighed. Now it was someone else's turn to keep an eye on Sam.

~

Three months earlier, our family made a trip to San Diego so Natalie could visit colleges during spring break of her junior year. We told a few people we'd be in town and mentioned that Sam would love to surf. After dropping Natalie off to continue on with a friend, we headed to the beach. Four grown-up men with the enthusiasm of golden retrievers at a dog park showed up at La Jolla. Each of them offered to assist Sam in satisfying his thirst for riding a board over the ocean's final ripple before it hits the sand.

According to Sam, something happens out there beyond the white foam. The water is quiet and the horizon feels near. The peace before the thrill. Sam takes in the beauty. He smiles softly. He expresses gratitude for the adults who believe the good things in life can be shared with like-minded companions, including a 15-year-old amputee with cancer.

The late afternoon sun and mild but surfable waves made for a welcoming time in the water while a few of us landlubbers chatted and watched with our feet in the hot sand. After an hour or so, Sam took a break. He had recently begun developing a cough, and my own chest clenched tightly every time I heard it. He landed on a towel to rest, and warm up a bit. I pulled out a bottle of eucalyptus and peppermint oil from my backpack and tipped into his cupped hands. He covered his mouth and nose to breathe it in. The coughing abated. His body relaxed.

Sean had remained on the sand, attending to his baby daughter in a front pack. One of his missions in life is to enrich the lives of disadvantaged young people by teaching them to surf. If it hadn't been for the Ebola virus, Sean would still be the founder and director of a surf-centered non-profit for the troubled youth of West Africa. Instead he was now living in San Diego, guiding kids with a different kind of disadvantage. Like Sam.

As soon as Sam's coughing fit subsided, Sean asked him,

"Hey, you're not going to believe this, but I just saw Rusty on the beach. Would you like to meet him?"

"Rusty?" Sam squinted. "Wait, Rusty? Like *the* Rusty?" Sam asked.

"Yeah, he's right over there. I can ask him to come meet you if you want." Since Rusty had personally shaped Sam's board, he knew about Sam, but they had never met.

Sean called Rusty over for a quick greeting and photos.

"Hey, can I be in a picture too?" said Sam's friend, Jeff. "Take one with my phone!" They conversed with Rusty and snapped photos while the sun sunk closer to the horizon. Everyone looked so happy, including Sam.

"I can't believe we saw Rusty." Jeff repeated it a few times. "It's wild that he was actually here."

"It's Sam." said our friend Nancy. "He's like an angel. Everywhere he goes these incredible things happen."

So much had happened with Sam's cancer since that visit to San Diego three months before. But somehow Sam had made it to surf camp, and he was ready now to hit the waves.

More or less.

"Hey Sean." I wanted to tell Sean about Sam's emotional state that morning in case he wasn't able to pull out of his funk.

"Hey Lorna! You guys made it! I'm excited to get Sam out there."

"Well, yeah. Sam is having a hard time this week. The cancer has been tough, but he's also really wrestling with the shootings that have been happening lately. With Bob being in police work, ya know, well I'm hoping this will pull him out of it but-"

Sean looked me straight in the eye, punctuated by a confident grin. "We'll keep an eye on him, but I really think today will be good for him."

"I hope you're right."

Sean said nothing about cancer, or police shootings, or prosthetic limbs. He just pointed to the water. Sam picked up his board and together they walked toward the ocean. I looked up to find a shaft of sunshine crack through the clouds. Sam turned back and shouted, "Hey, Mom! Take some pictures, okay?"

I gave him a thumbs up and watched him head into the water. When he turned away, I let out a big sigh to release my worry because suddenly I knew: Today Sam would be okay.

Over the course of four days, the surf camp became more than just a playground for waves - it was a launchpad for kids to dream big about a life shaped by the ocean. Each day brought new experiences, from field trips to casual conversations with mentors and friends. The kids didn't just learn to ride waves; they soaked up energy from seasoned surfers who shared their stories of thrills and wipeouts, inspiring the next generation to carve their own path on the water.

I watched Sam all the time. I tried not to let on that I was watching him, and once in I would wander away to give him some freedom. Sam was 15 now. The age of independence and identity. He shouldn't be at camp with his mom. My emotions fluctuated with his, and this week at surf camp put me at ease, only because I could see him smiling and leaning into a sense of belonging with other surfers.

The apex of the week was a day-long festival centered around the band, Switchfoot. It's called the BroAm. There were crowds on the beach and a surf competition with band members, followed by an outdoor concert in the evening. The camp kids were given an opportunity to surf with coaches while gobs of people watched and cheered.

They paired each kid up with an adult. The organizers had

their eye on Sam because they decided to pair him with the most famous surfer, Rob Machado.

Sam knew who he was, and I watched his face turn humble as he shook Rob's hand.

I had Bob on the phone, giving him the play-by-play of this very cool moment. They headed to the water when Sam turned back for a moment to say, "Mom! Tell dad I'm surfing with Rob Machado! Tell him he's basically the LeBron James of surfing!" I giggled on the phone with Bob and watched him head toward the water.

The first couple of waves didn't go well. Sam struggled to steady himself on the board and he fell into the sand below the shallow water, in front of a full beach of spectators. Rob decided to switch it up a bit and I tracked them as they paddled farther out to a bigger set of waves. Rob waited patiently with Sam, then they paddled into a lift in the water. The wave was much bigger than anything Sam had surfed before and they both stood on the same board with Rob gripping the back of Sam's rash guard. The beach audience started pointing and tracking the two of them.

Our friend, Jeff, stood next to me shouting as Sam and Rob rode that beautiful big wave. I recorded it on my phone with Jeff's enthusiastic exclamation, "Holy Shit! Holy Shit! Holy Shit! Look at that!"

This moment thrilled the people who organized surf camp. The spectators thought it was cool that Rob Machado was surfing with a disabled kid. While I'd agree it was an incredible moment on the beach that day with famous surfers and musicians and a large crowd of people cheering him on, the highlight of Sam's week happened later.

On the final day of surf camp, the kids had an opportunity to compete. Throughout Sam's six years of fighting cancer, I was attentive to his loss of opportunity to play sports. He was such an obnoxious winner when he was little - hard-wired to be a competitor. Aside from his one season in track, he'd been out of sports for six years now. He didn't get the chance to learn good sportsmanship, or feel the adrenalin of winning a hard-fought game. He didn't know teamwork or the honor of wearing a uniform with pride. I'm not much of a competitor, but I think that when people are born with a competitive spirit, they need to compete.

Two adaptive surfers sat in beach wheelchairs at the edge of the waves as official judges while the campers entered their first ever surf competition. There were no crowds, no impressive sound systems, no brand name sponsors or massive banners to draw attention to the event. It was nothing like the energy on the beach the day before.

When it was Sam's turn, he took to the waves with methodical determination. I watched his mind and body work in sync with the ocean on a level I had not seen before. He was focused, taking wave after wave and earning points with each ride. He was so bright that day; so alive. The heaviness he carried on arrival at camp had drifted away and was replaced with elements of the life he was designed to thrive in.

When his heat finished, I walked down to catch photos of him coming out of the water. He looked at me and said, "Mom, that was amazing! I felt like I surfed perfect!" I told him he looked fantastic out there and I asked him to smile and give me a shaka for a photo.

He tied for first place. That trophy still sits on a shelf in our home. It was the last time I saw Sam's spirit fully alive.

38
HIS EYES

Five weeks after surf camp, Sam started having that side pain again. He was easily winded. I thought, we'd better go get it checked out tomorrow.

We had lined up a new experimental chemotherapy to start in a few days. While pacing my backyard one morning, I had spoken with the clinical trial investigator on the phone. He answered my questions patiently, kindly inquiring with me more than once if there was anything else I wanted to know. I knew the protocol would make Sam nauseous, so as we approached his start date I boosted his cannabis dose.

Sam spent the evening at his friend's house. For several weeks he and Carter had been trying to find time to hang out while Carter was busy with the start of his freshman football season. At home later that night, Sam rested on the couch with his hands on his chest. "Mom, I laughed so hard tonight! Oh my gosh it was so funny. But, my chest really hurts." I gave him something for the pain. During the night, his discomfort got worse. I ended up sleeping beside him, massaging his shoulders and redosing him with meds on the schedule I knew all too well.

In the morning, I could tell by the way he moved around the

kitchen that the pain had become insupportable. We went right to the emergency room. An X-ray confirmed that tissue surrounding his left lung had filled up with fluid. Within a couple of hours he was wheeled into the procedure room to insert a tube to drain the fluid. His relief was brief.

The next few days were so disastrous I can only think or talk about them when I need to let my grief flow. There were medical mishaps, missing scans and botched communication with terrible consequences. I made calls to other doctors I'd come to rely on, and wondered if there was anyone in the medical profession in that hospital or the world that I could trust.

One night, in the darkened hospital room, Sam draped his thin pale body over five stacked pillows. He couldn't sleep but wanted to talk. Barely 15, his adolescent whisper was deeper and more resonant now, though he needed extra breaths with pauses to complete his sentences. He shared with me his travel dreams, "You know, there are a lot of countries I want to see."

"I do know that. Tell me about them again."

"I want to go to Belgium. And Germany. Switzerland is supposed to be a beautiful country. Georgia, in the former Soviet Union, obviously." He listed several more that I'd heard him talk about, "The problem is, I want to do it all before college."

I stroked his white hair and felt the weight of my own broken heart.

The next day contained multiple visits from teams of specialists unable to relieve Sam's pain or improve his condition. At one point, as they were checking the spot where a tube entered his side, in a mild panic Sam exclaimed, "Ow. Ow. Ow. I feel pressure. I feel pressure!" But the team didn't seem to be alarmed. They just stood there watching, as if to suggest his discomfort wasn't even noteworthy. Only later would we learn this faulty tube placement would cause irreparable damage to the right side of his lung.

Later, when a medical tech from the surgery team removed

the tube from his chest that was supposed to be draining fluid, a large quantity of cloudy yellowish-red fluid came gushing out of his side. Again, no one seemed alarmed.

Bob spent the next night in the hospital. Before bed I texted Sam: *I love you and I'm proud of you. Tomorrow will be another step in the right direction. Sleep well and heal.* In his text back to me he mixed up his words but conveyed his stress and pain: *thanks the two day was to this tough.* His incoherent text made me all the more determined to make tomorrow better. I wrote back: *Yes, it was. But you did it!*

When I woke the next morning, I called Bob, hopeful for any signs of improvement. Sam was about the same. Bob replied: *Not much sleep. Still on oxygen. Only a couple of bites of food.*

Still in my pajamas, I made it down the stairs and sat down on the bottom step. Most mornings were spent determining what I could do for Sam, but this was different. Today my adrenalin was primed. Today was going to be *our turn the corner day.*

I knew his deteriorating body was desperate for nutrition, so I pulled out some homemade bone broth from the freezer. I used it to cook rice. I set some aside for sipping as well. Sipping bone broth out of a bowl in the morning was another mini ritual for Sam and me, one I cherished because I believed it made him stronger. I was sure my preparations were setting us up for a successful *turn the corner day.*

I texted my nutrition friend, Melanie, to see if she could visit us to offer her insight on what ingredients might be added to Sam's IV to reinvigorate him, because I was certain the surgery team was not addressing his needs urgently enough. She said she'd come by in the afternoon.

When I arrived, Sam was awake. Nurse Tara attended to him with care and efficiency. A cold Starbucks sat on the adjustable rolling table next to him, with only a few sips missing. I kissed Sam's forehead and sat on the edge of his bed. I put my hand on his scarred foot, with just three toes, poking out from under the white hospital blanket.

Bob shared details about the night before. "Respiratory therapy came by. Sam tried to take a couple of deep breaths, but it was about the same. He still can't go long without oxygen, but I think it's getting a little bit better."

Sam's eyes kept closing for several seconds at a time. He wasn't using his phone or watching TV. He was simply existing in a hospital bed, waiting to improve. Like he had so many times before.

Bob remarked, "Aunt Pam came up to visit. We laughed so hard, right Sam?"

"Yeah," Sam replied, chuckling a little as he exhaled. "Aunt Pam is so funny."

As I listened to them converse, my gaze fixed on Sam. Away for the night, I had fresh eyes. Everything about him looked dangerously frail. His abnormally big pupils seemed to look through me. His chest was still bandaged up from the hole where the tube had been, with little rise and fall. His white hair and pale skin contrasted to his chafed red cheeks. The act of breathing seemed to exhaust him. For a moment or two he raised his head off the pillow, then tilted it back for a rest.

I thought to myself, *he looks like he's dying.*

I stared at his eyes and wondered whether I was seeing his death come nearer.

The thought echoed in my head. It didn't accelerate my familiar fight or flight mode. I didn't panic or cry or hyperventilate. I stood there gazing at Sam with a sudden sensation of cold fear that oozed from my heart and numbed my fingertips. Bob and Sam and Nurse Tara spoke but I didn't hear them.

I don't know how long I stood there silently in that hospital room. The thought *he looks like he's dying* transitioned to another thought. *If this is it, I am no longer trying to save him. Now, my most important task is to escort him all the way to heaven.*

Fighting for Sam had been the most difficult job of my life. I surrendered my career, and assumptions about faith and identity in order to fight for Sam. It was never a noble calling. It was the call that compelled me, out of a deep love for my son. I wanted him to survive more than my own breath. Suddenly I understood that I was confronting the transition that for six long years every cell in my body had fought to avoid.

It was his next passage - and mine, too - and as terrifying as it seemed, I wanted to be everything a dying child might need.

The terms had shifted, but I was still the mother bear instinctually fighting for his life. I needed to make sure the hospital did everything they could to keep him comfortable. I needed to arrange any last visits he might want. I would need to assure him that he was not alone. And that we would be okay. I would need to save my own agony for later. It was my bravest calling.

Tara left the room. It was quiet for a bit. I moved some things around on the counter. Sam lifted his head up off the stack of pillows. "Hey you guys. My pain is almost gone. On a scale of one to ten, it's like a 2." After a couple of more breaths he said something that still brings me close to the profoundness of death, "I'm not in pain anymore. I just wanted you to know that."

The oncologist came in and did the usual check-up of Sam's vital signs. Bob talked her through the events of the night. He told her Sam's pain was finally under control.

On her way out, I followed her out of the room. I shut the door. Tears fell from my eyes. It took me a long time to get the words out. "Would you tell us if this is the end? I mean, to me he looks like he's dying."

With a sigh, she offered "I think the next few hours will tell us whether he's going to turn the corner." She said sometimes it takes a while for the lungs to re-expand after the fluid is drained. However, I could tell that she too was worried that time might be different.

Bob came out of the room and noticed my tears as I consulted with the oncologist. I looked at him but avoided his eyes. My voice was shaky, "I think we need to consider the possibility that Sam might be leaving us."

"What?" He responded as if the idea had never crossed his mind. "Why? No! I don't think so. I think he just needs a little more time." But then he paused.

"Let's see what happens in the next few hours," the oncologist said.

Now Bob's face had the same blank look as mine when I first thought *he looks like he's dying*. I told the oncologist that Natalie was heading to the beach for the day with some friends in her school leadership class, and wondered if we should tell her to turn around and come back.

"Yes." she said. "I think you'd better do that."

I sat on the floor in the hallway, not yet ready to face Sam.

I glanced up to see Melanie, on her way to greet me. She sat down onto the floor next to me. The lanyard with her hospital ID was hanging from her neck, but what I needed now was a friend. Eye contact hurt, so I kept my forehead in my hands and stared at the floor. I said, "I don't think he's going to make it."

Then I cried and cried, while my friend sat quietly next to me and watched while my hope dissolved.

After that, Bob and I didn't talk about Sam dying. We called a handful of people who were close to us. I phoned my friend Sarah and right away she came to be with us.

That evening, Natalie sat next to him in tears. Sam's room gradually filled up with some of his closest friends, not one of them his age. It was a gathering of adults who considered Sam their friend. They shared his interests and style of humor. Years and maybe decades older, they admired him for his intelligence, his spirit and his resiliency. They told stories while I sat next to the window, out of view from his reclining bed, and cried quietly.

Sam acted as if this were just one more spontaneous gathering of friends around his hospital bed. He had developed a new oxygen-deficient laugh, which due to the onset of puberty might be high or might be low. A little addled by the medication, he offered up his random thoughts. "Hey Brad, we should go to a movie again some time. Yeah, we should see that new Marvel movie," Sam took another breath. "But maybe not right now."

Natalie hardly spoke. The people in the room loved her too, as much as they loved Sam. Her face was wet from crying. I have always thought that Natalie was put on this Earth to bring sunshine and sparkle to wherever she is, whatever she does and every relationship she embraces. This is her gift. But, just as the doctors couldn't fulfill their God-given purpose and cure Sam, this time Natalie couldn't guard herself from the intensity of grief, and she knew it. Her decision to simply remain by his side as her brother started to die was the most courageous in her life.

I've noticed how when one passes, the announcement will usually include how he or she "died peacefully, surrounded by friends and family." I wish I could find new words for the experience because the cliché has dulled the meaning of that experience. Surrounded by friends and family in the moment of a transition creates a supernatural cushion of love, upholding us in our darkest moment. Our shared love echoes. That love would carry us through the incomprehensible next thing.

Late that night, our friends left, and Bob and I remained in Sam's room. I extended the recliner out as far as it could go, down next to Sam's bed, while Bob took his place by the window.

We asked the nurse questions about how a child with cancer dies. They told us his breathing would change, and that would be a clue that his time was near. He hadn't arrived there yet. We trusted them to wake us if they noticed the signs and grabbed a few hours of sleep next to our son. I wished I could keep going and stay awake. The minutes we had together were so limited.

The next morning Sam hunched over his stack of pillows again. We hadn't spoken to him about dying. Bob and I sat at the foot of his bed. Sam lifted his head and asked, "How do you guys think I'm doing?"

"Well Sam," Bob did his best to respond to that impossible question. "Remember, we've got two battles on our hands: the fight to survive, and the fight to live well."

Sam's head hung from his shoulders. His thin bare back was marked with the scars of various shapes in the places a surgeon had cut into his body. The curve was made rounder by the thick masses of cancer just beneath the surface. He lifted his head again, and said breathlessly, "With the fight to live well, I'm doing really good." He took a few more breaths and added, "But the fight to survive..." He lifted up his hand and gestured a one-inch space between his index finger and thumb, "Only about this good."

Sam knew, it was finally time to surrender. His words pulled back the curtain on the last stretch of this exhausting, painful, beautiful journey. We cried at the foot of his bed.

I knew how to fight for Sam, but living without him was something I wasn't prepared to do. In a deeply shared love, the simple physiology of one heart continuing to beat after the other had stopped seemed like a malfunction, or a tragedy. I couldn't fathom how, in the days and weeks and years to come, my own broken heart would continue.

Tears dripped through Sam's oxygen mask and onto his pillows. I grabbed the tissue box. The three of us let the sadness flow, holding each other. Bob and I promised to stay by his side every minute. Sam confided, "I know that I'm dying, and I'm at peace with that. But I really thought God wanted me to live a long life. I really thought I was going to change the world."

After more shared tears and wet sniffles, with that wonderful, familiar sense of humor, Sam inquired, "When I die, I want one of those Viking funerals where they send the body out to sea and shoot flaming arrows at it to set the ship on fire."

Bob and I laughed and cried at the same time.

The moment when everything changed was a small window. Just a few hours earlier I was fighting for Sam. Now I had to walk Sam to heaven.

Bob was on the phone with someone when Sam said to me, "I want to be baptized."

"You do Sam?"

"Yeah. I do. I want to be baptized." Baptism is meant to be a public expression of one's faith in Christ. Bob and I felt it was up to the kids to decide if and when they would want to be baptized, and neither of them had chosen it yet. Right away, I called some dear friends in the ministry. They cancelled their appointments and meetings to come to Sam's bedside. When the pastors (also dear friends) arrived with their water and bowl to anoint him, we invited all lingering visitors into the room, and we gathered around Sam's bed. Our friend, Jason, baptized Sam with holy water and tears. Sam's voice became strong when he professed his faith. It was extraordinary to watch Sam confront his own death with a softness and love that turned toward the heavens. He wasn't angry. He didn't protest. He didn't curse God, he drew near.

I don't think this experience is unusual. There is a grace surrounding death that exposes to the world our most loving, soft, beautiful, and unadorned hearts. This is what I believe, but I won't know this for sure until I'm with him and have seen the things my son has witnessed before me.

The day filled up with visitors for as long as Sam could tolerate them. Friends and their parents appeared at his bedside with tissues pressed to their wet faces. They told him they loved him. They retold funny or poignant stories. They promised to remember him. Now and then, Sam requested a private moment alone with a certain person. I don't know how he had the inner strength and the mental capacity to be so intentional with his goodbyes, but he was.

While those closest to him had their final five minutes to say goodbye, the circle of friends in the lobby of the hospital was growing. They cried and held hands and consoled one another while their friend Sam faded away. Through it all they continued to tell stories. Much love was remembered, and minute by minute the love increased, love that was intimately intertwined with sorrow.

After a full day of goodbyes, Sam needed to rest.

Bob and I were left to be with our son.

With his consent, we agreed to make him more comfortable. The nurse sedated him, and the hallways got quiet. It seemed the whole of the universe swirled in Room 4 of the pediatric oncology floor. Bob laid down his head on Sam's bed, weeping. One hand gripped his fingers, while the other cradled his head. Sedated, Sam lay back against the pillows, his heart barely beating inside his frail and exhausted body.

The hours passed by, softly. Our dearest friends stayed with us around Sam, including my dad. We told more stories. Though he showed no signs, we felt that Sam was listening. I lay beside him in the bed, while Bob sat next to him. I stroked his hair and wiped the saliva from his lips. I held onto his fingers as they turned purple. Weeping, I prayed for him to rest, to be at peace.

All at once, I felt he was no longer there, even though his heart kept beating. His lungs had so little room to move yet he kept breathing and breathing and breathing. So slowly, there was hardly any oxygen moving through his lungs. Bob said it was all that nutrition I'd pumped into him, keeping his organs going. I didn't disagree. I needed to believe I'd helped Sam to fight the cancer with every resource and ounce of energy that we had. We promised to be strong and still remember him forever. I whispered to Sam, "It's all right. You can go now. We will be okay."

I watched his chest gently rise and fall with every breath. Then it would stop. Eight to ten seconds would go by while I wondered if he was finished. But as soon as I rested my hand on his chest, another rise of his lungs would bring in more air, as if he was reacting to my touch. While I lay next to him in his bed, Sam continued to breathe one slow shallow breath at a time.

After midnight, I suggested everyone move to the schoolroom down the hall for a bit, so Bob and I could be alone with Sam. They did. Bob and I sat in silence with Sam for another 45 minutes. Bob laid down his head next to Sam. At one point he jolted awake, afraid he'd fallen asleep and missed Sam's last breath. It was almost 1 am.

It seemed Sam was going to stay with us a little while longer. I walked down the hallway to tell our friends and family to go home and get some sleep. They each hugged me and expressed their love. Just as I was heading back toward Room four, my phone buzzed with a text from Bob. I didn't read it right away because I had just arrived at the door to his room.

"Lorna. He's gone."

I missed it. I missed Sam's last breath. I collapsed onto the bed and put my hand on his chest. He did not take another. I bent down and kissed his head on that spot on his temple that always felt like the perfect spot for me to kiss him. With my hand on his forehead, I kissed him again. I told him I loved him.

We used the call button to request the doctor, who came in to confirm there was no heartbeat. Our friends had not even left yet, so we brought them into the room to be with Sam for a moment. I sat on the window bench in a paralyzed daze. My dad put his arms around me and from somewhere deep inside his own terrible pain, he said, "I'm so sorry."

Sam died at 12:52am on August 27, 2016. Bob texted Natalie while I reached for my computer and typed into his Caringbridge page, "Sam is free."

39
LOST

After Sam's death, I spent some time being lost. My mental capacity was so altered that I had difficulty approaching the most routine daily tasks. I had wanted to free Sam from cancer more than anything in life. And while I hated how it controlled us, cancer gave me direction. After he was gone, there was no purpose to my days. This kind of grief - it is an inconceivable kind of pain. I didn't know how to live in it.

For a time, I lived aimlessly and it was exactly what I needed - to wake up each morning with the simple task of grieving, of getting food and water in me and resting. I walked and I did yoga, and I talked to friends when I knew that would help. I said yes to a few things because I didn't know until I tried them whether they would be good for me or not. I was so tired. To this day I still can't remember much of what happened in the first few months after Sam died.

Freedom hits differently after loss. I can think of very few circumstances where freedom is not understood to be liberating. The word suggests an unbound opportunity to pursue a more delightful life. But Sam *was* delightful. He was my heartbeat, and cancer was the thing that tethered us to a life consumed by illness. When Sam died, a new version of freedom emerged, and I feel it should be given a different name. Instead of embracing it like a gift, it was more like a blank page I needed to fill, but without the capacity to muster a single written sentence. While I once craved freedom from cancer's grip, I first needed to exist in the shadow of his death. It was there for me to take, but so offensive to even acknowledge. It would need to wait until I was ready. Meanwhile, I could embrace the freedom to stay in a dark place.

In spite of the hardships, our whole family also lived many, many good and beautiful moments because of cancer. There was fear but also the compassionate response of hundreds, or thousands, of people. There was suffering but also a deep relational connection with other parents who've been there. There was separation from my community, my colleagues, and my friends, but there was also a belonging inside those hospital walls. I had learned the language of oncology. I became brave, resourceful, and resilient. I loved deeply and carried more pride in my kids than I ever could have imagined. While I hated how Sam was living with cancer for so long, I had this immense sense of competence and of direction while he was sick. After he died, I was in between two worlds - the childhood cancer world and the other world where people had schedules and jobs and a clear purpose for their days.

The grocery story made me sad. When the casserole deliveries diminished, I pushed a shopping cart down the aisle of New Season's Market alone. My chest hurt and my throat was tight because the food I would buy was not for Sam. Even though I knew my way around, I was aimless. I spotted the usual items - coconut oil, sugar free chocolate chips, bundles of leafy greens, and boxes of local, organic berries, and I was indecisive about whether to drop them into my cart. Everyone has nuances about the foods they purchase at the grocery store. Ground coffee or whole bean, Gala apples or Honey Crisp, lean meats or firm tofu. We habitually reach for the preferences that our brains have mapped out, so we know exactly where to stop and reach and grab. I didn't even see the items that I never purchased, and I rarely wondered what I was missing. Each time I reached for a food item on the anti-cancer list there was a little hit of pleasure. Like placing a puzzle piece or ordering that clothing item from a favorite brand. When I shopped for Sam, I was always on a mission and could tackle the list with the efficiency and maneuverability that could win me a spot on a network game show. But without that clear and compelling mission, my grocery store demeanor wilted, and I felt lost.

I hadn't touched a cereal box in several years, but Natalie suggested, without making eye contact, that I bring it back into the house. So, I stood in front of that aisle-long section of the store, picking up boxes labelled "whole grains" and flipped it to the back to check the sugar content, and bristled at how cereal is still not a whole food. I knew too much now. I was judgmental. Processed foods, high glycemic foods, color added foods, and chemically preserved foods all bothered me. But I was also bothered that the whole food, anti-cancer plan didn't help save Sam's life. I'd vaguely remembered when my spice shelf consisted of lemon pepper, Morton Salt and a plastic container filled with several packets of taco and sloppy joe seasoning. I could never go back to that. But I also didn't know what kind of food shopper I was any more. I visited the fresh bread section. Adding carbs to our high fat ketogenic favorites would certainly lead to some unhealthy outcomes and I hadn't thought through what high fat foods we should eliminate, but it sounded comforting and didn't require any work. I could get sourdough or fresh focaccia. Cheese and crackers could be a meal. Maybe some grapes or sliced apples would round it out. The lump in my throat stayed with me for the duration of my trip through the store and I hoped the checker would not unknowingly ask, "How is your day going?"

There was no space for hope in my shopping cart anymore. I would need to spend some time being lost.

40
TROUBLED

In church I felt alone. The stirring I used to experience at a much younger age was replaced with an ugliness inside of me, because of how I reacted to the messaging. I hated how I felt. Yet I also feared that if I expressed my frustration about the church messages, I might offend and push away the people I cared about. I had little tolerance for the topic of sin when what was consuming my heart was a deeply felt anguish, unrelated to anyone's misguided choices. Ministers can preach to sin, or they can preach to woundedness, and I developed an acute belief that most of us need to be blessed instead of corrected. I came to church each week hoping that exposure to love and grace and the delightful things in life could nurture my wounded heart. While my own pain was so completely raw, each person in the church was carrying some sort of pain, and I longed for someone to preach to the quiet anguish we all experience on some level. Once I pinpointed what was bothering me about church, I became fixated on it.

In the darker moments of my grief, I imagined my own church sermon. I would tell them they're making things up. God is different from what they think, so stop believing that every little disappointment in life is really God guiding us to a better way. No. I would tell them that I'd seen the most remarkable child suffer and die. The certainty that God would always take care of them and their children is simply not true. There is risk in life, and God will not catch us when we fall. I'd say we need to find a new belief system that still recognizes the divine preciousness of life and love and beauty. One that acknowledges that pain and suffering don't have to have a kind reason behind it, because the world isn't the way it's supposed to be - like it was in the Garden of Eden. I'd tell people they should stop asking why people suffer and instead learn to tend to it. Let the questions go unanswered and the outcry go uncorrected. I want to tell people that their answers only offer peace to people who find a reward on the other side of their trials. When someone was healed - when things worked out. That didn't happen for Sam. He went through the hardest of times, and then he died. They would suggest he was healed in heaven and that should give me peace. I'd tell them to stop trying to make sense of everything and instead let grief and love find its way deep into our souls because if we don't do that, we could end up angry and offensive, pretending that every-thing happened for some mysterious reason we still haven't unveiled.

I didn't preach. Instead, I scheduled a moment with the two main ministers, both dear friends, and shared with them while my voice shook, and my throat turned tight. I told them how I felt, and they responded with exceptional kindness. "You have never been a better friend," one of them texted me later that day.

Even before Sam was sick, I was intrigued by the many places in the Scriptures where God answers a question with another ques-tion. These stories usually occurred as the backdrop of tremendous emotional turmoil. These unanswered questions were brought to my attention by a mentor I still consider a great influence in my spiritual life. She pointed me to the story in Genesis where Jacob was left alone at night in the wilderness, hours away from facing a battle with his brother who, he feared, would kill him. A man, believed to be an angel or some manifestation of God, appeared to him in the darkness while he was terrified. They fought. All night Jacob wrestled this angel with all of his might, and the angel would not let up. When they were finished wrestling, Jacob was depleted. The angel gave him a new name. Israel.

Jacob then requested, "Please tell me your name."

But the angel replied with a question, "Why do you ask my name?" Jacob departed the angel without answers, but he was given a new identity. He lived through the fight of his life and walked away with a limp. He was forever changed while a simple question was turned back for him to reflect on. The next day, Jacob's brother embraced him and they reconciled. I find that such a satisfying story, because of its mystery. A difficult experience, a change in identity, and questions left lingering as life moves forward with a deeply felt understanding of what matters.

I don't have an answer for why all of this happened to Sam. I don't want one. When well-meaning people offer me a reason for Sam's suffering and his death, it is invariably less satisfying than leaving it to wonder. It's been suggested that God never meant for Sam to be in this world for a long time. That idea triggers a sick feeling inside of me. I would rather be changed by the experience of being his mom, than settle on the certainty of a clear and tidy answer. The beauty is in knowing that a heart can become bigger, even when it is broken.

Today, I have peace. In the isolating months of the COVID pandemic, a new version of my faith emerged, freeing me from the tension I felt with traditional Christianity. A revised theology based on ancient tradition and a theme that allows us to trust the wisdom from within, as well as from the scriptures. Everything that has life, is sourced from the Divine, and we are on a journey to becoming all that we were made to be in the beginning. I rarely pray with words anymore, and find my deepest peace when I live with an awareness that God's light is all around me all of the time, and so is Sam.

41
HE SMILED

For several months after Sam died, I tended to my grief by visiting the places and events where Sam and I shared memories. I talked about him often, and spent time in his room, with his things. CAF named an award after him, so I went to San Diego to give a speech. Camp Ukandu invited us to a bereaved parents gathering where members of the camp community share their memories of the loved ones they've lost. As much as I wanted to stay connected to these communities, I had no lasting place in them without Sam. Instead, I sought more beauty and solitude in nature from sunrise hikes and starry skies. I fished. I wrote. I travelled. I practiced yoga. I rarely avoided crying, and usually chose to do so alone.

One day when I was sad, I indulged my emotions with wine and a movie. Sam and I had both read the book, Wonder, about a boy named Auggie who has facial deformities and goes to public school for the first time in 5th grade. He is teased and some students are repulsed by him. He is lied to by someone who he thought was a friend. Yet the boy has a sweetness about him - an innocence that should never be met with the cruelty of mean kids. I remember Sam talking through tears about how sad the story was, and how he related to the boy. The movie came out just a few weeks after he died.

I watched Wonder alone in the downstairs room at the back of our house, and I cried all through it. Sam understood the boy and I shared the heartache of his mother. But Wonder had an uplifting end. I wished for a different ending for Sam.

Tears wet my face for over an hour. I spoke to Sam and told him I was sorry and that I loved him again and again and again. Then I took a long nap in his bed. By evening, my heart felt lighter. Grief has affirmed the idea that sometimes we need to pass through periods of devastating weakness before we discover strength once again.

One morning, just days after Sam died, I started reading a book written by another mom, who had become a friend. Dana's daughter, Darah, also died of Ewing sarcoma. I knew from social media she had some sort of experience with signs, but I avoided the stories of loss until it became my story too. I stayed in my pajamas for a few hours and read most of Dana's book in one sitting. She wrote an account of the many signs she's received from Darah. They were everywhere. Especially feathers. I went to the internet and looked up feathers from those who have died, and sure enough, feathers were a common sign sent from people who have passed. After closing the book, I got dressed and took Cedar for a walk, wondering if it could even be true. Wondering if I should allow myself to believe this was possible. Back at the house, I pulled out my yoga mat and lay face down in a child's pose. The top edge of the mat was rolled up toward me, just beyond my forehead. I looked up and reached out to flatten the mat, and right in front of my face lay a little white feather. Goosebumps flooded my skin. I smiled, and I let myself believe.

I saw signs from Sam often. There were so many little white feathers, often in the perfect spot at the perfect moment. I had many other experiences with signs, even receiving a message from his Instagram account just days after he died. Numbers and songs, and even a couple of snakes appeared at the most opportune time, with the very person they were meant to startle. I'm certain Sam was giggling from above.

For several months after his death, I didn't want anything to do with cancer. It was too painful. But, eventually, my desire to support research re-emerged. I knew too much, and I understood the need. I missed having a reason to be hopeful.

Friends asked me if the Sam Day Soirée would continue, and I curiously began to pay attention to nonprofits engaged in the work of childhood cancer research. I thought maybe I could start a nonprofit and keep the Soirée going. It could be a part-time job. I could keep it small. This is not an uncommon step for a bereaved parent to take. We all need something to do with the love we still have for our kids, and we all know how neglected childhood cancer research is. Many nonprofits choose to supply gifts for kids with cancer, or financial support, or music programs or awareness. While the missions vary, there are many, many nonprofits around the country that exist in the name of a child that has died from cancer. But, in the Pacific Northwest, there was none focused on research for childhood sarcomas.

After much reflection and counsel from people I trusted, I scheduled a call with an attorney who had set up a few nonprofits and knew the process well. We talked for an hour. At the end of the call, I thanked him for his input and asked, "Is there anything I'm not thinking of that I should be asking you?"

"Yes," He paused. "I think you should ask me to do your startup work pro bono." Eight months later, on April 27th, 2018, the Sam Day Foundation became official.

In my preparation for stepping back into the childhood cancer space, I decided to expose myself again to the oncology unit at the children's hospital. On a Sunday afternoon, Bob and I visited the children's oncology floor at the hospital. As the double doors opened from the hallway into the unit, a touch of protest ran through my body. The receptionist gladly welcomed us in with no agenda other than to be in the space where Sam lived and died. Within minutes, the nurses greeted us along the back row of rooms, forming a little circle in the hallway. They acknowledged our loss, and talked about Sam. We laughed and cried at the same time.

As we left the hospital, Bob suggested we walk the full length of the upper parking lot, even though we parked down below, because he had walked that lot so many times with Sam. Sundays are quiet, so no one else was in the lot at that time. I heard the sound of a low flying helicopter, about to land on the roof of the hospital. I looked up, and just beyond the helicopter was something I'd never seen before - an upside down rainbow. I stopped. It wasn't a rainbow kind of day with the mix of sunshine and rain and a sky puffy with clouds. I never would have looked to the sky if the helicopter hadn't flown by. There was only a wisp of a cloud next to the completely blue sky, with a clear and colorful rainbow in the shape of a smile.

42
TODAY

It's now nine years since I've lost Sam. I close out this book knowing there are still many stories that weren't included. Today, most of my time is dedicated to managing the Sam Day Foundation. We've put $3 million into research for childhood sarcoma and brain cancers. A new clinical trial we funded opened last month, and another one is being written. I am no longer jealous of the families who will one day benefit from the treatments that will result from our work.

Many parents who have a child with cancer won't want to talk to me, or read this book. I represent the thing they are most afraid of and wholeheartedly honor the distance they need. I do my best to connect them to more hopeful stories than ours. Regardless, SDF is working hard to create a new future for those kids and one day the oncologists will be able to say to those families, *I have good news, the treatment is working.*

When I started the organization, I didn't realize how meaningful it would be to cultivate the culture and character of the Sam Day Foundation. I say all the time, Sam taught us three things: Dream Big, Laugh Often, and Live Well. Everything we do at SDF reflects the spirit of the boy we lost. Now we have this beautiful community of the most compassionate, generous and creative people who are not afraid to dream big and go for it. I'm surrounded by other parents who are walking a similar path. Leaning into the community of common experience has led to a deeper kind of friendship. I've known more families who have lost a child to cancer than I can keep up with, and I've learned to trust that my heart can handle it. We are capable of great capacity for love and pain and compassion and sacrifice. Sometimes we won't know real strength until we've known true, debilitating weakness. I wonder if it is an essential element of a deeper, more soulful kind of existence. Today, I hope to live my life in a way that expresses Sam's spirit and his own light. I hope to live equally, authentically me.

Bob is now the Chief of Police for the City of Portland. While favor toward the police has increased since the dark days of 2020, his job is quite public, political, and he could use a bit more sleep. After getting demoted in 2016, he went on a learning journey to understand the relationship and history between the police and people of color in America. Bob has evolved into someone who carries the difficult dissonance of competing views, and believes that the most promising way forward for us as a society is through curiosity, empathy and hope. Bob retired from officiating football in the Pac 12 when he became the Chief. He misses it.

Natalie stayed in southern California and is married and about to have our first grandchild. She is a minister at a church, caring for students through their youthful years, and they love her. She is mentored by a woman senior pastor in a community where everyone is welcome to worship. Natalie has continued to be a leader at Camp Ukandu, where her own grief can flow while having outrageous fun and a nearness to her brother.

Sam has a scholarship and an adaptive athlete award and an organization named after him. In 2017, his story and his photos took up multiple pages in the first publication of Adaptive Surf Magazine.

I've always been susceptible to sorrow, but I've noticed through the ups and downs of my story how my spirit can be shaped by a few specific components. People in my life who are loving and good, a purpose for how to invest my energy, and environments that are flooded with light and life and beauty. In the same way a plant grows by being exposed to light and water and nutrient rich soil, I had the sense that my heart could grow strong and good if only I could expose it to healthy sources of nourishment. This is what resilience looks like for me.

My hope for Sam to survive was crushed. But it got me through many difficult days when he was still here with us. Since losing him, hope has gently and graciously shown itself to me again. In the beginning of my life without him, I hoped to get through the first year without being completely incapacitated by grief. Somewhere along the way, hope reemerged, reincarnated as a companion to help me find a new way of existing in this world without my son. All of it would become a part of me. My sorrow, my love, my story, even Sam's spirit has become infused into my own soul. I want to live as an expression of all of it.

My heart will forever be broken, but it is also bigger, because I got to be Sam's mom.

AUTHOR'S NOTE

Starting a nonprofit has given me something to do with the love I still have for Sam. While it has been the most difficult and lonely job I have ever had, it is equally and profoundly meaningful.

In its first seven years, the Sam Day Foundation (SDF) has grown to four staff, and our budget is set to contribute $1M in funding for childhood cancer research this year, 2026. We intend to maintain that cadence, while leaving room at the table for bigger dreams too. When I started SDF, I chose to support research for the most destructive and neglected childhood cancers - sarcomas and brain tumors. The alternative would have been to focus all of our resources on Ewing sarcoma. The choice to be inclusive was all about hope. The hope I had each day Sam was alive was only because I knew someone was working on a cure. And yet, I met several families whose kids were dealing with different sarcomas, and research for those seemed to be non-existent. Every kid should know that someone is working on a cure for their cancer and every family should have a reason to be hopeful. Today we are challenging the research community to be inclusive of other sarcomas or brain tumors, to collect more tissue for study, and to explore how existing drugs can be repurposed for the most neglected childhood cancers. I want SDF to be the organization that says, *We're working on it.*

We now have a rigorous process for selecting research projects, guided by a committee of rather accomplished scientists. While we have funded researchers around the country, we favor the Pacific Northwest. Most clinical trials offered to kids are located on the eastern half of the country, and yet there are very few families with the resources needed to relocate. So, SDF aims to bring more clinical trials to this corner of the country, so kids can access the most hopeful options close to home.

A smaller portion of SDF's work is to offer wellness resources to families dealing with childhood cancer. A substack newsletter, Well ONE DAY, offers no-cost, evidence-based articles on nutrition, and mental health, plus essays written by someone who understands. We address topics that become difficult for young people who have had to endure cancer, and a place of understanding and support for their own well-being. We supply wellness boxes to patients in the PNW too - a few healthy snacks, recipes, fidget toys, games, stuffies, drinkware, gift cards, and a message that says, *we're working on it.*

When I started SDF, I didn't anticipate how enjoyable it would be to cultivate the character of an organization. Today I am protective of that character. I hope that when people step into the Sam Day community, they feel immediate belonging. I hope people know they can trust us with their support while we work tirelessly and strategically to accelerate better treatments for kids. Every fundraising event is intended to make people laugh, cry, and think, and I hope people don't want to leave when the program ends.

The most impactful element of SDF is the way in which we're connected to three groups of people in the ecosystem - patients and their parents, oncologists, and researchers. We seek to be a connector to elevate expertise and a sensitivity to the needs of patients. The unfortunate reality for this population is that relapse is common, and ineffective treatment plans often follow their bad news. I receive calls from parents with shaky voices, asking me if I know of any new clinical trials. I hate saying no. But if I can connect parents to researchers, or researchers to oncologists, and some degree of hope comes from that connection, I'll sleep better at the end of my days.

As SDF grows in influence and effectiveness, I look forward to the day when oncologists have more promising protocols to offer frightened families. One day, oncologists will have a different conversation with their patients, and they will be able to say, "I have good news. The new treatment is working, and your cancer is gone." I hope the Sam Day Foundation can help us get to that day.

Samdayfoundation.org
samdaynews.substack.com

ACKNOWLEDGMENTS

My husband is my number one champion. Bob and I walked this road together, and I'm convinced that his humor, his love for his family, and his willingness to step into hard conversations made our entire story more tolerable. Bob currently serves as Chief of the Portland Police Bureau. Surviving a police marriage is tough, and so is the loss of a child. I'm proud of the path we've navigated together.

Natalie has been the kid I worry less about. How she's maintained her sparkle through all of this is unreal. I had the gift of witnessing a deep and entertaining friendship grow between my kids and I'm proud of how she showed up for her brother. She's the kind of young woman people are drawn to. And so am I.

Thank you mom, dad, and Cathie - a true Scottish family with an abundance of good memories. Thank you for keeping me so deeply connected to my roots. Dad, thanks for extra edits and inquiries such as, "How do you feel about the oxford comma?"

Cody Luff, who taught me how to write when Sam was still here, and walked me to the finish line when my story was finally written. Susan Spitzer and Karen Polinski offered to help with editing, and they've both made me look smarter than I am. Kate McMahon, you have a gift of making me feel competent and interesting. It's been an honor to share my grief, my anger, and my heart with you.

Nancy Leedy and Barbara Feil, a long time ago you believed I had something to say and gave me a platform to do so. You helped me find my voice more than you know.

The Attic Institute got me organized and introduced me to mentors who knew how to teach with care - Wendy Willis and Whitney Otto made sure I pushed this project forward with some skill.

Sam's medical teams, it must be a difficult role, to try to save a child's life and yet to be so quickly criticized when things go wrong. Thank you for the banter, the hope, the extra hours you worked, and for seeing that I had a pretty cool kid.

Cancer parents have become my community of support, love, and shared grief. Loss makes love all the more profound, whether bereaved or living with a cancer survivor, our stories are intertwined.

www.ingramcontent.com/pod-product-compliance
Lightning Source LLC
Chambersburg PA
CBHW051141130726
47988CB00005B/1936